INHERITING POSSIBILITY

Thank You
for being you

Inheriting Possibility

· · · ·

Social Reproduction and Quantification in Education

Ezekiel J. Dixon-Román

University of Minnesota Press
Minneapolis
London

A different version of chapter 2 appeared as "Diffractive Possibilities: Cultural Studies and Quantification," *Transforming Anthropology* 24, no. 2 (October 2016); copyright 2016 by the American Anthropological Association.

Published by the University of Minnesota Press
111 Third Avenue South, Suite 290
Minneapolis, MN 55401-2520
http://www.upress.umn.edu

A Cataloging-in-Publication record for this book
is available from the Library of Congress.
ISBN 978-1-5179-0125-7 (hc)
ISBN 978-1-5179-0126-4 (pb)

The University of Minnesota is an equal-opportunity educator and employer.

UMP LSI

For Elijah Sage Román

Contents

Preface

A s a scholar interested in theories of reproducing power relations and processes of marginalization, I found my home in critical
theory and cultural studies. In my graduate student days my long-time
mentor, Edmund W. Gordon, introduced me to works such as Raymond
Geuss's *Idea of a Critical Theory* and Pierre Bourdieu's "Forms of Capital."
I became even more enthralled by works such as Bourdieu's *Outline of a
Theory of Practice*, Louis Althusser's famous essay "Ideology and the Ideological State Apparatus," Michel de Certeau's *The Practice of Everyday Life*,
Jacques Derrida's "différance," Judith Butler's *Gender Trouble*, and Ernesto
Laclau and Chantal Mouffe's *Hegemony and Socialist Strategy*, among many
others. I even had the opportunity to spend some time with poststructuralist, post-Marxist political theorist Ernesto Laclau during my postdoc. I
was fortuned with a theoretical toolkit that equipped me to make a sharp
analysis of reproducing power relations as well as deconstructing their
foundations.

Conversely, I have also maintained a seemingly schizophrenic intellectual existence as a scholar whose graduate training was in quantitative
methods and psychometrics. Not only did/do I enjoy the *art* of measurement and statistics, I also found the questions *how much* and *to what extent*
to be critically important for the analysis of power and marginalization.
Working on the intersections of critical theory and quantitative methods, however, has been an arduous task. While I found much of critical
theory to be apprehensive of the quantitative, the only theory used in my
psychometrics program was measurement and statistical theory, with
some splattering of psychological and cognitive theory. And, to be clear,
the psychological and cognitive theory covered did not include thinkers
such as Freud, Lacan, Fanon, Fromm, Kristeva, Gergen, or Žižek. In fact, I
recall asking in my History of Psychology course why we weren't covering

Du Bois and Fanon and the professor's answer was that Du Bois was not a psychologist and Fanon wasn't even worthy of his response.

Despite these very clear departures I produced a dissertation that used longitudinal multilevel growth models in order to examine research questions that were theoretically informed by Althusser, Gramsci, and Bourdieu. The committee endorsed their support of the work and the dissertation was selected for Fordham University's Graduate School of Arts and Sciences dissertation award that year. I already had a stellar postdoc lined up at Northwestern University and was ready to do the work that I became a scholar to do. But no one prepared me for what came next.

As I continued in the academy and began the ritualistic practice of the peer-review process I consistently encountered reviews that had a visceral response to postmodernism and its use with quantitative methods. These responses can be characterized in at least two related ways: ideological and paradigmatic.

It is said that one of the virtues of the peer-review process is that it is objective and free of ideology, with all theoretical perspectives and methodological approaches being considered. I not only found this to not be the case, I received commentaries from reviewers that were clearly ideological. One reviewer stated in response to my use of postmodernism that "this is the kind of ideological work that should not be published in sociology." It has also been more explicitly required by other reviewers to "get rid of the postmodernism." Although there are scholars who may have a vehement position against critical theories, this should not preclude their open consideration of these theoretical perspectives in the works of others, nor should it give them license to constitute postmodernism as ideological. The blind peer-review process is not safe from ideological contamination, and I had to learn this the hard way.

An argument can perhaps be made for the legitimacy of these ideological responses, particularly to the extent that they are also paradigmatic. As Kuhn (1996) reminds us, a scientific paradigm constitutes a set of assumptions and activities that attain sufficient popularity so as to displace all potential alternatives. The normal science of the positivist paradigm that quantitative social science has *become* has created the foundation for responses such as those above, as well as a hermeneutics of suspicion toward the quantitative on the part of critical scholars. The former is seen in reviewer requests to "take the theory out," while the latter has been expressed by critical scholars in such terms as "I don't know if Butler meant for her work to be quantified." These paradigmatic responses have left little room for alternative scholarly possibilities.

Thus, I not only found apprehension about quantitative methods among critical theory scholars but also an eschewing of critical theory among quantitative scholars. On both sides, the consensus seemed to be that the two were irreconcilable. It was through this very complicated and frustrating experience that I realized I had far more work to do than I thought, and this work would essentially be field formation where I would need to deconstruct, develop, and teach.

The current book project is one major instantiation of this program of research. Here, I concern myself with the dualism of nature and culture that has undergirded both theories of social reproduction and social science empiricism. Thus, the ways in which we have come to understand and produce knowledge about the reproduction of power relations have rested on an assumptive premise that nature is made up of fixed universals that are the stage or ground for the creative, intellective, and discursive play of culture. It is said that "truth" exists in nature and that culture often contaminates our access to "truths" of the natural world. This same dualism underpins theories and research on inheritance, social reproduction, and human learning and development. Given recent work in the physical and biological sciences as well as new materialist philosophy, *Inheriting Possibility* not only argues that nature is, in fact, culture, consisting of the same creative, intellective, and discursive processes, but that the assumed nature/culture binary has ultimately limited our understanding of the reproduction of power relations. Moreover, the limitations of knowledge production have also been due to the false assumptions about nature and the possibilities of unlocking nature's "truths" with quantification. Thus, I proffer an alternative ontology, epistemology, and methodology that attempts to carve out a space within critical inquiry for quantitative methods. Regardless of where you stand on these two topics, I invite you to take this pedagogical journey with me through *Inheriting Possibility*.

Enumerating Difference
beyond Anthropocentrism

Consider the following hypothetical SAT critical reading question:

Santiago, Chile, lies in the center of a _____ , a large bowl-shaped valley consisting of broad and fertile lands surrounded by mountains.

    a.) coulee
    b.) plain
    c.) fault zone
    d.) basin
    e.) delta

EVERY YEAR MILLIONS of college-bound high school juniors and seniors participate in the ritual practice of taking the SAT, where they respond to test questions just like the one above. How the students perform overall on the test can be a major determinant in whether they are considered for admission at one of the selective institutions of higher education and subsequently their chances for social mobility. But the answer to this multiple choice question will prove less important than how the response is produced.

Responses to questions like this in Western culture and ideology are assumed to be indicative of one's intellect. Despite the longstanding challenges to universal, decontextualized theories of human learning and development, responses to multiple choice questions like the one above and the subsequently estimated test scores continue to be privileged and trusted to represent the test-takers' "true" intellect or ability. Research has not only indicated that human learning and development is situated and multiplicative (Cole and Scribner 1974; Gutiérrez and Rogoff 2003; Lee 2001; Nasir and Saxe 2003; Rogoff 2003) but that these situated multiplicities materialize in their item responses and test scores (Freedle 2003; Santelices and Wilson 2010). The above sentence-completion item is not only situated in the language of the Western science of geology but also assumes each test-taker has the same familial resources and cultural history to deploy in response to the item, while also assuming universal experiences and understandings of the subject of the item. Arguably, it is the particularities of the multiplicity of situated experiences with the content of this item that produces multiple responses. Regardless of whether the test-taker responds correctly, the inherited sociocultural and historical conditions of structural relations that produce responses and subsequently the quantitatively estimated test scores are often overlooked.

To further illustrate this point, let's take two contrasting examples: Ayodeji Ogunniyi and Josiah Hornblower. Ayodeji is a public school teacher in Illinois whose story was featured on a National Public Radio series about the National Teachers Initiative, which I followed up with an in-depth interview. Josiah is one of the young heirs featured in Jamie Johnson's controversial 2003 documentary about growing up wealthy in America, *Born Rich.*

Ayodeji Ogunniyi is a first-generation immigrant to the United States from Nigeria. Although his parents were college educated in Nigeria, their degrees were not recognized in the United States. His father had to work as a taxi driver in Chicago and his mother worked for $3.25 per hour cleaning at a hotel. Their working-class existence made it difficult to afford test preparation and (as we'll learn in chapter 4) his public high school put their test preparation resources into the Illinois state exam. Thus, Ayodeji did not study for either of the commonly used college admissions tests, the SAT or the ACT. Moreover, his family lacked the resources to travel outside of the United States and experience the world beyond their Chicago community.

In contrast, Josiah Hornblower is one of the heirs of the Vanderbilt and Whitney families, two of the oldest and richest families in the United States. He attended St. Paul's School, one of the most elite private schools in the East, where, as we will see in chapter 4, they take the SAT very seriously. He also regularly traveled outside of the United States while he was growing up. In *Born Rich,* Josiah shares the following story of being quizzed by low-income coworkers in Texas about the capital of Chile: "In my mind, I knew it was Santiago but I went on a fly-fishing trip with my dad down there in the mountains and [remembered] going around on helicopters, going from pool to pool." Josiah didn't just know the capital of Chile as information committed to memory but also had a very personal and material experience with the city of Santiago. Similarly, the above SAT critical reading question would elicit profound memories for Josiah that would be aural, visual, olfactory, and affective; materially experienced within the terrain and climate of the ground and from a bird's-eye view of the topography of Santiago via the helicopter excursions; they would be socially and culturally familiar through his experiences of the sociocultural and historical conditions in Santiago during the visit and the ways Josiah and his father engaged the social, cultural, and geographic landscape. The relational ontology with the material place of Santiago profoundly affects Josiah's understanding of Santiago and its material and sociocultural particularities. Josiah's inherited resources provided him the opportunity to have an understanding and knowledge of the content of the SAT question that goes beyond the limits of the subject matter of the question by having an intimate relational experience with the ontology of the *matter* of the subject.

Again, the correctness of the response to the test item is less important than how the response is produced. The familial history of socioeconomic resources, sociocultural convergences, sociopolitical positions, geographic pathways, pedagogical opportunities, corporealities, and historical conditions all come together to enact a reading, interpretation, experience, and preconscious bodily response to the SAT question. Although often reduced to the transfer or gifting of material property, *Inheriting Possibility* theoretically and empirically demonstrates how inheritance is more of a process, one made up of myriad inseparable material and sociocultural (i.e., discursive) forces that are both producing and produced by the complex and differentiating influences of time and space. Ayodeji and Josiah's example illustrates the ways in which inherited economic resources, social privilege, and sociocultural practices materialize in pedagogical practices that contribute to legitimated and clandestine processes of social reproduction. The material and discursive power relations of this example haunt the potential responses to the SAT question and can be misinterpreted and misrecognized as a behavioral response that is reflective of Ayodeji's and Josiah's "true" ability.

Although the estimated SAT scores are assumed to represent, in part, "true" ability and knowledge, *Inheriting Possibility* argues that the estimated scores can be better understood as enumerating the myriad inherited forces of material, sociocultural, and historical power relations. The story of inheritance and multigenerational inequality undergirds the socially contrasting example of Ayodeji and Josiah's SAT experience. That story, along with the inextricable reproduction of marginality, the ways in which it is entangled with multiple forces of social difference (including race, gender, and sexuality), and the extent to which there may be cumulative effects on youth social and educational processes, is one of the main concerns of this book.

The phenomenon of persistent inequality has been a longstanding subject of social inquiry (Becker and Tomes 1979, 1986; Blau and Duncan 1967; Bourdieu and Passeron 1977; Bowles et al. 2005; Ermisch, Jäntti, and Smeeding 2012; Featherman and Hauser 1978; Piketty 2014; Rogoff 1953; Sharkey 2008, 2013; Smeeding, Erikson, and Jäntti 2011; Solon 1992; Warren and Hauser 1997). Increasing research shows the extent to which inequality has been reproduced across generations. For instance, Mazumder (2005) has estimated that as much as 62 percent of income inequality in one generation was reproduced in their offspring's generation. Conley and Glauber (2008) have also estimated that as many as 55 percent of the offspring of the top wealth quartile remained in the top wealth quartile by adulthood—and this pales in comparison to the less than 10 percent of the offspring from the bottom wealth quartile who actually attain the top quartile by adulthood (Conley and Glauber 2008). These are just examples of the growing mountain of data that indicate a strong rigidity in the reproduction of inequality in the United States. Thus, Ayodeji's working-class, low-resourced educational experience, in contrast to Josiah's familial history of multigenerational inherited wealth and privilege, is not unique. In fact, the data indicates that their contrasting example is much more emblematic of the normative process of social reproduction.

Social theorists have posited that inheritance is the medium and process of social reproduction. It is often thought of as the *gifting* or passing on of the material forms of wealth such as property, business, or assets from parents to offspring. But critical social theorists such as Pierre Bourdieu have also pushed the boundaries of inherited resources to include social relationships, symbolic status, language and dialect, dispositions of perceptions and appreciations, and corporeality and practices, among others. In so doing he opened up new ways to examine the more clandestine processes of social reproduction that are often missed by the panoptic purview of the State.

Regardless of what is inherited, I will argue that, as a *gift*, inheritance is an impossible possibility. As Jacques Derrida (2008) reminds us, the act of giving is not chosen by the heirs, it is imposed upon them. The imposition commands a response (whether conscious or not) that could never fully recompense or repay the giver. This lack of full recompensation ultimately annuls the gift and sets in motion a circular economy of exchange. Because the act of giving requires that there be no reciprocity, Derrida argues, the very condition of possibility for the *gift* is its impossibility. Thus, Ayodeji's inheritance, not just his material conditions and parents' practices but also his parents' desires and expectations, is an impossible possibility.

Despite the compelling nature of the data discussed above and related theoretical work, there continues to be an abyss between the work of cultural studies and critical inquiry and the dominant uses of quantitative studies on social reproduction. While the critical work of Bruno Latour or Pierre Bourdieu as well as the growing critical scholarship that employs statistics have dared to work within this contentious ontological and epistemological space, there continues to be a radical divide. On the one hand, scholarship in cultural studies and critical inquiry has maintained a hermeneutics of suspicion toward the critical possibilities of quantitative methods at the cost of not accounting for what is inherently, in part, a question of quantification: the materialist analysis of power relations. Thus, the above compelling data of reproduced inequality would not be taken up.

On the other hand, the dominant orientation toward quantitative social science research on social reproduction has eschewed critical theories, maintained a positivist posture toward the data, and assumed privileged access to the "truths" of natural phenomena via the logics of mathematics. As a result of its almost atheoretical lens, the positivist orientation tends to interpretively misrecognize the underlying structural relations of the data, often falling into the trap of pathology, deficiency, and depravity narratives of the marginalized. From a Western cultural perspective of individualism where social problems are understood to inhere within persons or groups, the ideological interpretive misrecognition of the marginalized as morally wanting, socially deficient, or intellectually unable is quite easy, especially since the measured unit of analysis is often individuals or families and the comparative lens of statistics necessitates the interpellation of identity and difference.

Where both of these perspectives do agree is in their paradigmatic centering of the human, which assumes a fixed "nature" as the stage of human cultural processes and sociality. Although one could work on creating a methodological space for quantitative methods within critical inquiry from this anthropocentric starting point, this has ultimately limited the produced knowledge and understanding of reproducing power relations by not taking up the lively and vibrant forces of matter and materializations. Moreover, in chapter 2 we will consider that a new materialist lens frees the quantitative from the logics of representationalism, moving from questions of meaning toward asking "what it functions with, in connection with what other things it does or does not transmit" (Deleuze and Guattari 1987, 4). Thus, a new materialist deconstruction of the nature/culture binary is necessary in order to rethink and reconsider the possibilities of quantification for cultural studies and critical inquiry.

Recent work in posthumanist studies, deconstruction, and new materialist feminist science studies has pointed toward the ways in which the matter of nature has always been *mattering* (Alaimo and Hekman 2008; Barad 2007; Coole and Frost 2010; Kirby 2011)—that is, matter has always engaged in the processes of communicating, interpreting, scripting, and inventing. As Barad states, "*matter is a substance in its intra-active becoming—not a thing but a doing, a congealing of* agency" (2007, 151). Matter is not a product but rather an ongoing process of materializations that are continuous material reconfigurings of the world. New materialist reconceptualizing and reontologizing of matter has had important implications for the ontology of the human.

New materialists have also postulated that the processes of culture are merely an inheritance from nature where the human is one entangled ontological expression of Earth's becoming, what Vicki Kirby (2011) has called quantum anthropologies. Kirby pushes the humanities and social and natural sciences to rethink and requestion the inherited assumptions of the Cartesian split that have reinscribed binaries such as that between mind and body, nature and culture. Kirby challenges us to consider the ways in which the very processes of communication and intellection assumed to be of culture have always been nature. She wants us to consider how nature and culture are inseparable and profoundly entangled, where the existence of either does not predate the other. Quantum anthropologies is a new materialist theory of the entanglement of the world, of which we are not outside viewers, but rather always inside intra-acting observers of the world's in-process ontological fabric. How do quantum anthropologies challenge philosophical and scientific understandings of the supposed category of the human? In what ways does this approach challenge the binaries of empiricism such as subject and object, subjective and objective, and qualitative and quantitative? And what are the implications for how the social sciences research inheritance and social reproduction? These new materialist deconstructions of nature and culture have imploded the foundations of many theories and philosophies of (social or natural) science.

The socially contrasting example of Ayodeji and Josiah's SAT experience highlights how power and social reproduction *matter* in ways that have been traditionally overlooked by the cultural constructionist lens of poststructuralism. Poststructuralist theories of social reproduction, for instance, continue to separate the material of wealth and property from the so-called nonmaterial, the symbolic resources of the social and cultural (e.g., Bourdieu 1986). Even the treatment of the matter of "nature" as including the corporeal has been limited to symbolic and discursive constructions. This separation between the material and the symbolic, I argue, is merely one of the symptomatic theoretical expressions of the nature/culture binary that has undergirded philosophy and social science's understandings of inheritance. The matter of nature has been assumed to be made up of prefixed essential properties, immutable, and predating the human processes of culture. The constructing, inventing, imagining, interpreting, and communicating of culture has also been assumed to be proper to the human. The discursive acts of Josiah's traveling to Santiago, Chile, with his father to go fly-fishing would be treated as cultural, and the ontology of the material place of Santiago, Chile, would be treated as a separate matter with prefixed characteristics. But is the symbolic so separate and irreducibly different from the material? How might Josiah's experience not simply be about discursive formations but also the materialization of mattering matter? In what ways has the assumed irreducible difference limited our theoretical conceptualizing of inheritance, social reproduction, and human development? And in what ways has the haunting influence of the nature/culture binary constrained both how we have investigated these processes and how we have come to know and understand social reproduction? These are the main questions that I seek to interrogate in the following chapters.

My own intervention then is to critically reconsider and rethink how the nature/culture binary has undergirded various theories of inheritance and social reproduction. I seek to proffer a new materialist alternative that considers what I see as three of the major forces of inheritance: material-discursive processes, timespace, and assemblages. With this new materialist framing I discuss the implications for quantitative inquiry and offer an alternative lens and process of inquiry. Following this theoretical work, I demonstrate a theoretical shift for critical social inquiry by examining two phenomena that have substantial implications for the reproduction of social inequality: parenting practices and the SAT. Both have been extensively examined for their endogeneity to social, racial, and gender inequality as well as their exogenous influence on the same forms of relational difference. These theoretical reconsiderations have implications both for how we conceptualize the processes of inheritance and how we go about social inquiry more broadly. In the following I will expound in more detail on the implications for social inquiry, beginning with a review of some of the seminal works on inheritance, intergenerational inequality, and social mobility and reproduction that form the backdrop of this work.

Social Science Literature on Inheritance, Social Mobility, and Reproduction

Social science studies on intergenerational inequality and social mobility go back several decades (Becker and Tomes 1979, 1986; Blau and Duncan 1967; Bowles et al. 2005; Ermisch, Jäntti, and Smeeding 2012; Featherman and Hauser 1978; Piketty 2014; Rogoff 1953; Sharkey 2008, 2013; Smeeding, Erikson, and Jäntti 2011; Solon 1992; Warren and Hauser 1997). Dominated by the quantitative, many studies have focused on stratification and mobility from the parents' generation as it affects the offspring's educational attainment, occupational status, or income. While there have most certainly been important qualitative studies (e.g., Carter 2003; Khan 2011; Lareau 2003; Willis 1977), they have often been in the service of these privileged quantitative works. Thus I focus my review here on some of the seminal quantitative studies.

Work on social mobility has not always put into question the ideal of the so-called American Dream. Some earlier studies, for instance, suggested that there was greater social mobility in the United States than in the United Kingdom (Blau and Duncan 1967) and that the intergenerational income elasticity (an estimate of the proportion of inequality reproduced from the parents' generation to their offspring) was around 0.10 in the United States (Becker and Tomes 1979, 1986). This estimate would indicate that 10 percent of the inequality in the parents' generation was reproduced in their offspring's generation. While the evidence on both of these lines of work has been challenged (Solon 1992; Erikson and Goldthorpe 1985), more recent work has taken advantage of better measures of income over a longer period of time in order to account for transitory shocks to the market. Using the Panel Study of Income Dynamics (PSID) and a parent income measure over sixteen years, Mazumder (2005) estimated an intergenerational income elasticity of 0.62, indicating that 62 percent of the inequality in the parents' generation was reproduced in their offspring's generation. Additionally, other recent work has indicated that the United States leads all developed nations in the persistence of inequality (Smeeding, Erikson, and Jäntti 2011).

These more recent challenges on the persistence of inequality have led to many studies examining how inequality is inherited and how policy may enable greater social mobility. Using the PSID, Bowles and Gintis (2002) not only found that the contribution and transmission of genetics (as measured by mother's IQ) is less important, they also found that wealth, race, and schooling are the more important factors in the inheritance of economic status. Duncan et al. (2011) focused on the durable effects of economic deprivation in early childhood in both the United States and Norway and found that not only were there unfavorable correlations between early childhood income and adult outcomes but that the associations were larger in the United States than in Norway. They suggest that the more egalitarian welfare state of Norway may aid in mitigating the effects of early childhood economic deprivation. Similarly, Mayer and Lopoo (2008) examined the variation of state government spending within the United States in association with intergenerational economic mobility. They found that states with high spending had more mobility than low-spending states. In his monumental work *Capital in the Twenty-First Century* (2014), Thomas Piketty argues that under market capitalism, inequality has historically increased across generations because it rewards the owners of capital. He finds that the flows of inheritance (i.e., the total gifts and bequests as a rate of total private capital) have been rising since the 1970s, when in the United States inherited wealth comprised about 50 to 60 percent of all private capital. What has reduced inequality, Piketty argues, has been moments of government intervention such as war, policies of taxation, or greater investments in increased quality education. These more recent works point to the importance of race, wealth, and public policy in the degree and persistence of inequality.

More studies are considering the role of family wealth and racial stratification in the persistence of inequality. Indeed, parental liquid assets have been found to have an effect on offspring outcomes such as educational attainment and labor market participation over and above parental permanent income, educational attainment, and occupational prestige (Conley 1999). Additionally, parental liquid assets accounted for a substantial proportion of the racial differences in offspring outcomes. For offspring adult educational attainment, no racial differences remained when parental liquid assets was added to the model. Other work has examined the family background factors of racial differences in adult wealth holdings. For instance, Keister (2004) found that both family structure and family size were substantially associated with the trajectories of adult wealth accumulation. The role of racial stratification and family wealth also begins to point toward the importance of the assemblages of "difference" in the persistence of inequality.

In related work, substantial research has considered the importance of neighborhoods in reproducing inequality both socially and racially. While studies such as the Gautreaux Program (Rubinowitz and Rosenbaum 2000) and Moving-to-Opportunity (Goering and Feins 2003) provided evidence of the importance of neighborhoods for social mobility, a more recent study by Patrick Sharkey (2008) estimates the most robust and compelling results thus far. Sharkey argues that neighborhoods can be understood as another mechanism of social and racial stratification. Using PSID data, he found that more than 70 percent of black children who grew up in the poorest quarter of American neighborhoods remained in the poorest quarter of neighborhoods as adults, compared to 40 percent of whites. These data further underline the rigidity of intergenerational inequality and the influence the material and discursive phenomena of racialized structural relations have on social reproduction.

Each of the studies discussed above is based on two generations. Other studies have examined the extent to which there are cumulative or time-lagged effects of multiple generations of inequality. That is, how much of the inequality in offspring is attributable to the grandparents' inequality net of the parents' inequality? Investigators have examined the direct effect of grandparents' socioeconomic factors on grandchildren's socioeconomic outcomes in earnings and occupational prestige, with many of these studies finding little to no direct effect (Cherlin and Furstenberg 1992; Peters 1992; Ridge 1974; Warren and Hauser 1997). As an attempt to examine the inclusion of grandparents in social and economic stratification, Warren and Hauser (1997) used regression and structural equation modeling methods to analyze three generations of the Wisconsin Longitudinal Study. Their results provided little evidence of grandparents' direct effects on grandchildren's outcomes net of the parents' direct effects. Thus, although the grandparents indirectly affected the grandchild they added little meaningful explanatory power to the grandchildren's adult socioeconomic outcomes.

Despite the lack of evidence of lagged grandparent effects in previous studies, others have more recently conceptually explored and empirically examined the potential social processes of multigenerational effects. Some scholars argue that by not accounting for grandparent or multigenerational inequality we may be underestimating the persistence of inequality across generations (Chan and Boliver 2013; Mare 2011). There are good reasons to consider social processes of inheritance beyond the traditional Markovian inheritance process where it is assumed that all of the exerted familial influence is via the parents. Mare (2011) suggests that analyses across multiple generations must employ an institutional analysis since institutions often outlive individuals. Among the institutionalized mechanisms that enable the transmission of affluence or poverty are the legal arrangement of generation-skipping trusts, the legacy system of Ivy League schools, wealth accumulation and transfer, and segregation and housing discrimination, to name a few. In fact, although not accounting for a specific institutionalized mechanism but rather a different geographic, historical, and policy context, a recent study using three-generation data from Great Britain found that net of parental occupational class, the grandparents' class position directly affected the class position the grandchild entered (Chan and Boliver 2013). As Mare suggests, Chan and Boliver's (2013) results indicate that multigenerational effects may depend both on the geographic and historical context in which the study was conducted, as the institutional mechanisms of inheritance may be more mobile or rigid.

While this literature provides useful information on social reproduction, its conceptual, methodological, epistemological, and ontological shortcomings lead toward overly determined narratives of the data. Conceptually, much of this work is informed by an overdetermining structuralist perspective or a strict positivist perspective that ideologically hides behind the data of the models. More concerning is the above-mentioned Western cultural tendency to interpret this data atheoretically, rendering the poor and marginalized as socially deficient, culturally depraved, and intellectually inferior. The narrow methodological lens of the quantitative only provides a limited slice of information for knowledge production, leading toward the construction of singular narratives at the cost of masking the multiplicity of forces that are expressed by the data. In addition, as we see from the review of the literature, the work is very sensitive to the when, how, and what of measurement. Even when the qualitative data have been incorporated or brought to bear to understand the estimates, the result is often a reduced narrative that does not take seriously the ways in which the data are in tension and contradict one another and how those tensions and contradictions refer to the myriad of forces at play in their statistical production. I will expound further on this in chapter 2.

Epistemologically, not only has the positivist lens dominated this work, it has maintained an anthropocentrism, assuming a fixed and immutable nature that is the predated stage for the cultural inventions, intellections, and communications of the human. Relatedly, an ontological separation is maintained between the dispassionate, all-knowing researcher (subject) and participants and phenomena of study (object). Not only is the researcher not understood to be deeply entangled and part of the world and phenomena of study, the effect of the produced knowledge on the researcher is not considered. It is for these reasons that I depart from the traditional quantitative approaches of social inquiry on inheritance and reproduction. At the same time, we have to wonder about the mysterious predictive possibilities of statistical estimation. For instance, how is it that we are able to predict, with some margin of error, what a test-taker's SAT score will be based on a host of relevant covariates? Thus I not only maintain a hermeneutics of empathy toward quantification but, more important, I offer a new approach to Barad's (2007) diffractive methodology that frames social inquiry, including the quantitative, as a process of intra-acting performativities (discussed in chapter 2).

Organization of the Book

Inheriting Possibility employs data from multiple methods and sources, including film media, biographical memoirs, Internet sources and media interviews, ethnographic participant observation, and the quantitative modeling of national probability samples. I begin by engaging in a new materialist deconstruction of the nature/culture binary in order to rethink and reconceptualize the processes of inheritance and social reproduction that account for the entanglements of quantum anthropologies. This theoretical retooling then frames the rethinking of quantitative methods and informs the analysis in the rest of the book.

In the second chapter I discuss the dominant perspectives of the social sciences on social inheritance: genetic heritability, culture and social context/constructionism, and interactionism/epigenetics. By leaning on Vicki Kirby's (2011) new materialist deconstruction of nature/culture and her thesis "there is no outside of nature," I deconstruct these perspectives and consider a posthumanist alternative that assumes nature as culture and culture as nature, where the human is an entangled ontological expression of Earth's becoming. This will then frame my reconceptualizing of inheritance by discussing three major forces of inheritance: material-discursive forces, timespace, and assemblages. Material-discursive forces consider the double injunctive process of inheritance whereby the heir is chosen while the performative act of being chosen simultaneously enables the possibility of the heir's materially and discursively shaped choice. More important, material-discursive forces do not assume the matter of nature to be fixed or immutable but rather dynamic and intra-active and, as such, producing an ongoing (re)configuring of the *matter* of the heir's body and inheritance. The material-discursive forces not only occur with/in the entanglements of time and space but are both produced by and producing timespace. Finally, I employ the notion of assemblages as a way to conceptualize the inheritance of the multiplicity of social difference in the social events and situations of timespace. I argue that it is no longer enough to study an evolving and growing human organism in the backdrop of an assumed fixed, *pre*-scripted and predated nature. The ecologies and matter of "nature" are mattering on/in/with human learning and development.

In the third chapter, I discuss how a belief in the methods of quantification has not been widely shared in cultural studies. On the one hand, the dominant orientation of the quantitative continues to hold on to positivist assumptions of objectivity and the privileged access to the "truths" of natural phenomena via the logics of mathematics. On the other hand, cultural studies has radically rejected quantification due to positivist logics of representationalism; being an instrument of governmentality; its fixity and essentialism; an assumed privileged access to the metaphysics of internal mental processes; and an assumed privileged access to nature and "truth." But, to what extent does this radical rejection of the quantitative compromise the deconstructive project of cultural studies by falling into the trap of the quantitative/qualitative and nature/culture binaries? This chapter builds on the previous chapter's new materialist deconstruction in order to rethink and reconsider the possibilities of quantification via a diffractive methodology. A diffractive methodology, as articulated by Barad (2007), is a transdisciplinary approach of putting the theories of different disciplines in conversation. I extend this method to include the reading and analysis of data from multiple methods. It is via a diffractive methodology that the possibilities of quantification are enabled for cultural studies and critical social inquiry.

The third chapter is the first of two demonstrated diffractive analyses. The chapter begins by examining primary socialization and the extent to which the performative practices of parenting are enfolded sedimentary historialities both drawn from and enabled by the social conditions/conditionings in which the parents grew up. And, given the ways in which the forces of race, gender, and class are often empirically found to converge in the performativities of parenting, I also (re)consider how the lenses of diffraction and assemblages can be helpful for comparative analyses in critical social inquiry, particularly with quantitative methods. This chapter will lean on three forms of data: (1) the structural equation modeling of the Panel Study of Income Dynamics data on parents' and grandparents' socioeconomic resources and the parents' material-discursive practices of parenting; (2) a materialist analysis of sources from film media such as Dee Rees's independent film *Pariah* and the viral YouTube video "How Not to React When Your Child Tells You That He's Gay"; (3) a literary analysis of Anne Lamott's *Operating Instructions* and *A Journal of My Son's First Son*, Alfred Lubrano's *Limbo,* and Common's *One Day It'll All Make Sense.* Each of these provides a different lens, a different window, and a different perspective on the processes and forces of inheritance in parenting practices. While the structural equation models will provide more generalized data, the materialist and literary analyses will provide a more fine-grained situational, material, and discursive view of these processes, where we are likely to locate the multiplicity of forces that make up quantum anthropologies. With a particular interpretive focus on the assemblages of statistical "difference," this chapter will present the data in conversation with each other, diffractively reading each through the other with a particular focus on both the comparabilities and the tensions and contradictions of difference in order to illuminate the multiplicity of forces that come to *matter*.

The United States has rested its values of progress and democracy on ideologies of meritocracy. It has been via ideologies of meritocracy that selection, inequality, and social im/mobility have been legitimated. Meritocracy is institutionalized and evaluated in symbolic signifiers such as awards, credentialing, degrees, valued experiences and opportunities, and various measures of achievement such as standardized assessments. One of the historically constructed and epitomical measures of merit has been the SAT college admissions test. The fourth chapter examines the ontology of the apparatus of the SAT and its association with conceptions of "meritocracy"; how the apparatus is socially understood by test-takers and how that influences preparation (if any); and the effect of enfolded sedimentary historiality of grandparent education with grandchild SAT performance.

This chapter begins by briefly discussing the social history of the SAT while putting into question the democratic aims of meritocracy. I then review the body of literature on family background and SAT performance in order to discuss the persistent social distribution of SAT scores. Because grandparent effects on SAT performance have not been examined we cannot know if an applicant's chances at admission are partially a trace of their grandparents' social position. The recent body of research on the effects of grandparent social and economic resources on the human learning and development of their grandchildren (Dixon-Román, forthcoming; Phillips et al. 1998; Sharkey and Elwert 2011) suggests so. Most of the results of this research suggest that the grandparents do have an enfolding effect on the standardized test performance of their grandchildren over and above that of the parents. This chapter extends this work by examining the effect of grandparents' education on their grandchildren's SAT performance.

Then I put in conversation the data of film media from the series *Gossip Girl* on elite youth from an elite private school in the Upper East Side of New York City; biographical narratives from Alfred Lubrano's *Limbo* and Shamus Khan's *Privilege*; the structural equation modeling of National Longitudinal Survey of Youth 1997 data; and the excavation of Internet sources on the SAT scores of entertainers and public figures. Through this diffractive analysis it will be demonstrated that the notion "from shirt sleeves to shirt sleeves in three generations" can be reinterpreted and

understood as the rigid materialization of poverty and lack of social mobility, putting into question the ideals and possibility of meritocracy.

I conclude by critically considering how social policies of social mobility have delineated both what is possible and impossible. As an intervention into critical policy studies, I demonstrate the import of diffraction
as an analytical approach to reading and analyzing that which is said to
regulate and enable justice: the law and policy. I will discuss the history
and ontology of two admissions policies: the social mobility policies of
first-generation college admissions, and the conservative policies of legacy admissions by elite colleges and universities. By diffractively analyzing one through the other I seek to show how first-generation admission
policies fall short and how the intra-action of the two produce new forms
of inequality and power that seemingly mask the impossibility of social
mobility.

I then put myself into the larger ontological fabric of this book project. Rather than "reflecting," as if I were a distant observer, I discuss more
broadly how this work has ontologically affected my thought and understanding of questions on social reproduction and social inquiry. I discuss
what I learned both from theoretical interventions as well as empirical results. Finally, I will provide some remarks on the enfolding possibilities
of where I think critical inquiry *must* go. The ubiquity of digital technology and the ways in which the ontologies of algorithms are reconfiguring
timespace as well as reshaping material and discursive realities has made
quantification ever more relevant. I will contend that the critical theoretical and cultural studies concerns of deconstruction and new materialist
analyses of power relations are at stake and must work from within in
order to implode the reproduction of power and structural relations.

Inheriting Possibility

Quantum Anthropologies and the Forces of Inheritance

The idea of heritage implies not only a reaffirmation and a double injunction, but at every moment, in a different context, a filtering, a choice, a strategy. An heir is not only someone who receives, he or she is someone who chooses, and who takes the risk of deciding.

—Jacques Derrida, *For What Tomorrow . . .*

The investment in the identity of the limit, a limit that separates human exceptionalism (with its cultural misrepresentations) from the substantive reality that it can't know and can't be, has prevented us from appreciating that our corporeal realities and their productive iterations are material reinventions. Life reads and rewrites itself, and this operation of universal genesis and reproduction is even internal to the tiny marks on this page, which are effective transubstantiations.

—Vicki Kirby, *Quantum Anthropologies*

INHERITANCE HAS BEEN UNDERSTOOD as one of the necessary and significant processes of biology, more broadly, and of the human organism in particular. The evolution of various species, material phenomena, and living organisms, for instance, necessitates their reproduction. The survival of language, culture, and knowledge rests on the process of inheritance. *Inter vivos* and bequest transmissions of symbolic and material phenomena are what reproduces language for communication, transmits knowledge, maintains social orders, and enables the continued advancements of technologies. That is, without intra- and intergenerational transmissions phenomena would cease to exist. However, inheritance is not an all-or-nothing process nor is it something that we independently choose. From the very moment we are born into the world we are named, gendered, racialized; we are born into particular social spaces with social positionings; and we are immersed in the symbolic order of the dominant language of that social space (among other forces). Each of these social and cultural forces existed before us and interpellated our bodies upon our advent into the world. Thus, we did not initially choose these forces, they chose us and appropriated us to be the heirs of their legacy in order to keep them alive. Moreover, while the process of inheritance is necessary for social and cultural life, Bourdieu and Passeron (1979, 47) remind us that "differences that derive from social origin are passed over in silence, while those that are deliberately expressed in opinions and tastes are manifest and manifested." The reproducing and transmitting process of inheritance also enables the clandestine reproduction of social power, "difference," and inequality—each of which constrains human possibility.

Although human possibility is structured and constrained by inheritance, Derrida's quote above points toward the enabling and necessary process of inheritance. That is to say, the inheritance occasions the possibility for the heir's already constrained choice or decision about what he or she will do with that inheritance. We choose at various points in our lives how we will re/appropriate that which has been both bestowed and imposed on us for our own lives and interests. Moreover, because phenomena like language and culture are not pure, essential, or material entities it is impossible to fully appropriate them and each is constantly open for re/interpreting, re/comprehending, and re/casting in order to make sense for our own social histories and ontologies. Thus, even though there are always traces of our inheritances, there are always moments of possibility as we re/interpret, re/comprehend, and re/cast that which has chosen us.

Various perspectives on inheritance have been articulated in the social and biological sciences. This chapter seeks to begin by briefly discussing the broader perspectives on inheritance. These include genetic heritability, culture and social context/constructionism, and interactionist and epigenetics perspectives. I ultimately will argue that while they all have something of value to offer they each ultimately miss the mark and fall prey to the continued anthropocentric perspectives of the human sciences. I will then turn toward new materialisms, beginning with a development of new materialist thought and its intellectual background. I lean on work in new materialisms, in particular Vicki Kirby's deconstructive thesis "there is no outside of nature," in order to deconstruct the nature/culture binary that plagues each of these perspectives on inheritance. This will point toward an alternative posthumanist perspective on the nature/culture binary that assumes the human organism as merely another ontological expression of Earth's becoming.

Following the deconstruction of the nature/culture binary I will then discuss three forces of inheritance. The first force pertains to the double injunctive operations of the material–discursive forces of inheritance. The double injunction of inheritance holds that while what one inherits chooses and appropriates one's body, this simultaneously occasions the possibility for one's constrained and material–discursive choice. This will frame my discussion on the role of inheritance in the social production of space, the inherited products of space, and the spatially producing context of lifelong and intergenerational forces. I move toward the entanglement of time and space by considering the ways in which inheritance is a trace of complex, differentiated, and enfolding sedimentations of historiality. The third process I discuss considers the ways in which the inheritance of a multiplicity of social differences is always a complex, sticky, and shifting assemblage that emerges as a confluence of myriad forces in the time and space of social events. Each of these processes is discussed not necessarily as parts in a coherent theoretical whole but rather as part and partials of theoretically understanding the phenomena of inheritance.

Finally, I will conclude this chapter by discussing how this conceptualization of inheritance has implications for both theory and research on social reproduction and human development, as will be empirically demonstrated in later chapters of the volume.

Social Science Perspectives on Inheritance

The processes by which life is reproduced have been a concern of the social sciences since their inception. Disciplines such as anthropology and psychology arose to examine them (Gould 1981). Anthropometrics and psychometrics, for instance, go back to the middle of the nineteenth century. Interest in the reproduction of life and the human organism, in particular, has varied from developing a better understanding of the transmission of living organisms over time to trying to document the superiority of particular species or categories of species over others. A philosophical and empirical engagement of the processes of reproduction has deep importance not just for enhancing understandings of the human organism but ultimately to inform the design and implementation of social policy.

Much has been learned and many social policies have been informed by countless investigations into human heredity and reproduction. The perspectives taken on these processes have varied, however, and each has been structured by a binary that has plagued the social sciences from its inception: nature versus culture. On the one hand, nature refers to the fixed, essential, pre-scripted, and predetermined characteristics of matter in the world; and, on the other hand, culture refers to the processes of meaning-making, communicating, learning, and practices. While theory and research in recent decades have recognized that it is not simply nature or simply culture but a complex interaction between the two, I will argue below that these perspectives continue to be grounded in and structured by this binary. I will begin by discussing separately three general perspectives of the social sciences on nature/culture—genetic heritability, culture and social context/constructionism, and interactionism and epigenetics—then move toward a deconstructive questioning of all three that begins to proffer an alternative perspective.

Genetic Heritability

The desire to understand the variability of human phenotypes and behaviors goes back centuries. In Plato's *Republic,* Socrates engages the question of justice and explains that the differences in human behavior are an expression of their essence, the stuff that the human is made of. Although the concept of genes was far in the future, this idea helped inform the biological and genetic determinism of the nineteenth and twentieth centuries (Gould 1981; Selden 1999).

Some of the earliest work on inheritance and biological determinism was by an Austrian monk and mathematician, Gregor Mendel. In 1857, Mendel studied the variability of the garden pea (e.g., wrinkled, smooth, yellow, or green) and the heritability of each of these traits based on the cross-fertilizing of different variants of a pea plant. From these experiments Mendel developed mathematical ratios for what the expressed phenotype would be for any subsequent generation and what type of cross-fertilizing occurred in the previous generation. It is from this work that terms such as dominant and recessive elements (now called genes) were developed and, more famously, Mendel's laws of inheritance. Mendel's laws of inheritance were later appropriated by U.S. eugenicists in order to develop their social theory of heredity and genetic determinism (Selden 1999).

The social theory of heredity and genetic determinism undergirded the eugenics ideas of genetic heritability. The ideas of eugenics have their roots in Darwin's theory of natural selection and the anthropometric work of his cousin, Francis Galton. Galton coined the term eugenics and sought to develop an empirical basis for the genetic heredity of human mental capacity (Gould 1981; Selden 1999). Others later continued his work by incorporating psychophysics to develop measures of mental ability and intelligence in order to continue the empirical pursuits of genetic heredity and human development. Unfortunately, the social theory of the eugenics movement fueled ideologies of racial superiority, masculine domination, social class respectability and elitism, and heteronormativity, as well as bodily constructions such as able, feebleminded, retarded, defiled, inappropriate, and deviant. While the construction of human "difference" existed well before, eugenics provided the social theory to legitimate ideas of genetic heritability in policy and practice. Much more can be said about eugenics but I merely want to discuss the historical backdrop that gives rise to social science perspectives on genetic heritability. (Readers interested in a more thorough review of the eugenics movement should see Gould 1981 and Selden 1999.)

It is important to draw a distinction between genetic determinism and genetic heritability. Genetic determinism refers to the structure of genotypes that cause phenotype expressions. Although offspring genetic structures are copies from their parents, there are DNA copy mistakes. DNA copy mistakes produce genes that are not from either parent. An example of this would be Down syndrome, where there is a third copy of chromosome 21 instead of the usual two. Genetic heredity refers specifically to the variability of differences expressed in human characteristics within a population. Thus, the statistical study of heredity is based on populations and not individuals and, at best, the proportion of variance in the population can be estimated but not individual likelihoods. This distinction is important. One would be very hard pressed to argue against the material existence of genetic structures that are part of the makeup of the human organism. This molecular structure makes up the materiality of the human. From this perspective, it is plausible to talk about someone's behavioral characteristics as genetically determined, but genetic heritability can only estimate the variation of differences in a population. This variation is often due to DNA copy mistakes or environmental influences on genetic variability. While genetic determinism is more often used in common discourse, genetic hereditability is the concern of social science research and policy.

In the past fifty years, the fields of genetics and behavioral genetics have made rapid advancements while also making appeals to public policy. It is now a widely accepted convention that at most human behavior is 50 percent genetic and there are usually multiple genes that make up that genetic structure. Despite this widely accepted convention, studies still exist that empirically search for "the gay gene" (Hamer et al. 1993; Hu et al. 1995; Mustanski et al. 2005), for example. Other studies have also weakly argued and, though faulty, empirically suggested that while they acknowledge the environmental, the influence of genetic heredity strongly determines the variability of differences in human behavior and intellect (Hernstein and Murray 1996; Jensen 1969, 2000). They have deployed this argument to put into question the viability of social policies such as Head Start. The estimated group differences in IQ are assumed to be due to genetic heredity and not unmeasured environmental characteristics such as the discursively formed ontologies of being black, for instance. They also often ignore the greater within-group variability than between-group variability. And, more concerning, this literature commonly assumes that intelligence and its IQ measure are predominantly determined by genetics, fixing and essentializing the processes of reasoning that the instruments purport to measure.

In fact, the IQ measures themselves are cultural products that engage in discursive practices with the measured subjects. (Chapter 2 will more fully expound on the performativities of measurement.) The genetics are unobserved, yet assumed. Genetics in these studies is merely a construct of metaphysics that can be likened to a theology that preys on the "blind faith" of its ideological believers. While much of the theoretical and empirical legitimacy of this work has been put into question (Kincheloe, Steinberg, and Gresson 1996), other areas of research (e.g., epigenetics) have evolved with enhanced technology to observe these processes more directly. As I will discuss later, while both of these areas of work are making substantial contributions to the social science knowledge base, they both tread the fine line of continuing the ideological agenda of biological determinism and genetic hereditability over and against the importance of culture and social context.

Cultural and Social Context/Constructionism

Where genetic hereditability was a more common perspective of the late nineteenth and early twentieth centuries, cultural and social perspectives emerged in stark contrast in the early to mid-twentieth century. These ideas can be traced back centuries in philosophy. One of the earliest perspectives of social constructionism was put forward by Immanuel Kant in his postulation that the world that we know is merely our own interpretations of our perceptions and experiences of it. These perspectives of social and cultural influences are in no way uniform and, in fact, vary substantially.

Arguments of genetic hereditability opened the way for the depravity or deficiency argument. The framing for the line of argument was already set. If genetics didn't explain group differences in inheritance and human development then it had to be environmental, and if it was environmental then there must be something wrong or deficient about the environment of the assumed inferior group. Depravity or deficiency may be by way of economic resources, physical environmental conditions, social relationships or norms, or cultural knowledge or practices, and the marginalized are measured against dominant group standards. That is to say, the dominant group's social and cultural norms are universalized to the population and it is the marginalized who are depraved or deficient. Under this perspective, exposure to conditions of depravity or deficiency during primary socialization leads to issues of child development, maladaptive behaviors, deviance, or social and psychological pathology. The respectability of heteronormative familial structures is upheld as are the values of the dominant group. What also became known as a "culture of poverty" suggested that the cycle of poverty from one generation to the next was inherent to the poor and their values (Lewis 1966). Some leading works informed by this perspective were E. Franklin Frazier's (1939) *Negro Family in the United States,* the so-called Moynihan Report (Moynihan 1965), and Kenneth Clark's (1965) *Dark Ghettoes,* as well as later works such as William Julius Wilson's (1987) *The Truly Disadvantaged.* The depravity or deficiency lens can also be read in more recent modernist appropriations of social and cultural capital theory. In fact, it has been argued that cultural capital theory is merely a cloaking of the culture of poverty perspective (Varenne and McDermott 1999). Later in this chapter, I interrogate more extensively cultural capital theory and Bourdieu's theory of social reproduction.

While the variability of culture has been viewed in the pejorative sense, other streams of thought have focused on the transmission of language and the social construction of reality. On the one hand, Ferdinand de Saussure's (1910) seminal work on linguistic structuralism posited that language is made up of an arbitrary relation between signifier and signified and that it is in and through the difference between signifiers that signification is produced. In other words, the world is made up of a differential relation of signs that we construct meaning onto. Moreover, structuralism held that human being and doing was completely determined by social structures. Thus, who we are and how we have come to know, understand, and interact in the world was constructed for us in and through the symbolic systems of the world. The structuralist perspective was appropriated into anthropology, sociology, history, religious studies, psychoanalytic theory, and literary studies. On the other hand, phenomenology postulates that through language the objects of the social world are constructed but not the subject. The human subject is left intact as a fully rational and totally conscious and present being. It is in and through our interaction with the world that we construct the world around us and our ongoing process of becoming is enabled. Thus, although we are born into an already existing world we have full agency to make of it what we want. Although both of these perspectives recognized the variability of culture they both were central to the debates on structure and agency.

Both structuralism and phenomenology had limitations that were eventually deconstructed. Derrida questioned the dualism between objectivity and subjectivity, pointing toward the ways in which the two contaminate one another, need one another, and call into question any singular or unified understanding of either. While difference is still understood to produce signification, a sign may have multiple referents giving way to the *play* of language. It is this play that, as we will see later, gives way to moments of possibility. The deconstructive questioning of the above dualism also gave way to what became known as the "death of the subject," where the case for singular objectivity was put into question, also implying the (de)construction of the idea of a unitary and singular subjectivity that was assumed by phenomenology. The deconstruction of both structuralism and phenomenology enabled the developments of poststructuralism and postmodernism and new theories of inheritance and social reproduction.

One of the most commonly employed theories of inheritance and social reproduction is Pierre Bourdieu's habitus. According to Bourdieu, the process of reproduction occurs, in part, as the objective social world produces a scheme of dispositions which, in turn, produce individual and collective externalized actions and practices. That is to say, given one's social and economic conditions of existence, a scheme of thoughts, perceptions, appreciations, and actions is produced. This scheme of dispositions externalizes a homology of practices that is socially classifiable and, ultimately, reifies their social location. This description of the process of reproduction in and through inheritance is what Bourdieu (1990) referred to as habitus. Habitus is the conditioning of socioeconomic conditions of existence and the produced dispositions as well as the distinction in externalized practices that subjectively constitute social structures and inequality (Bourdieu 1977) and reproduce intra- and inter-generationally. One's social location is predicated by the possessed volume of the various forms of capital (i.e., economic, social, and cultural capital) of a particular social field which are accumulated via inheritance and over the life cycle.

Although Bourdieu's theory of reproduction deals with the dualism of objectivity and subjectivity it has been the subject of criticism for other concerns. For instance, Michelle Lamont and Annette Lareau (1988) argue that cultural capital cannot perform its theoretical functions. For example, educational degrees and certifications, as Bourdieu employed them in his work, cannot be a signal of class culture because these are variables that apply to members of all social classes. I also argue that despite his efforts to consolidate between the dualisms of structure/agency and objectivism/subjectivism, Bourdieu still overdetermines the schemes of dispositions and externalized practices that reproduce social structures. Even though Bourdieu's lens on the reproduction of power can be helpful, his ardent push back against Sartrian existentialism, economist human capital theory, and the political project of neoliberalism led him to overlook the potential moments, spaces, and processes of discursive agency. Bourdieu gives more attention to social space and not enough attention to the practices situated within social space (de Certeau 1984).

In addition, Bourdieu's lack of attention to temporality and historicity leads him to overlook the ways in which structures do change, and as such the restructuring of them also changes (Calhoun 1993). Lastly, Bourdieu provides an alternative view on consolidating the Cartesian split between mind and body via the embodiment of the socially structured dispositions or cognitive structures of habitus. Although he never attempted to measure these unobserved interiorized structures, several studies in sociology and education have done so (e.g., Dumais 2002; Lee and Bowen 2006). Each of these studies fall into a modernist trap by measuring a metaphysical construct via subject survey question responses, assuming a structuralist perspective to the reading of the survey question(s) while applying a mental realist interpretation to the subject's responses. These methodological interventions epistemologically compromise Bourdieu's poststructuralist concerns about the Cartesian split, the dualism of subjectivity and objectivity, and an assumed real construct.

Despite these criticisms of Pierre Bourdieu's theory of reproduction and the empirical employment of it, there has been and continues to be substantial and meaningful theoretical import in research on social reproduction. With the exception of work in deconstruction and other works informed by deconstruction such as queer studies and feminist studies, however, the majority of the views and theories of the cultural constructionist perspective try to radically account for the cultural at the cost of ignoring, not accounting for, or not deconstructing the "natural," or failing to see the interaction and interplay between the two.

Interactionism/Epigenetics

As mentioned earlier, many social scientists have accepted the idea that genetics at most accounts for 50 percent of the variation in human behavior, which has led to theories and empirical work that assume an interaction or interplay between nature and culture. These can be characterized in two related areas: interactionism and epigenetics.

The interactionist view assumes that expressed human behaviors and characteristics exhibit some degree of genetic influence. These theorists try to account for genetic influence in their work but tend to focus more of their attention on the social and cultural forces of influence (Gordon 1999; Selden 1999). They assume the genetic to be fixed and believe that by developing a better understanding of the social and cultural dynamics they can begin to better inform policy in ways that might be more meaningful and productive. This can be found in theories of multiple intelligence, such as Cattell and Horn's fluid and crystallized intelligence (Horn and Cattell 1966).

Another widely employed theory that assumes an interaction between genetic and cultural influences is human capital theory. Initially developed by economists in the early 1960s (Becker 1964; Schultz 1961), human capital, generally speaking, is the (innate or developed) skills, credentialing, and characteristics that an individual possesses that can be attributable to that individual's productivity. Some of the influences on the variability of human capital that have been examined include schooling, school quality, training, peer effects, noncognitive processes, and innate ability. In fact, innate influences are assumed.

The assumed influence of innate ability in human capital theory has led to many studies—in human development and social reproduction—that have used mothers' Armed Forces Qualification Test (AFQT) scores to control for hereditary influences. While generally used for military enlistment, the AFQT is used here as a proxy measure of intelligence with the assumption that the estimated correlation between the mother's AFQT scores and the offspring's behavioral outcome accounts for a proportion of variance in genetic influence. This means of accounting for innate ability attempts to avoid omitted relevant variable bias, a statistical concern that arises when variables that are theoretically correlated with an outcome are not accounted for in a model. However, this approach makes at least two fatal assumptions: (1) the correlation between the mother's AFQT scores and her offspring's behavioral outcome is assumed to be the covariance of genetic heredity, and (2) the AFQT is assumed to measure some degree of genetic influence on intelligence. However, even if the AFQT were measuring some degree of genetic influence, how do we know the estimated correlation is not measuring similarities in social context and cultural processes between the mother and her offspring? Is it not plausible that the estimated covariance might be due to the overlapping variability of cultural influences on human development? This is not only plausible but, based on the next point, I would argue it is unquestionable. The AFQT is based on a discursive process and the measured subject's responses are very much a product of her cultural history and understanding of the language and tasks in the test. Thus, the subject's response is always contaminated by her cultural location and understanding, to say nothing of the universalized particularities of definition and operationalization of the construct(s) of measurement. The latter critique is less concerned with cultural differences in the measured subjects and the problematic of bias in measurement, but rather conceives of the practice and products of measurement as cultural. Thus, the correlation between the mother's AFQT scores and her offspring's behavioral outcomes more likely controls for other processes of the cultural world and not innate ability.

In fact, when we consider the entanglement of nature and culture in the next section this argument will be further complicated.

What is more troubling about human capital theory is that it is still stuck within the modernist binds of the Cartesian split, the subjectivity/objectivity dualism, and economic determinism. By maintaining a split between mind and body, the theory assumes a fully rational and totally conscious subject. While an individual may be constrained by a lack of resources, human capital does not account for the objective structuring of the social world on the human subject. In the end analysis, the determining forces of focus are labor market outcomes and economic productivity, making human capital an epitomical theory of neoliberalism. Thus, individual decision-making is understood as an investment practice into one's human capital in order to maximize one's utility function and perceived potential productivity. The human capital theory has been widely employed in social science research and has also influenced public policy and the development of private human capital consulting firms. Thus, despite its modernist assumptions about the subject, subjectivity, and the objective social world, it has become accepted in *popular* culture.

While generally informed by modernist assumptions, the growing field of epigenetics examines the interplay between genes and their environment. More specifically, in multicellular organisms where each cell contains the same gene structure, variability in the expressed phenotypes still occurs due to nongenetic forms of cellular memory. The field of epigenetics seeks to better understand the conditions, processes, and mechanisms that drive the interplay between genetic and nongenetic forces. For biology and genetics, this *is* the study of inheritance and evolution. And from some perspectives, epigenetics is moving even closer to seeing the inseparability between genetic structures and culture and context. Some work, for example, has considered the long-term influence of cultural practices and social environment by studying multigenerational prenatal effects during pregnancy. In the case of a female fetus, the eggs she will have for the rest of her life are produced just a few weeks after conception, indicating that the eggs of a mother's grandchildren are in her bodily environment for nearly nine months. Work in epigenetics suggests that there may be intrauterine or environmental effects on the grandchildren's health and development (Gluckman and Hanson 2005). This work more importantly suggests that genes are not exogenous to the environment but, in fact, endogenous.

Although the interactionist and epigenetics perspectives take both nature and culture into account they still, for the most part, rely methodologically on the premises of modernist empiricism and objective truth.
They also tread the fine line of contributing to ideologies of genetic heredity, particularly when the influence of the genetic is privileged over and
against the cultural. More important, both of these perspectives treat the
categories of nature and culture as separate, maintaining their identities
and the problematic Cartesian split, upholding anthropocentrism and the
assumed irreducibility of their difference.

Toward New Materialisms: A Posthumanist Intervention

The three general perspectives of the social sciences on nature and culture
have continued to treat these categories as separate and irreducibly different. While most scholars will take an interactionist approach that at least
acknowledges the existence of nature, this still assumes that nature is the
separate and pre-scripted space that predates the cultural inventions of the
human. However, none of these perspectives interrogates the assumed difference between these two categories or critically considers the ways in
which they may be entangled. Here, I begin by intellectually situating and
developing new materialist thought and then lean on new materialist deconstructions of the nature/culture binary. I discuss the ways in which the
identities of nature and culture are coconstitutive, entangled, and variable
cuts from the same larger fabric and point toward new questions and possibilities in the study of inheritance and social reproduction in education.
    While the radical division between nature and culture goes back to
early philosophical thinkers such as Plato, Descartes and his idea of the
cogito, and Newtonian physics, the social sciences inherited these modernist assumptions in Auguste Comte's philosophical and political project
of positivism. The "social physics" that Comte developed was situated on
not just the Cartesian split between nature and culture but also the definition of matter as "corporeal substance constituted of length, breadth,
and thickness; as extended, uniform, and inert" (Coole and Frost 2010). It
was this definition of matter that became constitutive of the natural world
and the basis of quantification for both the natural and social sciences. As
understood in modernist social science, the "truths" of the social, cultural,
and psychological world are accessible via the rigorous study of the materiality of human phenomena, as that materiality is said to be fixed and

pre-scripted, predating human symbolic consciousness and sociality. The material of human phenomena includes not just the solid, inert forms of physical matter but also the corporeality of human social behavior. Based on this logic, mathematical reasoning about that which is quantifiable is necessary in order to unlock the "truths" of the social world. As will be discussed further in chapter 2, Comte's positivist philosophy forged what later became known as the quantitative imperative in the social sciences. The modernist philosophy of social science not only rests on the division between nature and culture but, in fact, necessitates a conception of matter and human materiality that is a corporeal substance with fixed and uniform properties and that predates human ontology.

The positivist conception of matter and the assumed nature/culture binary was challenged in the mid-twentieth century by work in the sociology of science (e.g., Berger and Luckmann's *Social Construction of Reality*) and postmodern philosophy. Deconstruction and poststructuralism, in particular, interrogated the binary between nature and culture, moving in promising directions that put into question matter, the body, truth, the metanarratives and models of science, and the instrumentation and interpretation of the products of science. Jacques Derrida posited the aphorism, "there is no outside of the text." Similarly, Judith Butler recasts this thesis as "there is no outside of culture," while Michel Foucault argues that "there is no outside of power/knowledge." Each of these postulations extends the reading, scripting, and meaning-making of culture beyond the written text to have no limits. That is, even things that are understood to be the objects of nature become signifiers whose reading and interpretation is always contaminated or obscured by culture. This provokes the questioning of the scientific and, by extension, the possibilities of ascertaining truth via the logic and instruments of the scientific method. The assumed natural division of the sexes, as an example, becomes bodily signifiers for the cultural construction of gender. In other words, this powerful theoretical move reconfigured the ontology and the epistemological possibilities of nature, rendering the objects of science unintelligible, incomprehensible, and incalculable.

While the deconstructive workings of these aphorisms put into question the foundations of both science and the nature/culture binary, they still preserved the separate identities of the two. They extended the limits of culture, making everything a symbolic text of the cultural landscape, but ultimately failed to interrogate the identity and ontology of nature. Nature remained ontologically preserved with fixed essential characteristics yet epistemologically inaccessible due to the ubiquity and inescapability of culture. Thus, the specters of Cartesianism reared up again in the culture (mind) and nature (body) split.

In order to push the envelope in considering the ways in which the categories of nature and culture are entangled, Vicki Kirby raises the following provocative question: "To what extent is nature culture and culture nature?" More specifically, Kirby reappropriates Derrida's aphorism to consider "there is no outside of nature." In this thesis, she makes two important arguments: (1) nature has always engaged in cultural processes of communicating, reading, meaning-making, and decision-making, and (2) the human organism is one of the infinite expressions of Earth's ontology. Both of these arguments reconfigure the ontological and epistemological entanglements of nature and culture, pushing the limits of the cultural fabric of life while reconsidering the powerful language of science and technology.

The entanglement between nature and culture and the ontological reconceiving of matter has been taken up by several scholars of new materialist feminisms. Thinkers such as Stacy Alaimo, Karen Barad, Jane Bennet, Diana Coole, Samantha Frost, Donna Harraway, Susan Hekman, and Vicki Kirby, among others, have taken seriously the remarkable theoretical and empirical developments in the natural and physical sciences that challenge modernist and postmodernist understandings of the matter of nature. These developments fall into two main areas: ontologies of more-than-human organisms, and new theoretical and empirical understandings of matter.

Ontologies of More-Than-Human Organisms

The processes of discernment, decision-making, reading, scripting, and communicating have traditionally been assumed to set the human apart from other living organisms, with symbolic consciousness and language separating the human from the nonhuman, or "animal." Work in complexity science and biosemiotics has demonstrated a process of reading and discerning that takes place all the way down to the cellular level, a process of decision-making wherein the decision to open up to the wrong cell may result in death. Swimme and Tucker explain:

> In a simple but elegant form, awareness appears in unicellular organisms. The capacity for discernment resides in a thin outer layer of each cell, called its membrane. The membrane, through

its receptor and channel proteins, selects what is of interest and what is not, what will enter and what will not. Each cell encounters a wide spectrum of atoms and molecules and other organisms floating alongside it. Each time the cell makes contact, primitive discernment emerges.

In the vast majority of these interactions, the membrane remains tightly sealed in order to block a novel molecule from its inner life. However, in encounters with molecules of particular configurations, the cell responds very differently. The molecules of the cell's membrane latch onto this new molecule. The cell then alters the structure of its own membrane so that this molecule can be drawn in. Because of this discernment, the new molecule becomes part of the cell's internal milieu. In this way the cell finds and captures its "food"—the energetic molecules it can digest.

Discernment is crucial. Mistaken decisions can lead to death because the inner coherence may be broken by the strange new guest-molecule. Thus, at the edge of its body, each cell makes an elemental choice. Is this a risk worth taking? Is this food nourishing? Will this increase the chances of remaining alive? (2011, 50–51)

Despite the anthropomorphizing, these are the plausible decisions a cell must make for its survival. This describes the cellular-level discursive processes that take place in the traditionally constituted natural world. There are many other examples of these semiotic processes (I would refer the interested reader to Hoffmeyer's 2008 *Biosemiotics*).

Work in biosemiotics has not only pointed toward the communicative and interpretive processes of nature but also the forming, storing, and passing of information. Storing and passing information is one of the most critical and ingenious processes of life, as it is here that living organisms not only reproduce themselves but enable development, creative adaptability, and survival. The best-known biological example of this is DNA. New research has discovered that genes do not determine phenotype, psychic, or behavioral characteristics (Hoffmeyer 2008). Genes are merely passive codes of information or instructions. The actors, readers, and translators of these passive codes are the membranes of egg cells, which interpret the coding system of genetic structures as situated in time and space. In other words, reading and interpreting the coding system is very much contingent on the temporal and spatial context in which the interpretation takes place, which results in material effects that occur in often unpredictable ways. Even the genetic code is not singular but, in fact, a code-duality based on the interplay and message exchange between both digital coding (i.e., code for memory) and analog coding (i.e., code for action or behavior). The code-duality as situated in a temporal and spatial context highlights the creative brilliance and adaptability of living organisms while further complicating the translational process of life. Life is a semiotic process; life is semiotic survival.

The simple deterministic DNA narrative has never been an accurate account of human behavior. This became ever-more clear with the work of the human genome project (Coole and Frost 2010; Wynne 2005). Initially it was believed that each gene produced distinct corresponding trait characteristics and that once these were clearly determined, greater genetic interventions could prevent or produce these particular trait characteristics. To the surprise of many, geneticists found a much smaller number of human genomes than expected, overturning the preexisting paradigm of simple genetic determinism and accepting the idea that the variability in human phenotypic characteristics must involve much more complex interactions between genes and several other factors such as hormonal and neurochemical processes, diet, and environment (Coole and Frost 2010; Wynne 2005).

Developments from the human genome project, complexity theory, and biosemiotics indicate that the social sciences have overlooked the creative brilliance and adaptability of life (Coole and Frost 2010; Hoffmeyer 2008; Swimme and Tucker 2011; Wynne 2005). More important, these developments challenge conceptions of the corporeal body and the assumed materiality of the natural phenomena that is the human. The vibrant and acting organisms that compose the human corporeality *are* ontologies that *do* read, create, discern, and act in nonfixed and situated ways. To assume fixed, uniform, and pre-scripted bodily substance is to miss not only the creative subtleties of the body but the ways in which they covary, adapt, and shift with the material conditions of socioeconomics, race, gender, disability, or sexualized structural relations.

New Theoretical and Empirical Knowledge of Matter

The developments in the biological sciences have paralleled and been influenced by discoveries in the physical sciences. Complexity theory,

quantum physics, and chaos theory have all challenged modernist conceptions of matter. New materialists have taken these developments seriously,
moving away from conceptions of matter as an inert substance subject to
the forces of predictable causal processes. For new materialists, matter is
active, vibrant, creative, productive, and unpredictable (Coole and Frost
2010). Agency is no longer understood to be simply situated within the
realm of the human.

   New materialists have revisited twentieth-century theories and research
that challenge assumptions that matter is solid and inert. Einstein's theory
of relativity, for example, demonstrated that matter and energy are equiva-
lents, challenging the previous view that inert matter was set in motion
by the external forces of attraction and repulsion. Einstein's theories also
shifted our understanding of atoms. As Coole and Frost (2010) describe it,

> Vast numbers of atoms are assembled in the kind of macrostruc-
> tures we experience in the "condensed matter" of the perceptible
> world, their subatomic behavior consists in the constant emer-
> gence, attraction, repulsion, fluctuation, and shifting of nodes of
> charge: which is to say that they demonstrate none of the comfort-
> ing stability or solidity we take for granted.

The complex, shifting, and nonfixed properties of atoms push us to recon-
ceive of the matter of modernist social science empiricism that assumes
that "truth" is lodged within the solid, inert materiality of the natural
world. A reconceived understanding of atoms as nonstable and elusive
suggests that fixed, foundational "truth" can no longer be understood simply by unlocking the logic of material phenomena.

   Particles have also been reconceived in radically new ways. Although
we theoretically know little about the existence of particles, it is agreed
that their short-lived and fluctuating existence must be accounted for in
any conception of matter. Particles are "like vibrant strands of energy,
strings that oscillate in eleven dimensions" in and out of existence (Coole
and Frost 2010, 12). Thus, it is not accurate to refer to or characterize matter as having fixed properties, nor is it acceptable to assume it to be a solid
substance. The understood ontology of the particles of matter as fluctuating and short-lived energy further underscores the porous, nonstable ontology of matter.

   Putting theoretical and empirical work in quantum physics in conversation with poststructuralist theories of the discursive, Karen Barad (2007) reconceptualizes the ontology of matter and the iterative process of materialization. She rethinks the discursive as a process of *material* reconfigurings of the world via a process of iterative intra-activities. Intra-action (rather than interaction) is a process of mutual constitutions between objects or agencies within phenomena. For Barad, matter *"is substance in its intra-active becoming—not a thing but a doing, a congealing of agency. Matter is a stabilizing and destabilizing process of iterative intra-activity."* She continues, "Phenomena—the smallest material units (relational 'atoms')— come to matter through this process of ongoing intra-activity. 'Matter' does not refer to an inherent, fixed property of abstract, independently existing objects: rather, *'matter' refers to phenomena in their ongoing materialization."* All bodies come to matter, not just human bodies or the contours of the human body, but the atomistic ontologies that make up the composite materialization of the body. As an entangled expression of the world, the material conditions of the body matter "because *matter comes to matter* through the iterative intra-activity of the world in its becoming" (Barad 2007, 151–52).

The shifting conceptions of matter in the natural and physical sciences highlights the ways in which the traditional assumptions about matter in the social sciences are outdated. The above examples are only a few that new materialists pull from. Other authors have discussed further developments and discoveries in quantum physics, chaos theory, and complexity theory (see for example Alaimo and Hekman 2008; Barad 2007; Bennet 2010; Coole and Frost 2010; Kirby 2011). A raft of theories and research in natural and physical science have already challenged and continue to challenge the modernist conceptions of matter that the social sciences continue to rest on. The materiality of nature is not fixed, stable, or simply subject to causal forces. Manifold vibrant, elusive, and self-transforming ontologies contain far more complexity than meets the eye.

How Culture Is Nature and Implications for Inheritance

While the above describes the cultural processes of nature, what about the ways in which culture is nature? In order to engage this question Kirby (2011) considers a geo-logy of the human organism. That is, she develops a perspective that understands Earth as Being where the human organism is merely another expression of Earth's becoming. She states:

My suggestion is to try a more counterintuitive gambit, namely,
to generalize the assumed capacities of humanness in a way that
makes us wonder about their true content; after all, what do we
really mean by agency, distributed or otherwise, or by intentionality and literacy? . . . When we explain away this social complexity
as an anthropomorphic projection whose comparison diminishes
what is specific to human be-ing we automatically secure the
difference of our identity *against* the insect (Nature) and reiter-
ate that agrarian cultivation and animal husbandry (Culture) first
appeared with Neolithic people. We hang on to such assumptions
by insisting that natural "smarts," clear evidence of engineering
intelligence, social complexity, ciphering skills, and evolutionary
innovation, are just programs, the mere expression of instinctual
behaviors. . . . But what is a program if it can rewrite itself? Certainly not *pre*-scriptive in any fixed and immutable sense. Surely,
the point is not to take away the complexity that Culture seems
to bring to Nature but to radically reconceptualize Nature "alto-
gether." (2011, 87)

Indeed, the human is not just another animal that relationally exists on
Earth, but in fact is one of a myriad of expressions of Earth's ontology. This
perspective is in line with contemporary complexity theory and evolutionary biology (Swimme and Tucker 2011) and, moreover, further pushes
the entanglement between the cultural and natural. Thus, the study of the
human organism is analogous to the study of one aspect of Earth, a geo-
logy. In fact, Kirby asserts that if the categorical boundaries of culture and
nature had never been instituted then their identities would not exist,
would be one and the same, and would radically change our understanding of the world.

Because the identities of matter (nature) and meaning (culture) have
been instituted in opposition to one another we have to requestion and reconsider the implications for our understanding of the world, the human
organism, the study of the human organism, and inheritance in particular.
This geo-logical understanding challenges us to further consider nonfixity,
fluidity, and shifts in time and space. The ontology of the human organism
goes beyond the discursive processes of the mind to the material body
as well. This has direct implications for what questions we take up in the
study of the human (further discussed later in this chapter).

The process of inheritance, in particular, must be reconsidered in both biological and human sciences. On the one hand, biology has been assumed to consist of fixed and predetermined characteristics and processes of the natural world. Darwinian natural selection assumes an amorphous Being that has essential characteristics and engages in calculated, fixed, and logical causal processes. This assumes that there is a precise calculus of the natural world that can be deciphered and ascertained. The biosemiotic perspective and the entanglement of the nature/culture binary have undermined the foundations of these assumptions. The biosemiotic perspective, in particular, suggests that the natural world is not fixed and running on a calculated logic based on an amorphous Being but rather made up of a multiplicity of organisms with relational ontologies that navigate the world by reading, interpreting, and translating the various signs and codes in the natural world within temporal and spatial contexts. Although regularities do emerge and exist in the world they are not fixed, nor are they void of context or nonmalleable. Thus, the study of inheritance is not about the study of possible predetermined characteristics and causal processes of the world but rather the myriad of material and discursive forces that enable reproduction.

This focus also challenges the paradigmatic view of how nature, biology, or the genetic is understood in the process of inheritance. From this perspective, the body, matter, and biology are important and entangling aspects of the larger reproducing forces of inheritance. In other words, to examine the discursive processes of social reproduction in the human without accounting for the entangled material forces is to consider only a swatch of the larger ontological fabric of life.

Much has also been written about the cultural nature of social reproduction and human development (Bourdieu 1977, 1979, 1986, 1990; Bourdieu and Passeron 1977; Cole and Scribner 1974; Lave and Wenger 1991; Rogoff 2003). In fact, it has long been understood that human learning and development are situated in an ecological context. However, understanding human development in context also, like the interactionist perspective, assumes a fixed and predetermined biology of being human. The biosemiotic lens, in contrast, suggests that not only are the social and cultural processes of being human developed in situ but that the semiotic processes of the body are also situated in temporal-spatial context. This "hypercontextualizes" the processes of inheritance and human development and pushes the social sciences to reconsider not just the ecological and cultural dimensions of context but also the bodily context and the ways in which it is entangled with the particularities of time and space.

Among the myriad ontological forces of inheritance, I have chosen to focus on the study of inherited everyday practices as human expressions of material–discursive forces situated in time and space. The always-already mattering matter of the body and the materiality of everyday practices is assumed. Thus, DNA is understood to be merely a passive code-duality that is read, interpreted, and translated in nonfixed, nondetermined, and often unpredictable ways in situ. Positioned within this framework of inheritance, also, are the double injunctions of material–discursive forces and their situating in time and space. The geo-logy of inheritance even more closely aligns the being, doing, and development of the human organism as entangled within phenomena. It is to these forces of inheritance that I now turn.

Forces of Inheritance

The previous deconstruction of the nature/culture binary opens up new possibilities for rethinking the relational ontology of human bodies and the necessary process of inheritance. Here, I seek to theoretically lean on new materialist work to explore three entangled forces of inheritance as a way to rethink how we understand inheritance and, in particular, social reproduction. These forces include double injunction and the material–discursive force of inheritance; the timespace of inheritance; and the assemblages of inheritance. More specifically, I employ new materialists' work to re-think *through* these three processes of inheritance.

As discussed above, new materialist feminist Vicki Kirby (2011) pushes the humanities and social and natural sciences to rethink and requestion the inherited assumptions of the Cartesian split that has led toward reinscribed binaries of nature and culture, mind and body, subject and object, and structure and agency. Rather than assuming a pre-scripted, immutable, and fixed nature that predates culture and is inaccessible to and confounded by the cultural processes of the human, Kirby challenges us to consider the ways in which the very processes of communication and intellection always assumed to be of culture have always been nature. She wants us to consider how nature and culture are inseparable and profoundly entangled. To this end she states that entanglement "suggests that the very ontology of the entities emerges *through* relationality: the entities

do not preexist their involvement" (76). In other words, cultural processes
are not predated by nature but rather *are* nature. This entanglement of the
world, of the world's in-process ontological fabric, which we view not from
outside but rather always as inside relational observers, is what Kirby refers to as quantum anthropologies. The challenge both ontologically and
epistemologically is how we understand and produce knowledge of the
category of the human in the world. Given that existing critical theories
of inheritance and social reproduction have assumed an immutable nature
with essential truth that is veiled by culture, the implications of quantum
anthropologies are far reaching. I will discuss these implications in more
detail below.

Double Injunction and the Material–Discursive Force of Inheritance

Theories of inheritance and social reproduction are widely employed in
educational research, particularly as a way of understanding how educational inequality is reproduced both intra- and inter-generationally.
While there are many theories of inheritance and social reproduction, arguably the most widely employed and referenced is some form of Pierre
Bourdieu's social theory. Although the concepts of Bourdieu's framework
of power and social reproduction comprise a theoretical whole, his concepts of social capital, cultural capital, economic capital, habitus, and field
have been applied independently or in different conjoint configurations
in educational research. Bourdieu's work has substantially contributed to
more sophisticated understandings of how educational inequality and in-
equity are both a product and process of social reproduction.

Bourdieu's practice theory is a key component of his overarching framework of social reproduction and one of his greatest contributions. It is a
major critical intervention aimed at escaping the dualisms of the Cartesian split between object and subject, objectivity and subjectivity, and
structure and agency. For Bourdieu (1990), the structuring structures
formed and shaped the structured structures of what he called habitus. As
he states,

> The *habitus,* a product of history, produces individual and collective
> practices—more history—in accordance with the schemes gener-
> ated by history. It ensures the active presence of past experiences,

which, deposited in each organism in the form of schemes of
perception, thought and action, tend to guarantee the 'correctness'
of practices and their constancy over time, more reliably than all
formal rules and explicit norms. This system of dispositions—a
present past that tends to perpetuate itself into the future by reac-
tivation in similarly structured practices, an internal law through
which the law of external necessities, irreducible to immediate constraints, is constantly exerted—is the principle of the continuity
and regularity which objectivism sees in social practices without
being able to account for it; and also of the regulated transforma-
tions that cannot be explained either by the extrinsic, instantaneous determinisms of mechanistic sociologism or by the purely
internal but equally instantaneous determination of spontaneist
subjectivism. (1990, 54)

The socially structured cognitive structures of habitus materialize in embodied practices ranging from language, dialect, and vocabulary to what
one wears, bodily comportment, and tastes and preferences. These materializations are not just the materiality of social structures but ultimately
reproduce social structures. The repetition of the structuring forces that
individuals are born into eventually socially concretizes the social divisions of the world so they are taken for granted, what Bourdieu referred
to as doxa. Where one is positioned based on the relations of power in
multidimensional social space is determined based on the volume of the
different forms of capital one has accumulated.[1]

One of the important advancements of Bourdieu's theory of social
reproduction is the collapsing of the assumed irreducible difference between objective structures and subjective acts by making them one and
the same. For instance, the embodied (subjective) acts that are situated
in a hierarchy of social power and privilege also collectively comprise the
objective structures that structure habitus. This theoretical lens provides
a sharp analysis of the reproduction of social relations in education while
also thwarting any biological determinist or humanist explanation. It also
captures the intergenerational (and even multigenerational) dynamics of
social stratification and mobility that are not accounted for in meritocratic
ideology or policies. Despite the critically important and helpful contributions of Bourdieu's theory there are two predicates that his theory rests on
that need to be given closer reading and questioning.

The first is the extent to which the circularity of habitus rests on an overdetermination or oversaturation of structuring context. As a product and producer of history, habitus "tend(s) to guarantee the 'correctness' of practices and their constancy over time, more reliably than all formal rules and explicit norms" (Bourdieu 1990, 54). While Bourdieu relies on a history and repetition of social practices as enabling them to function, he also seems to over-determine and saturate their structuring context: "the *habitus* [italicized in the original] makes possible the free production of all the thoughts perceptions and actions inherent in the particular conditions of its production—*and only those* [italics mine]" (Bourdieu 1990, 55). By constraining social practices to "*only those*" inherent in the particular conditions of production, to what extent is there no room for alternative possibilities or subversive acts or disobedient behavior that disrupt the boundaries of the existing order?

The second predicate is that in his formulation of the objects of inheritance (i.e., the different forms of capital), Bourdieu posits material (i.e., economic capital) and nonmaterial (i.e., social, cultural, and symbolic capital) resources. This critical intervention was developed, in part, as a way to account for the more clandestine forms of transmitting privilege, advantage, and power. As Bourdieu (1986) has suggested, the more redistributive and ideologically meritocratic policy mechanisms are, the more the privileged engage their nonmaterial capital in order to reproduce their social position. Although habitus was, in part, Bourdieu's way out of the specters of the Cartesian split, he reinscribes that dualism by formulating resources as material and nonmaterial (or symbolic) and, as such, nature and culture. This reconfiguring of the split between material and symbolic resources has consequential implications for the analysis of social reproduction. I expound on both of these problematic predicates in turn.

In order to analyze the extent to which habitus rests on an overdetermination or -saturation of structuring context, I'd like to begin by considering a few Derridean (1982) concepts: iterability, citationality, and break (in context). Derrida and Bourdieu would agree that what makes language, speech acts, or social practices effective, intelligible, and communicable is repetition. However, where Bourdieu assumes a simple (and arguably linear) repetition Derrida posits the repetition to be an iterability. Building on the Sanskrit meaning of the prefix iter- (or more correctly itara-) as "other," Derrida conceptualizes iterability as repetition with alterity; that is repetition with differentiation and not uniform sameness. First,

the functionality of language in the general sense "must be repeatable—
iterable—in the absolute absence of the addressee or of the empirically
determinable set of addressees" (Derrida 1982, 315). Second, in order for
the structural context to exhaustively determine within the limits of produced conditions of a speech act or social practice there must be full conscious intention and presence. Without this there is no way to enclose or
harness the multiplicity of fleeting and drifting effects. As Derrida argues,
"For context to be exhaustibly determinable . . . it at least would be necessary for the conscious intention to be totally present and actually transpar-
ent for itself and others, since it is a determining focal point of the context"
(1982, 327). While Bourdieu and Derrida would agree that full conscious
intent and presence are an impossibility Derrida would be suspicious
of the overdetermining of the structural conditions. In fact, for Derrida,
every sign or act can be cited, and removed from its "originary" context.
As such, the citationality of a social practice is a *break* from the given context and thereby can be redeployed in a new context in a nonsaturable way.
Thus, it is not that context doesn't matter but that speech acts and social
practices are not totally determined by context, enabling the emergence of
new meanings when cited in new contexts.

Bourdieu's (1991) theory of speech acts and practices (i.e., habitus)
suggests that performative acts are situated in fields of hierarchized social
power, where both the social institution of language and the social position of the speaker legitimate or de-legitimate the speaker's performative
utterances. Thus, the force of social context always underlies the effectiveness of embodied acts. As embodied acts, the norms and ideologies
of context form and structure the bodily hexis. However, as Butler (1997)
argues, Bourdieu's structural overdetermining of speech acts and failure to
account for iterability do not leave open the possibility for future forms
and resignifications:

> The oversight has consequences for his account of the condition
> and possibility of discursive agency. By claiming that performa-
> tive utterances are only effective when they are spoken by those
> who are (already) in a position of social power to exercise words
> as deeds, Bourdieu inadvertently forecloses the possibility of an
> agency that emerges from the margins of power. His main con-
> cern, however, is that the formal account of performative force be
> replaced by a social one; in the process, he opposes the putative

> playfulness of deconstruction with an account of social power that
> remains structurally committed to the status quo. (Butler 1997, 156)

Thus, it is at the site and social interstice of the iterable possibility of speech acts that the possibility for a constrained and ambiguous agency is enabled—a double injunction that is "in the context of an already circumscribed field of linguistic possibilities" (Butler 1997, 129).

As that which is simultaneously product and producing, inheritance is a discursive process of double injunctions: for example choosing and not choosing; (re)appropriating and being appropriated; being faithful and unfaithful; autonomy and heteronomy; presence and absence; keeping alive and putting to death. Each of these double injunctions is a critical operation of the process of inheritance. Derrida's double injunction of inheritance rests on his notion of the "break" or the force of rupture between a performative utterance and the "originary" context in which it is deployed. In contrast to Bourdieu, Derrida argues that each performative utterance is distanced from its given social context and institution, opening the possibility of future forms in new context. In fact, the double injunctive operations of discursive processes are arguably one of the most important operations of inheritance because although always-already formed and shaped they enable alternative and new possibilities. Inheritance is that which both constrains and enables, maintains and evolves the ontological fabric of life.

The object of inheritance is a gift. As we learn from Marcel Mauss (1990), the gift is never free or pure but rather always assumes recompense. The assumed recompense in the gift produces an economy of exchange that does not enhance solidarity but, in fact, contradicts its possibility. In a deconstructive reading, Derrida argues that what underlies the gift is a double injunction. Because the motives, interests, desires, or value of the gift can never be fully recompensed, the very condition of the possibility of the gift is simultaneously its impossibility. This deconstructive operation that Derrida applies to the gift is also what he extends to inheritance.

Inheritance, according to Derrida, is a double injunction of both choosing but not choosing. The double injunction of inheritance holds that one does not choose one's heritage. It has chosen, even imposed itself on the heir. Yet, the imposition of the gift of heritage conditions the possibility of an obliged and constrained choice to keep it alive. As Derrida states, to reaffirm "means not simply accepting this heritage but relaunching it otherwise and keeping it alive" (Derrida and Roudinesco 2004, 3). The imposed obligation of inheritance is part of a constant iterative process of life rewriting itself that ultimately is not able to fully recompense the giver. Through the discursively formed choice and process of reaffirmation of what (violently) chooses (or appropriates) the heir, one must not just accept (or appropriate) the gift, one must (re)appropriate it in order to maintain its legacy.

Because of the nonpure and nonessential character of the gift the appropriation is never fully or completely appropriable: "there is no natural property of language, language gives rise only to appropriative madness, to jealousy without appropriation" (Derrida 1998, 24). There is always a contextual *break* between the intentions of that which is given and the heir's appropriation(s) of it. Thus, the (re)appropriation of the gift is always-already an unfaithful gesture. It challenges the gift by creating a difference between the gifter's intentions and the gifted's appropriation of it. However, it is the unfaithfulness of the reaffirming act which keeps that heritage alive and maintains its faithfulness to the legacy. Derrida also reminds us of both the multiplicity of language and the bestowing (and lack of choosing) of language. He states the following antinomy: "1. *We only ever speak one language—or rather one idiom only. 2. We never speak only one language—or rather there is no pure idiom*" (Derrida and Roudinesco 2004, 8). It is the iterability, the multiplicity, and the nonfixed nature of language that enables the discursive *play* of inheritance.

Although the law may enable proprietary ownership of material land, products, assets, knowledge, and ideas (i.e., copyright laws and intellectual property), culture, language, and meaning-making cannot be owned or possessed. Culture and language do not belong to the subject, the marginalized, the master, the parent, the colonizer, or the Other. Culture is not propertied because (1) there is no pure, fixed, or essential culture or language, and (2) as such, culture is not fully or totally appropriable. "It is the monolanguage *of* the other. The *of* signifies not so much property as provenance: language is for the other, coming from the other, *the* coming of the other" (Derrida 1998, 68). It is, in part, because of this inability to fully appropriate culture that there is a *break* and the subject is always engaging in a (re)appropriation of language and culture. Thus, inheritance is always a product of the tensions and contradictions of the interests and intentions of the gifter and the heir's (re)appropriation of the gift.

There are no limits to the symbolic. As discussed earlier, Derrida's aphorism "there is no outside of the text" suggests that every object (whether material or nonmaterial) in the world is symbolic. In line with Bourdieu's theory of symbolic capital and habitus, the symbolic world has no limits in what is included as an inheritance. This theoretical lens has the virtue of including even those traditional material forms of inheritance such as properties or trust funds. These forms of inheritance are often assumed to have fixed and essential characteristics. However, a symbolic theoretical lens places even those material forms of inheritance under the obscuring purview of culture and the meaning-making the heir places on them within the context of inheritance.

Although the double injunctive operation of inheritance is a helpful way of rethinking the process of social reproduction it still assumes a fixed, pre-scripted, and buried nature which the playful and messy vagaries of culture are working separate from, on top of, or beyond. Kirby's aphorism "there is no outside of nature" pushes us to (re)think further the ways in which nature, as inherited forms of matter, is always-already "mattering." As a way of moving beyond such representationalist thinking of matter and meaning, Karen Barad argues that matter is not fixed or immutable, passive or a blank slate; nor is it the product of linguistic constructions. For Barad, matter has an ongoing historicity. She states that "matter is a dynamic intra-active becoming that is implicated and enfolded in its iterative becoming" (2007, 151). As Barad defines it, intra-acting (in contrast to interacting) is the relational acts within entangled entities, not between them. Thus, like Kirby, Barad postulates that the materiality of nature or the body has always engaged in an intellective, communicative, and relational process and cannot be understood apart from the performative acts and social practices of culture.

> *Matter(ing) is a dynamic articulation/configuration of the world.* In other words, materiality is discursive (i.e., material phenomena are inseparable from the apparatuses of bodily production; matter emerges out of, and includes as part of its being, the ongoing reconfiguring of boundaries), just as discursive practices are always already material (i.e., they are ongoing material [re]configurings of the world). (Barad 2007, 151–2)

By reading Foucault's discursive theory and Butler's theory of performativity via Bohr's conception of matter and vice versa, Barad develops a material–discursive theory of the performative.[2] Via Barad's reconceptualizing of performative acts, matter comes to matter through the ongoing reconfiguring of material–discursive processes as the inheritance comes to rewrite, reinvent, and re-create new possibilities for life. Inheritances are material–discursive forces that are continuously reconfiguring the boundaries of both possibility and impossibility. The material conditions of inheritance come to matter in and through the ongoing iterative intra-acting performative acts.

The inseparable entanglement between materiality and the discursive presses us to rethink the material conditions of the inheritance. On the one hand, the inheritance is often thought of as a passive object that is merely subject to the constructions of the cultural world. Regardless of what the inheritance is, the material human body is also assumed to be a passive, mediating entity for the intellective interest and will of the mind. The material–discursive lens assumes the inherited object is always intra-acting with the receiving ontologies of the heir's body. The understanding and use of inheritance is never fixed and even when there is an intra-active performative choice and decision, the inheritance intra-acts and -reacts back on the heir in complex and sometimes mysterious ways. In addition, a material–discursive theory accounts for the materiality of the body and how it *matters* for/in/through inheritance. In other words, the composite of ontologies of the body and the material–discursive forces of the inherited object are deeply entangled in the intra-acting process of inheritance.

A material–discursive theoretical lens has the virtue of opening up three veins of understanding of inheritance that go beyond the material/nonmaterial binary of inherited resources and processes (as conceptualized by Bourdieu). First, as a material–discursive theory, this includes the double injunction of how the inheritance simultaneously acts on the body of the heir and enables the possibility for the heir's performative intra-action. In fact, as elaborated above, it is within the material and discursive tension and interstice of the inheriting moment that the possibility for the heir's intra-acting agency is occasioned. Agency, here, is not understood to be something possessed by agents but rather a matter of intra-active process. "Agency is 'doing' or 'being' in its intra-activity" (Barad 2007, 178). *It is through intra-actions that the boundaries between what is possible and what is excluded from mattering are enacted and reconfigured.* Second, the entanglement of material and discursive forces positions inheritance in situations rather than being linearly gifted from one generation to the next. In fact, those intergenerational gifts can also be understood as situated within the moments of the intra-active acts of inheritance, where their use and value is always deferred. While inheritance is often thought of as the *inter vivos* or bequest gifting from parents to their offspring, material–discursive forces of inheritance have the effect of not universalizing or essentializing the inherited and rather shift the focus from the meaning-making of these gifts to the situated and multiplicative doing of these gifts. Third, posthumanist performative practices provide a way for understanding the process of social reproduction that accounts for the mattering of material conditions. The local cultural and historical material conditions that both constrain and enable possibility are forces that both materialize social reproduction. We will see in the next section how socially reproducing processes are more fully enacted in the entanglement of time and space.

Although inheritance is often thought of across generations, I argue that it is always lodged in time and space; the material–discursive forces and performative intra-actions are always contingent on the material conditions and particularities of time and space. It is to these entangled temporal-spatial processes that I now move.

The Timespace of Inheritance

Many have turned to social space as a critical force and process of social reproduction. Space as a concept has long been theorized and studied in philosophy, the physical sciences, and the social sciences. In fact, the early dominant approaches to the study and practical understanding of space began in the physical sciences with astronomy and mathematics, particularly geometry. Unfortunately many social scientific approaches have fallen short by appropriating the paradigms of the physical sciences study of space, such as geography. Although not conceptually agreed upon, space—understood as distinct from place—has become understood as one of the critical dimensions of human existence and social reproduction.[3]

To account for the social reproduction of space, one of the foremost theorists on space, Henri Lefebvre (1991), draws a distinction between the production of *things in* space versus the production *of* space. He posited that social space is a social product: the social production of *perceived, conceived,* and *lived* physical place and nature. Space is both produced and producing, constituted and constituting, structured and structuring. As Lefebvre states, "social space *per se* is at once *work* and *product*"

(101–102). He conceptualizes the production of space as the dialectical process between spatial practice (i.e., perceived), representations of space (i.e., conceived), and representational space (i.e., lived). Spatial practices, in particular, are in dialectical relationship with space. They are produced by space while also simultaneously (re)appropriating space. Social space is inherited and the spatial practices that are constituted are simultaneously constituting space.

These inherited spatial practices are situated in a political economy of space that produces not just things *in* space but, more important, the *knowledge of* space. Following Marx's critique of political economy, the political economy of space also needs biological reproduction, the reproduction of labor power, and the reproduction of the social relations of production. Biological reproduction (not to be confused with a separate category of nature) consists of the reproduction of the biophysical and the familial; it is that which ensures the material reproduction of society from generation to generation. The reproduction of labor power maintains the existence and supply of the working class; whereas, the reproduction of the social relations of production produces and sustains the social division of labor. These social relations of production become critically important in thinking about and understanding the political economy of space. For instance, who are the producers of the *knowledge of* space? Who is authorized to conceive of and become the architect or social engineer of the dominant spaces of society? How do these constructed dominant spaces legitimate particular spatial practices, symbolically exclude particular actors and communities, and coconstitute marginalized spaces?

Underlying these questions is inheritance and the reproduction of power and inequality over the individual life cycle and from generation to generation. Social space is both inherited and (re)constituted via the (re)appropriating practices of inheritance. As Bourdieu reminds us, the structuring forces of social space go undetected while the materiality of socially hierarchized "differences" are the objects of power and surveillance. Thus, the structuring force of the social context and institution of space needs the medium and process of inheritance to reproduce and maintain its structure in both material and symbolic form.

Similar to Lefebvre's political economic theory of space, Bourdieu (1990) also conceptualizes space as socially produced and structured as a hierarchy of the relations of power—what he refers to as social fields. Social fields, Bourdieu explicitly posits, are what social subjects are born

into and inherit. The accumulation of the different forms of capital determines where one exists in the power relations of social fields. Bourdieu
defines fields as analogous to games, objective spheres of action with produced and reproduced power relations that have particular logics, rules
of engagement, and structured taken-for-granted human behavior (i.e.,
habitus). Habitus, according to Bourdieu, is situated in, a product of, and
particular to social fields. Bourdieu states:

> In the social fields, which are the products of a long, slow pro-
> cess of autonomization, and are therefore, so to speak, games 'in
> themselves' and not 'for themselves,' one does not embark on the
> game by a conscious act, one is born into the game, with the game;
> and the relation of investment, *illusio,* in investment, is made more
> total and unconditional by the fact that it is unaware of what it is.
> (1990, 67)

Social fields are multidimensional spaces based on volume and type of
capital and consist of different types of field (cultural, educational, economic, religious, etc.). Each social field's rules of engagement are particular to it. The rules of engagement include who is authorized with authority
and has social power. The objective social structures of education, for example, condition, structure, and produce a competitive market of institutions, dispositions, and practices of pedagogical processes that are socially
distributed and classifiable.

Despite Bourdieu's advancements of Lefebvre's theory of space, social
fields still rest on the place and matter of nature and a linear conception
of time. Place and nature are merely the stage for the reading of space and
the practical logics of reproducing power relations. The matter of nature is
not conceived or configured as *mattering* in the production of space. Not
only does this reinscribe the nature/culture binary, it also fails to account
for the ways in which the matter of nature is reading, conceiving, and producing space. Moreover, although Bourdieu (1990) accounts for the joint
structuring effect of time and space, his conception of time is still linear
and sequential: "those properties of practice that detemporalizing science
has least chance of reconstituting, namely the properties it owes to the fact
that it is constructed in time, that time gives it its form, as the order of a
succession, and therefore, its direction and meaning" (98). The sequential ordering of practices as a "system of dispositions—a present past that

tends to perpetuate itself into the future" (156) reifies both a linear succession that unfolds in time and space as well as the identities of past, present, and future by an assumed interval that distances future supplementary unfoldings. In fact, the communicative, intellective, and discursive processes of matter, others argue, are inseparable from time and space.

The appropriated and (re)appropriating process of inherited spatial practices does not adequately account for the entanglement of space and time. Inheritance always has the markings of residual pasts and the expectations of receding futures, which constitute its nonsimple present. As Derrida postulates, meanings, intentions, and interests are always-already divided and deferred, a becoming-space in time and a becoming-time in space. These markings or imprints of the always-already absence of presence and the differed and deferred signification of the inherited are the traces of inheritance. A trace refers to the retentions and protentions of what was and what's to come. It is a symptomatic expression of enfolding (not unfolding) retentions and protentions, a nonsimple and fractured imprint of the seeming present. Inheritance is a trace, an entanglement of timespace that points toward the retentions and protentions of what was and what's to come, a historical specter and bio-graphical marking.

What Derrida doesn't account for are the mutually constituted material reconfigurings of timespace. The material reconfigurings of the intra-activities of inheritance are not simply the markings of time but simultaneously are the making of time. For Barad, temporality "is produced through the iterative enfolding of phenomena marking the sedimenting historiality of differential patterns of mattering" (2007, 180). Like the rings of a tree or the wrinkles on a face, intra-activities ingrain markings of material reconfigurings of sedimented historialities. The iterative intra-active reconfiguring of matter marks and produces the entanglement of time and space. Space is not based on Euclidean geometrics of fixed coordinates and boundaries, nor is matter situated in space. Rather space is produced from the iterative intra-active reconfiguring of the world. Through iterative intra-actions, the world continuously marks determinate boundaries of what matters and what is excluded from mattering. As we'll learn in chapter 2, this is the process of the world trying to become intelligible to itself. As Barad states:

> What matters is marked off from that which is excluded from
> mattering but not once and for all. Intra-actions enact specific

boundaries, marking the domains of interiority and exteriority, differentiating the intelligible from the unintelligible, the determinate from the indeterminate. Constitutive exclusions open a space for the agential reconfiguring of boundaries." (2007, 181)

The forces of inheritance are implicated in this mutually constituted and intra-active dance between time, space, and matter.

Building on Derrida and Barad, Kirby (2011) further deconstructs the identity of origin, challenging conceptions of time that assume a basic unfolding of time (e.g., Bourdieu). The entanglement of the categories of timespace, such that the traces of inheritance are the reconfiguring markings of always-already enfolded sedimenting historialities of differential patterns of mattering, challenges the assumed linear logic of causality. In fact, Kirby argues that "the 'future' would more accurately reflect the origin's complex identity, its discontinuities or differentiations *with/in itself*" (30). And, more astutely, she states in a footnote,

> If the ontology of time is internally entangled, if it is an enduring deferral/referral to itself, then discovering the present in the past is not a sign of hermetic enclosure and retrospective projection—a mistake—but something considerably more complex. (2011, 142)

The implication of Kirby's (de)construction of timespace points toward the way in which the (re)appropriations and material reconfigurings of inheritance are always the origin's complex and differentiated identity with/in itself.

As forces of inheritance, the material reconfigurings of timespace more concretely refer to the situational nature of inheritance. The iterative intra-actions with/in timespace produce lifelong situational processes of becoming, a material–discursive process in timespace that is the *re*writing, *re*creating, and *re*inventing of life. As a trace, inheritance is a partial and imperfect ingraining of what's possible and impossible.

The Assemblages of Inheritance

If inheritance is a material–discursive process with/in moments, events, and situations of timespace that always entails the (re)appropriation of the inherited, then how do we begin to make sense of the ongoing interpellations and constitutions of the body that are the effect of social reproduction? How might we make sense of those inherited (re)appropriations in the social ontology of the human? As mentioned earlier, when we are born into the world we are named, gendered, raced, classed, dis/able bodied, and eventually sexualized and nationalized, and the iterability of these interpellations is situational, but how can we understand the ontological complexities of the multiplicity of forces of becoming, particularly in light of the posthumanist challenge of the human organism being another expression of Earth's becoming?

These questions have often been theoretically understood from intersectionality theory's struggles with second-wave feminism and critical race studies. As a theory to understand the multiplicity of "difference," the intersectionality lens was a black feminist intervention to subvert the hegemonic configurations of race, class, and gender as well as sexuality and dis/ability among other categories of socially constituted "difference" (Cohen 1999; Collins 2000; Crenshaw 1993). Intersectionality has had tremendous influence in the social scientific study of identity and "difference" and has made important interventions in discourses on identity politics and social movements, theories of marginalization, and research on marginalized groups and intersectional subjectivities. While helpful and important, the intersectionality lens also has the theoretical misfortune of reifying "difference" while making the socially constructed essentialist categories of marginality the prosthetics to the categories of power (Puar 2007). As an anti-essentialist project, intersectionality ironically reifies the essentialist renderings of the categories of "difference" in the interests of resisting, subverting, or challenging them. Intersectionality neatly recenters the center without accounting for the complex, messy, and shifting nature of being with/in social events, acts, and situations.

As a way to rethink these concerns, others have considered the concept of assemblage as put forth by Deleuze and Guattari, who posit a system made up of the organization, arrangement, relations, and connections among actualities, objects, or organisms that seemingly appear as a functioning whole. This is not a collection of actualities, as would be understood in the English definition of assemblage, but rather a sticky constellation of a multiplicity of forces producing an event, situation, or composite grouping or body. It is a process that functions in relation and connection with other assemblages.

> There is no longer a tripartite division between a field of reality . . .
> and a field of representation . . . and a field of subjectivity. . . .
> Rather, an assemblage establishes connections between certain
> multiplicities drawn from each of these orders. (1987, 23)

Thus, it is less about the content or meaning of the assemblages, in the
sense of a signifier and signified, but rather the relations and connections
between forces and multiplicities. Although assemblages are not inten-
tional, they are purposive. Bennett (2005) further explains that assemblages are "a web with an uneven topography: some of the points at which
the trajectories of actants cross each other are more heavily trafficked than
others, and thus power is not equally distributed across the assemblage"
(445). Scholar Donna Harraway (1985) understands the body as unstable
assemblages that cannot be partitioned into the multiplicity of identity
formations as would be suggested by the intersectionality lens. Moreover,
Puar (2012) argues that assemblages have the theoretical virtue of (a) not
treating the human body as a separate and unique phenomenon but rather
directly connected to all matter beyond it; (b) deconstructing the human/
nonhuman division by acknowledging the bodies that live with/in and
with/out the human body such as bacteria and bodies of water; (c) understanding that the meaning of a substance is not only from signification but
rather a *doing* in matter, a "mattering"; and (d) social categories such as
race, gender, and class are situated in events, acts, and situations rather
than characteristics of human subjects. Puar does not want to render the
intersectionality lens useless but rather reread it via assemblages.

An assemblages rereading of intersectionalities is a promising home for
the becoming, reconfiguring processes of inheritance. As a material and discursive process situated with/in the timespace of events and situations, the
(re)appropriations of inheritance are part of the relational and connective
process of assemblages. The identitarian categories of intersectionality are
not attributes of the actors but rather the enfolding of sedimented historiality of inherited material–discursive forces in events, actions, and situations.
Iterative intra-activities lead to the sedimenting historiality of identities,
understandings, and corporealities in the world; a new materialist account
of Bourdieu's doxa. The (re)appropriating multiplicities of assemblages
are not limited to the interpellations of social categories but include the
reading and perceiving of every object within the timespace of events or
situations. As archiving and remembering beings, each material–discursive

event or situation exponentially complicates the existing arrangements and connections of objects, giving rise to (re)newed iterations and traces that come to matter. It is, in part, the in-process arrangements and connections of assemblages that render inheritance ontologically irreducible.

As an example, Lareau and Horvat (1999) demonstrate in their ethnographic study how cultural capital becomes racialized in and through the differential responsiveness of school service providers to black parents; they found that even black middle-class parents who were assumedly privy to the cultural norms of how to navigate the dominant institutions of schooling were treated differently from their white middle-class counterparts. In effect, these repetitive events of being treated differentially produced different orientations and practices by the black parents in order to ensure or advocate for the equitable treatment of their children. Differences in institutional responsiveness may be a product of what Jackson (2008) describes as a sense of racial distrust and even paranoia that produces these unintended consequences. The iterability and repetition of the affects of racial paranoia, fear, and social distrust produce preconscious bodily actions and responses to racial difference in social situations. It is important to recognize that the racialization of these social situations is not due to an attributable character of the actors but rather the discursive readings of the actors in connection with other multiplicities such as the ontology of the school, the authority of the institutional actors, the arrangement of institutional practices, and the material ontology of each actor's bodily flesh. More important, each parent's response will vary exponentially because each of them, as a body, is an assemblage of multiplicities that includes their prior experience with similar events or situations. Their understanding of the arrangement and connection of objects and categories with/in the situation will vary; and as such the significance and effect of the school's differential responsiveness will be manifold. It is the performative iterability of the materialization and discursive formations of race that gives rise to the racialized reading of these social situations.

While racial and class difference is given primacy in Lareau and Horvat's analysis, the implicit discursive formations of difference functioning in these events also include gender, sexuality, dis/ability, and linguistic categories as well as previous experiences with school institutional service providers. The assemblages of all of these discursive formations and experiences for each parent vary, producing variation in how each has been affected and affecting the situation. What would happen if the parents of a

black child were white? How might the school service providers respond
to their modes of advocacy? In what ways is class not rendered irrelevant
but functioning differently for black and white parents in these situations?
In what ways does the child's and/or parent's racialized gender complicate the situations? What about the parent who doesn't read and interpret
the assumed racial interpellations of the space of the assemblage? Is it not
plausible that there was a classed, racial, linguistic, or ideological reading
by the service providers or racialized dis/able bodied interpreting and
subjectivity? In other words, Lareau and Horvat's seemingly intersectional
analysis (that did not account for gender) misses the much more complicated, messy, and nuanced dynamics of the inherited events and situations
through falling into ontological reductionism. This reductionism misses
how the racialized trap of *doing* in these situations is both complicated and
queered by the explicit and implicit social categories and experiences of
the situations. The assemblages of inheritance with/in timespace provide
better insight into the complexities and differentiations of inheritance and
social reproduction.

Inheritance and the Ontologies of Life

As assemblages of material–discursive forces with/in timespace, inheritance complicates how we think about and research the processes of social
reproduction and human development. On the one hand, inheritance can
most certainly help to theoretically understand how power and inequality
are reproduced in society. Despite the several limitations, this has been
one of the theoretical contributions of Bourdieu's work and his theory of
social reproduction. On the other hand, the articulation of inheritance
developed here also points toward the ways in which inheritance reconfigures material–discursive possibilities. In fact, the double injunctive operations of the material–discursive process, the enfolding of sedimented
historialities with/in timespace, and the assemblages of inheritance each
point toward the empirical complexities and ontologies of social inquiry.

For social constructionists, inheritance would imply critical questions
about the conditions of discursive agency and the possibilities of empirically observing them. For instance, what are the conditions, forces, and
processes that may lead up to a resignifying or (re)appropriating act? Is
there any way of knowing or predicting an act of discursive agency? And,
are there any parameters to these performative acts? Not only are these

questions concerned with the privileged accessibility of the metaphysical inner workings of human intentionality, which are ultimately inaccessible, they point more directly toward questions of meaning and value rather than process and function. This approach remains stuck within the interpretive (and reflexive) lens of social constructionism, reinscribing the dualisms between object and subject, nature and culture. The new materialist focuses more on the relational and connected forces that produce an event and its effects. Thus, new materialist approaches are not about a search for meaning or truth but rather a recognition of process and function. These assemblages are, in part, what speak to the temporal-spatial contingencies of inheritance.

To this point I have discussed the (re)appropriating and reconfiguring possibilities as based on the iterative intra-actions between bodies, but what about the events and situations of chance, luck, tragedy, or serendipity? What about those uncontrollable and unexpected conditions and situations that have the power to profoundly affect us? Both tragic and serendipitous events are uncontrollable and unexpected events of assemblage. They both disrupt the continuity of life. They are the events of life "when life happens," when life blows in like the wind. You never know when, where, or how it will hit you but its effects are purposive. It is precisely our inability to expect, calculate, or predict these very moments, events, and situations that give them such profound power to affect us (Žižek, 2014), for if we could expect or predict them they would be within our scope of reason and understanding in the world. But change necessitates the tensions and contradictions of life and it is the unexpected and the unpredictable that both exceed and challenge the prescribed boundaries of reasoning. Impregnated in the transrational is always the possibility for the transformative. The inherited events and situations of the tragic and serendipitous will always push the boundaries of the rational but the question in each and every moment is the extent to which the heir will be faithful or faithfully unfaithful to their pre-scripted rationality. Being faithful would mean choosing the familiar and comfortable, whereas being faithfully unfaithful opens up the risk of the unfamiliar and uncomfortable. It is the movement, flow, and event of the assemblage that produce the unfamiliar and the uncomfortable and create the possible conditions for transformation.

As an example, I'd like to refer to a story told by Ayodeji Ogunniyi on an NPR broadcast of *Weekend Edition Sunday* featuring the stories of public school teachers. Ayodeji Ogunniyi emigrated from Nigeria to the United States with his family in 1990. His father worked as a cab driver in Chicago, Illinois, and wanted Ayodeji to become a doctor. Following his father's dreams, Ayodeji went to college and enrolled in a premed program. Then one evening there was a knock on the door. The police had come to inform Ayodeji, his mom, and his brother that his father had been murdered on the job. The news devastated the family.

Ayodeji was working as a tutor at an afterschool program at the time to make some extra money. The youth in the afterschool program, Ayodeji explains, were from the same conditions as the youth who murdered his father. He goes on to tell how one day a youth around the age of sixteen joined them and the activity for the day required everyone to read. The sixteen-year-old went storming out of the classroom and, not understanding why, Ayodeji went to talk with him. The youth broke down crying because it was hard for him to read. Ayodeji says, "There are many people that cry because they're hurt, they've been neglected, but to cry because you couldn't read, that spoke volumes to me." He enjoyed working with the youth and wanted to give more of what he had to "heal." As a result of the intra-acting performatives of these events, the material reconfigurings opened up alternative possibilities for Ayodeji: "Everybody at some point sits in a classroom. That could be the foundation for everything else." Ayodeji explained that, for him, the murder of his father was not going to be in vain. He changed his academic and professional trajectory to become a teacher.

If we understand the above narrative as a complex and differentiated account of Ayodeji's life events, it can be discussed as an example of how a tragic event in relational confluence with the forces of other events with/in timespace can reconfigure the material possibilities of one's inheritance (i.e., becoming a teacher rather than a doctor). These are not meaningless material–discursive events; rather, they are purposive assemblages. We all encounter events of tragedy and serendipity at various unpredictable moments in our lives. They are inescapable. Although they disrupt the continuity of life, tragic and serendipitous events are meaningful unavoidable forces in the complex and imperfect memories of inheritance. In connection with myriad other forces, they have the power to reconfigure the possibilities of our life trajectories. These multiplicative and relational forces of inheritance have implications for both theory and research.

Spontaneous events affect their subjects' lives and often the events contain social structures, and some afflict particular bodies and communities more than others. Neighborhood gun violence kills thousands of black and Latinx youth in urban centers every year. This is particularly the case in low-income neighborhoods of color. The early taking of a life is always a spontaneous event of tragedy. As parents, family, and peers we almost never anticipate young loved ones losing their life due to a violent crime, let alone predict or expect the timespace of the material event. However, these tragic events have afflicted poor urban marginalized communities of color far more than any of their wealthier counterparts. And, as we will see in chapter 4, the spontaneity of these tragic events has a profound material–discursive effect on the lives of these marginalized urban youth and their assemblages of becoming. Urban neighborhood gun violence is one example of many possible inherited spontaneous events that are socially structured and have a profound effect on the asymmetrical distributions of power within intra-acting ontologies. Even when a material event does afflict many (e.g., a natural disaster such as Katrina), there are always structural relations among the effected/affected bodies and to the State's response. In other words, the mattering force of natural disasters materially reconfigures the mutually constituted bodies of land, buildings, and humans, where some bodies are more infrastructurally vulnerable than others. The State's response, already impregnated with/in the enfolded sedimented historiality of the differential patterns of existing bodies, often reconfigures the determinate boundaries of bodies by designating which bodies matter and which are excluded from mattering. Thus, the tragic and serendipitous events in timespace, though unplanned or unpredictable, always-already have imbued structural relations that underlie how bodies are affected and come to matter.

As discussed earlier, theories of social reproduction often overestimate the influence of the social world on human behaviors and development. From the perspective of social reproduction, accounting for and understanding the reproduction of power and inequality in society is of critical importance. A vast amount of research suggests that inequality as measured by a host of social, economic, and educational indicators is substantially reproduced in subsequent generations (Bowles et al. 2005; Conley and Glauber 2008; Ermisch, Jäntti, and Smeeding 2012; Mazumder 2005; Piketty 2014; Sharkey 2008, 2013; Smeeding, Erikson, and Jäntti 2011). This has especially been the case in recent years where both income and wealth inequality have been found to be increasing (Piketty 2014) and the transmission of both income and wealth inequality to be very rigid (Conley and Glauber 2008; Mazumder 2005; Piketty 2014). For instance, Mazumder (2005) found that 62 percent of the income inequality in the parents' generation persisted in the offspring's generation and Conley and Glauber (2008) found that as much as 58 percent of offspring from the bottom quartile of wealth distribution remain in the bottom quartile by adulthood, while 58 percent of the offspring of the top quartile remain in the top quartile by adulthood. This empirical evidence most certainly speaks to the intergenerational rigidity and persistence of inequality in the United States. My intention is not to challenge or question this evidence but rather to provide a more nuanced theoretical account of these processes; to move away from the overly determining and reducing narratives that are produced as a result of such statistics by thinking about the intra-acting ontologies of being human; and to point toward the various ways in which this work is limited—for instance, how forces of inheritance and social reproduction are not just from generation to generation but located in material–discursive forces of assemblages with/in the reconfiguring dynamics of timespace. The conceptual lens employed in much of this work has led toward methodologically limited studies that often overlook the processes within discursive situations (to be discussed further below). It is the iterability of the intra-active performativities and the assemblages of the event that give rise to the rigidity of intergenerational inequality.

Intergenerational inequality has also been the interest and focus of work in human learning and development. Given human development's longstanding influence on and contribution to the debates on nature and culture, many of the conceptual frameworks on human development have emerged out of this binary. While the more recent work has assumed an interactionist perspective or is grounded in work on epigenetics, it still has not moved toward the new materialist or biosemiotic perspective where the processes of culture emerge out of the *matter* of the natural world. How might this have implications for research on human learning and development? What does this do to the existing categories and objects of research? In what ways might this ontological shift complicate and open up new possibilities in the study of human development? For instance, not only are fixed and essentialist theories of intelligence put into question in new ways but the genetic structures that are assumed to be in intra-play with the environment are conceptualized and understood to be remembering, discerning, and learning structures themselves. In fact, just as language and practices are understood to be different manifestations of culture so too are genetic expressions. Biomarkers can no longer be understood to have essentialist characteristics and would have to be studied more closely for their discursive processes (in a posthumanist sense) and the ways in which those discursive processes are relationally evolving with other categories and processes of human development. It is no longer enough to study an evolving and growing human organism against the backdrop of an assumed fixed, *pre*-scripted and predated nature. The ecologies and matter of "nature" are mattering on/in/with human learning and development.

Human development and the social sciences have long been concerned with subject formation and identity. Theoretically, inheritance helps add to our understanding of this process more fully. As discussed above, the double injunctive operations of the material–discursive forces of inheritance and the assemblages of inheritance frame how we make sense of what the subject inherits; the ways in which the inheritance intra-acts with the heir; how the inheritance reconfigures what is possible and what is excluded from mattering; and in what ways the (re)appropriated and reconfigured affects the enfolding sedimented historialities of differential assemblages. This new materialist perspective of subject formation and identity understands identity to be a continuously reconfiguring process of enfolding sedimented historialities of differential patterns of mattering assemblages. Moreover, it is not just what is given but how the heir's body intra-acts, (re)appropriating and reconfiguring the world. One instantiation of the ambiguities of the assemblages of subject formation and identity can be found in *National Geographic*'s September 2013 article titled "Visualizing Race, Identity, and Change." Asked for a six-word summary framing their identity, subjects gave such varied responses as: "I'm only Asian when it's convenient"; "Not 'bi-racial,' not 'mixed,' just human!"; and "What would make you more comfortable?" These responses speak to the complicated, shifting, and messy assemblages of being, to how identity is materially and discursively produced with/in timespace and ontologically irreducible. The assemblages of inheritance provide substantively meaningful insights into the processes and nature of subject formation and identity.

The theoretical articulation of inheritance put forth here has profound implications for research on social reproduction. On the one hand, the forces of inheritance are always multiplicative. As discussed above, there is substantial and ongoing research on social reproduction that underlines the determining force of original social position or primary socialization. Much of this knowledge has been produced from quantitative inquiries. The generalizability and interpretive virtue of the statistically produced numerical signifiers grants them great import in narrativizing the social problem and producing the warrant for policy intervention. However, as mentioned above, given that quantitative inquiry is an assemblage with/in timespace, some relational forces are always overlooked or missed. Inherently, quantitative inquiry can only examine certain processes and functions. Statistical estimation can measurably indicate information on quantity and intensity of processes and relationships of those (re)appropriations of the material–discursive, the assemblages, and those tragic or serendipitous events. These are processes that are more readily examined by the meticulous orientation and attention to detail that the ethnographic lens provides. Yet, as de Certeau (1984) argues, some processes even miss the purview of the ethnographic and, as cogently argued by Jackson (2013), the Geertzian "thick description" that explains both behavior and context has always been an impossibility. In particular, the chance and unexpected events of the tragic and serendipitous are often missed. Furthermore, this fails to take into account the increasingly new modes of ontology that are developed and produced with new media technologies. In this context, the (re)narration of film media and biographies or memoirs can provide productive forms of data that need to be employed and brought to bear in studies on social reproduction. These are cultural productions that have privileged (in)sight into the profound effects tragic and serendipitous events can have in ways that the quantitative inherently cannot speak to and the ethnographic misses. Thus I employ both film media and biographies and memoirs as forms of data in the subsequent chapters along with the quantitative analysis of national probability samples.

Because the identities of matter (nature) and meaning (culture) have been instituted in opposition to one another, we have to requestion and reconsider the implications for our understanding of the world, human ontologies, the study of the human, and inheritance in particular. This geo-logical understanding of inheritance challenges us to further consider the nonfixity, fluidity, and shifts in timespace. The ontology of the human organism goes beyond the discursive processes of the mind to the material body as well. This has direct implications for what questions we take up, and how, in the study of the human. For instance, while critical theoretical understandings of race lodge the construct in the performative and

ideological work of discursive situations, this does not preclude questioning the "biologizing" of race. If the communicative, interpretive, and
translational processes of the body are situated in timespace then there
are plausible questions of the biosemiotic, material effects of the racially
performative acts of the assemblages of events, actions, or situations. As
Hames-Garcia suggests,

> (1) Race has a material-economic reality in the immediate effects
> and legacies of racism. (2) Race has a social and psychological
> reality as an existing system of beliefs and attitudes with material
> effects (this would include certain epistemic effects on the produc-
> tion and acquisition of knowledge). (3) Race exists in a physical or
> biological form, as bodily matter. (2008, 321)

In other words, what are the nonfixed and non-predetermined material
consequences of the ideological hailing of race in material–discursive
situations? I take this question up more directly in chapter 3. This is one
example among a myriad that will need further reconceptualizing to account for the entanglement of matter and meaning.

The social sciences would also have to deal with the entanglement of
ontology and epistemology, what Karen Barad calls an onto-epistemology,
the study of practices of knowing in being, in social inquiry. The dominant
epistemological approaches to existing social science research continue
to be stuck within the oppositional confines of subject and object. This
suggests that there are social phenomena (i.e., objects) that are of interest
for further understanding, and the research actor (i.e., subject) is understood as an outside onlooker objectively examining and analyzing. Even
when research actors are understood as social subjects who hold their
own ideologies of the world and who necessarily must engage in reflexive
practices of inquiry, they are still positioned as outside onlookers who are
attempting to represent or mirror the world. This is taken up more directly
in chapter 2.

The ongoing divide between the quantitative and the qualitative is put
into question in the current work, particularly given the deconstruction of
the nature/culture binary. More specifically, the sciences of modernism
and the privileging of the quantitative have rested on two assumptions:
(1) the philosophy of science assumption that underlying the processes of
the natural world there are mathematical laws and (2) because of this the

quantitative is more closely aligned to the fixed, pure, and essential characteristics of the natural world. From there emerged what became known as the quantitative imperative in the social sciences. The quantitative imperative suggests that in order for any discipline that studies the human to be legitimated as a science it has to employ the methods of mathematical reasoning. Only in and through these forms of empirical reasoning could knowledge about the human be produced. Both of these assumptions rest on the longstanding Cartesian split between nature and culture. As deconstructed earlier, the meaning-making, discerning, and communicative processes of culture emerge from what has been constituted as nature entangling the categories of culture, with nature imploding the assumptions of the quantitative. In fact, the new materialist perspective would suggest that the quantitative has always studied both material and discursive processes and produced material–discursive data. Thus, not only does this make the quantitative simply a special case of the ethnographic but renders such produced material–discursive data as mutually constitutive.

The study of inheritance and social reproduction requires a repertoire of methods in order to produce the various forms of data for knowing in being. But, how can this be done without falling into the trap of representationalism? How might quantitative methods be reimagined for the new materialist analysis of power relations? And, in what ways might a repertoire of methods be engaged so as to analyze the processes and functions of material–discursive phenomena rather than meaning and value? It is to these questions that I will turn in the next chapter.

2

Cultural Studies and Quantification

Toward a Diffractive Methodology

The number is no longer a universal concept measuring elements according to their emplacement in a given dimension, but has itself become a multiplicity that varies according to the dimensions considered. . . . We do not have units (unités) of measure, only multiplicities or varieties of measurement. The notion of unity (unité) appears only when there is a power takeover in the multiplicity by the signifier or a corresponding subjectification proceeding.

—Gilles Deleuze and Félix Guattari, *A Thousand Plateaus*

NEW MATERIALIST DECONSTRUCTIVE interventions on nature and culture have profound implications for the philosophy of science and the assumptions made about the methods of social inquiry. The quote that opens this chapter speaks to one of them. Deleuze and Guattari (1987) posit that the "number" can no longer be understood as a universal or abstract concept but rather must be reconceived as a multiplicity, a substantive entity that emerges from the enfolding of other elements, particles, or multiplicities. They imbue number with ontology: not a simple signifier representing the measurable social world, but possessing an ontology that is not fixed or reducible. Their reconceiving of number as a multiplicity not only challenges the modernist philosophy of science assumption of mathematics as an abstraction of natural phenomena but also puts into question the paradigmatic assumptions of social science's logical empiricism.

The twentieth century was marked by two major paradigmatic shifts in social science and educational research. The first was that of positivism and the associated quantitative imperative and the second was the discursive turn that put objective knowledge and the accessibility of "truth" into question. Although the latter challenged the epistemological possibilities of quantitative methods, the more recent paradigmatic shift toward relational ontologies and new materialisms opens up new possibilities for quantitative methods, particularly for cultural studies and critical inquiry in educational research. By engaging the implications of new materialisms, I seek to reconsider the relevance of quantification for critical social inquiry and cultural studies as I argue that the identity of the limit has constrained the possibilities for deconstruction. Building on new materialist ideas, I develop an ontological reconfiguring of measurement and statistics that is informed by Barad's (2007) posthumanist performativity and diffractive method. The diffractive method that I develop assumes the quantitative to be a special case of the ethnographic imagination and seeks to read the data of each method through each other method, with a particular focus on the discontinuities and disjunctures between the methods. In accord with Kirby (2011), I want to push the deconstructive boundaries of the cultural studies lens in order to consider the "unreasonable effectiveness" of the quantitative. This is particularly important given cultural studies' commitment to the materialist analysis and deconstruction of power relations, analyses that arguably necessitate the inquiries of quantification. At the same time, I want to destabilize the social scientific privileging of numerical data, revealing the dangers of such a myopic lens of inquiry. The diffractive lens enables the possibility of quantification while addressing the ontological, epistemological, and methodological implications of posthumanist deconstructive interventions on nature and culture. I begin this chapter by discussing the major paradigmatic shifts in the philosophy of science that have laid the foundations for social science empiricism and the methodologies of quantification.

Paradigmatic Shifts: From Positivist Empiricism to the Discursive Turn

Social science empiricism has always been a subordinate heir to the natural sciences. Many of the paradigmatic assumptions, activities, and practices of the social sciences are some form of reappropriation of the natural sciences. As Kuhn (1996) put forward, a scientific paradigm constitutes a set of assumptions and activities that attain sufficient popularity so as to displace all potential alternatives. This can include the normative theories taught in the disciplines, the methods students are trained in, the kind of questions considered, as well as the "disciplining" of both language and the corporeal, especially for the performative presentation both in writing and verbally—these all constitute "normal science." Here, I'd like to discuss what I see as the major paradigmatic shifts of the social sciences— positivist empiricism and the discursive turn—as a way to frame the more recent shift toward relational ontologies. Given the vast amount of work under both of these paradigms I focus this discussion on some of the seminal thinkers and works that were associated with the major shifts, beginning with Auguste Comte's positivist philosophy.

The emergence of positivist philosophy in the early nineteenth century was one of the earliest forces to enable and legitimize the scientific investigation of metaphysical human phenomena. Particularly in the writings of Auguste Comte, positivist philosophy was an appropriation of the scientific method to the study of the human mind and the social world. Comte not only believed that the scientific method could be applied to study the mind and social life but that this was necessary for the development of societies. Positivism was not only a radical idea but a paradigm shifter, as it had been widely held that the only thing that could be studied scientifically was the "natural" world. Positivism was taken up by major philosophers and social theorists from John Stuart Mills to Emile Durkheim, facilitating the advent of disciplines such as economics, sociology, and psychology. This appropriation of the scientific method also led to the foundations of the social sciences being built on the tenets and assumptions of the natural sciences:

1. Universals do exist for the human organism and the social world.
2. Universal truths can be established through the rational application of the scientific method.
3. Empirical observation is the only rational means of exhibiting the laws of the social world.

In addition to each of these tenets and assumptions, Comte (1988) privileged the mathematical sciences as the key analytic tool for achieving precision and certainty in the pursuit of "truth." As Comte states, "mathematical science is of much less importance for the knowledge in which it consists . . . than for constituting the most powerful instrument that the human mind can employ in investigating the laws of natural phenomena" (66). He continues, "It is, therefore, mathematical science that must constitute the true starting point of all rational scientific education, whether general or special" (67). It is from this logic that the quantitative imperative in the social and behavioral sciences was then created (Michell 1999). Thus, although mathematics and probability existed well before positivism (as will be discussed below) and were not always associated with the objective, rational reasoning of the scientific method, the call for quantification led to the later allied development of both measurement and statistics in the social sciences (Hacking 2006; Poovey 1998; Porter 1995). Quantification became an essential goal for the objective study of mental and social life. In the twentieth century, the positivist tenets were incorporated into the logical positivist and later postpositivist movement in the philosophy of science. The scientific method and quantification *became* central features of the guiding paradigm in contemporary social and behavioral science. Under these terms, the positivist paradigm became normal science, an almost taken-for-granted epistemological lens for knowledge production in the social sciences, with quantitative methods as its chief hallmark.

Despite its great acceptance as the "normal science" of the social sciences, the epistemological assumptions of positivism were put into question in the twentieth century. The emergence and influence of social constructionism and the discursive turn began to challenge the assumed objectivity and privileged accessibility of the "truths" of natural phenomena. Beginning with Saussure's linguistic structuralism and later Berger and Luckmann's (1967) phenomenological social constructionism, the accessibility of the "real" was put into question. In Ferdinand de Saussure's linguistic structuralism, we learn that language is a system of signs with governing rules. The referent to those signs—the signified, meaning, or idea—we are told, has an arbitrary relationship with the sign. Meaning or signification emerges from a system of differences, such as the difference between day and night. Thus, there is no natural relationship between the sign and its referent aside from social function. In contrast, Berger and Luckmann teach us that human perceptions and interactions with one another in social systems over time lead people to create concepts, mental representations, and meanings for the objects of "reality"—that which is said to be the object of scientific study. Thus, it's not that no "real" material world exists; the dilemma that Berger and Luckmann pose to social science empiricism is an issue of *accessing* the "truth" or "reality" of the world. Although many works associated with both lines of thought could also be discussed, these seminal works offer two different perspectives of social constructionism and their epistemological implications for positivism.

Both of these perspectives influenced a raft of works in the social sciences but were clearly disparate in their approach. On the one hand, linguistic structuralism tells us that the subject is already socially determined by the social world; on the other hand, the phenomenological social constructionism of Berger and Luckmann teaches us that the object of "reality" is socially constructed. The binary between the signifier/signified and object/subject that was imposed by these two perspectives came under the deconstructive lens of Jacques Derrida (1982). The sign, Derrida states, is said to stand in place for the signified, the referent, or the thing the sign is said to presently represent. In language, the sign merely takes the place of the absence of presence of the referent. Thus, the sign is the deferred presence of the thing that is being signified, which can never be fully present. Also, the absence of presence of meanings that are produced from difference is always deferred and differentiated. Moreover, difference is not naturally pre-scripted but is, in fact, an effect. Lastly, the deconstruction of the full and total presence of the signified also puts into question the conscious subject:

> Most often, in the very form of meaning, in all its modifications, consciousness offers itself to thought only as self-presence, as the perception of self in presence. And what holds for consciousness holds here for so-called subjective existence in general. Just as the category of the subject cannot be, and never has been, thought without the reference to presence as *hupokeimenon* or as *ousia*, etc., so the subject as consciousness has never manifested itself except as self-presence. (16)

Consciousness is merely a perception of presence and an effect of a myriad of absently present forces. Not only are the identities of the limits of the signifier and signified put into question but also the analogous object and subject. Thus, both the object of reality and the perceiving subject are rendered partial and deferred, further putting into question epistemological possibilities.

In related work, Foucault's (1972 and 1980) theory of discourse in the human sciences and the production of power and knowledge also substantially reconfigured the conception of knowledge. He postulated that when a claim is made by an authorized authority and circulated in society, it becomes believed. The belief in that knowledge not only legitimates it as truth but also creates the conditions to act in accordance with that knowledge. Given that the claim is made by an authorized authority it generally will serve the interests of the structural relations of power. Thus, as society is acting accordingly they are also participating in the reproduction of power relations. In this way the produced knowledge from the social sciences, including social statistics, becomes part of the enumeration of power.

A whole line of scholarship was also influenced by Foucault's interventions, particularly in the cultural history of quantification, including the work of Ian Hacking, Theodore Porter, Mary Poovey, and Jonathan Crary, among others. Hacking's was the first work available in English that put Foucault's archaeology to work. As a philosopher of science, Hacking (2006) examined the concept of probability and its emergence as a form of evidence. Tracing the concept prior to the Renaissance, he concludes that probability was conceived of then as *opinion*.

> Probability pertains to opinion, where there was no clear concept of evidence. Hence 'probability' had to mean something other than evidential support. It indicated approval or acceptability by intelligent people. Sensible people will approve something only if they have what we call good reason. (22)

As defined by St. Thomas Aquinas, opinion, or *opinio,* referred to "belief which results from some reflection, argument, or disputation" (22). It was during the Renaissance that a new understanding of evidence emerged. Renaissance thinkers such as Newton and Galileo proclaimed that natural phenomena were understood to be "signs" of the grand book of the universe and that mathematics was the language of those signs. Hacking explains:

> A new kind of testimony was accepted: the testimony of nature which, like any authority, was to be read. Nature now could confer evidence, not, it seemed, in some new way but in the old way of reading and authority.... Probability was communicated by what we should now call law-like regularities and frequencies. Thus the connection of probability, namely testimony, with stable law-like

frequencies is a result of the way in which the new concept of internal evidence came into being. (44)

Probability went from being constituted as opinion to becoming evidence as the measured reading of the signs-of-evidence. Here, sign refers to the signs of the natural world. The burden of proof for what constituted evidence shifted from approval by "intelligent people" to the unquestioned author(ity) of "nature": God.

Other work that was influenced by both Foucault's and Hacking's work considered why "numbers" hold such discursive power in society and how statistics have become taken-for-granted forms of objective facts. In speaking to the faith in objectivity as a cornerstone to political democracy, Porter (1995) states:

> Quantitative estimates sometimes are given considerable weight even when nobody defends their validity with real conviction. The appeal of numbers is especially compelling to bureaucratic officials who lack the mandate of a popular election, or divine right. . . . A decision made by the numbers . . . has at least the appearance of being fair and impersonal. Scientific objectivity thus provides an answer to a moral demand for impartiality and fairness. Quantification is a way of making decisions without seeming to decide. Objectivity lends authority to officials who have very little of their own. (8)

Where Porter argues that the discursive authority of numbers is in their assumed objectivity, Mary Poovey questions the assumption that statistics is value- and theory-free in her 1998 *A History of the Modern Fact*. Poovey delineates the historical distinction between positivist description and theoretical interpretation, particularly in the use of statistical evidence for governmentality. She traces the conflation of numerical representation and objective knowledge to the mathematical practices of double-entry bookkeeping in sixteenth-century Britain—not as its beginning, but as the inaugurating period and practices that could now be associated with modernity. Because of the reconceived value of numeracy as objective knowledge products of natural phenomena and the unquestioned nature of these signifiers, Poovey explains, these practices were appropriated by the State in order to legitimize practices of governmentality.

More important, Poovey examines how the modern fact was appropriated by the sciences of wealth and society (i.e., economics and the social sciences). With numbers as epistemological units, she argues, the social sciences came to rely on quantification because numbers could be understood as simple descriptors of the particulars of natural phenomena. As products of invariably governed rules of mathematics, numbers provided a seeming resistance to bias, and were imbued with an assumption of systematically produced knowledge due to the deductive tendencies of mathematics. Both Porter's and Poovey's projects interrogate the assumed epistemological objectivity of numbers and, as such, the social science imperatives and privileging of quantification.

Although not a project about statistics or quantitative methods per se, Jonathan Crary's (1990) *Techniques of the Observer* examines the historical backdrop and philosophical assumptions that undergird vision, observation, and the body of the observer. He traces the various philosophical uses of the concept *camera obscura,* which "is part of a field of knowledge and practice that does not correspond structurally to the sites of the optical devices" (8). While his project focuses on vision and the reconstitution of the observing subject, he also discusses the implications of the necessity for observable proof in the role of the measurable as that which is visible.

> What is important, then, is that these central components of nineteenth-century "realism," of mass visual culture, *preceded* the invention of photography and *in no way required* photographic procedures or even the development of mass production techniques. Rather they are inextricably dependent on a new arrangement of knowledge about the body and the constitutive relation of that knowledge to social power. These apparatuses are the outcome of a complex remaking of the individual as observer into something calculable and regularizable and of human vision into something measurable and thus exchangeable. (16–17)

Crary's interventions on vision and the observing subject reposition the apparatuses of measurement and quantification as "visionary" practices that enable the seemingly objective observation of the world. Analogous to photography's aim to represent the world it seeks to capture, the observing practices of quantification were appropriated for logics of representationalism; as a way of reconstituting the observer; and as practices of surveillance and the legitimation of power relations.

Many more works have taken a critical orientation to positivist quantitative methods (Daston 1988; Dixon-Román and Gergen 2013; Gergen and Dixon-Román 2014; Steinmetz 2005; Walter and Anderson 2013; Wyly 2009). The current work seeks to move beyond a hermeneutics of suspicion. By leaning on new materialist interventions, in what ways might there be (re)new(ed) critical possibilities for quantification? How might assumed objectivity and the observing subject be reconceived? Can measurement be conceived beyond the logics of representationalism? How might "number" be reconstituted? And, how could we make sense of the "unreasonable effectiveness" of mathematics?

The Ontological Turn: Nature/Culture, Object/Subject, Quantitative/Qualitative

In *The Cultural Studies Reader,* Simon During (1999) says the following:

> Cultural studies . . . has mainly used qualitative research in order to avoid the pitfalls of sociological objectivity and functionalism and to give room to voices other than the theorist's own. The problem of representativeness has been discounted. For cultural studies, knowledge based on statistical techniques belongs to the processes which "normalize" society and stand in opposition to cultural studies' respect for the marginal subject. (18)

Simon During's criticisms from the cultural studies perspective still resonate in critical social inquiry and cultural studies. The problems of normalizing and representativeness in statistics are important concerns that need to be held in tension. But to what extent does this radical rejection of the quantitative compromise the deconstructive project of cultural studies by falling trap to another binary: quantitative/qualitative? In what ways does this binary assume an inextricable alignment between the quantitative and positivism? And, how might the assumptions of this binary rest on the pillars of the nature/culture binary? New materialists' deconstructive interventions on nature and culture not only attack the pillars of theoretical frameworks on inheritance, they also put into question both positivist and postmodern arguments on the philosophy of science and the methods that have been falsely aligned with them.

On the one hand, as discussed earlier, the assumption of the modernist philosophy of science that says mathematical laws underlie the processes of the natural world is what informed Comte's positivist paradigm. These philosophical postulations gave way to what became known as the quantitative imperative. In fact, this imperative has become most prevalent in studies on social reproduction, where the quantitative has become the dominant methodological orientation for knowledge production. However, mathematician and cultural studies scholar Brian Rotman (2000) argues that the Platonic assumption that mathematical logic is the language of nature assumes a metaphysical deity. Rather, he postulates that mathematics is a semiotic system and a human cultural invention and practice no different from the symbolic systems of the alphabet. Thus, according to Rotman, mathematical laws do not ascertain the "truth" of natural phenomena but rather the cultural inventions based on human perception.

On the other hand, the social constructionist and postmodern perspective has also been critically interrogated for its lack of adequate accounting for matter, ontology, and the entanglements of subject(ive) and object(ive), among other sharp critiques (Barad 2007; Haraway 1985; Kirby 2011). As discussed in chapter 1, the "standard" postmodern argument, that it is the obscuring and contaminating constructions of culture that make nature empirically inaccessible, left the identity of nature intact. Work in posthumanist studies and biosemiotics reveals the ways in which matter is *mattering* and how cellular organisms engage in intellective, communicative, interpretive, and inventive processes. Kirby's lens of quantum anthropologies suggests that culture not only predates the human organism but that the human inherited culture from nature as another entangled expression of Earth's ontology. Entanglement suggests inseparability and that the ontologies of the various expressions of Earth do not preexist their involvement (Barad 2007). In other words, nature does not predate culture but rather they are inseparable expressions of the same. Quantum anthropologies then assumes that we are not outside viewers of the world but rather always inside intra-acting observers of the world's in-process ontological fabric. As Barad defines it, intra-acting (in contrast to interacting) refers to the relational acts within entangled entities, not between them. Quantum anthropologies is a challenge, both ontologically and epistemologically, to the knowledge production of social inquiry. Given that existing critical theories of inheritance and social reproduction have assumed an immutable nature with essential truth that is veiled by culture, the implications of quantum anthropologies are profound. Not only are nature and culture entangled but so too are subject and object, and subjectivity and objectivity. The entanglements of quantum anthropologies push the project of deconstruction beyond the limits of social constructionism and postmodernism.

In pushing these boundaries, Kirby leans on Brian Rotman in order to consider the "unreasonable effectiveness" of mathematics. She argues that the Platonic imbuing of a theology, a deity, behind mathematics as the language of nature is undermined by the notion of math being a cultural invention. But, Kirby asks, what gives mathematics its "unreasonable effectiveness"? How do we make sense of the impressive functionality of advanced technologies that all have some mathematical algorithm(s) that inform their theoretical engineering and enable for example my digitalized writing of these words on the computer screen? Leaning on Rotman, Kirby argues it is the power of perception as "empirically originated patterns, processes, and regularity." However, Kirby wants to question whether this cultural invention begins with the human rather than being inherited from nature. Thus, Plato's notion of mathematics preceding human inquiry and creation would include their fabrication and nonfixed prescription in time and space. To state this more clearly, During's criticisms of the quantitative (mis)place and (mis)recognize the process of intra-acting performativities of measurement and statistics at the cost of excluding the "unreasonable effectiveness" of quantitative inquiry from the deconstructive project of cultural studies.

The Performativity of Measurement and Statistics

Numerical products and methods of measurement and statistics are discursive and material practices of the world. The semiotic perspective would suggest that it is via the systems of difference that meaning(s) and signification(s) are constructed and constructing. These in-process constructions can be understood as a product of what Althusser (2001) referred to as interpellation. Interpellation is the ideological naming or hailing of bodies into social existence. When those ideologically named bodies recognize the call they simultaneously recognize and affirm ideology.

For instance, a statistical mean has no social meaning until it is placed in contrast to another element by naming or labeling it as, for example, black males. This labeling or naming also discursively forms the sign of the numerical estimate as the seemingly observed statistical mean of black males, which then acts on others in mysterious and tricky ways by reconstructing their existing understanding of black males, particularly when placed in contrast with other group means. Moreover, this statistical mean will further act on those human bodies that are socially constituted as black males. Institutions will intra-act with them in particular ways and those who discursively self-identify as black and male will also both be appropriated by this statistical mean and reappropriate it from their own situated position. This discursive process of interpellation is part of what gender and queer theorist Judith Butler refers to as performativity. A performative is "that discursive practice that enacts or produces that which it names" (1993, 13). Performativity, for Butler, is not interested in the metaphysics of presence of ideology, meaning, and intention but rather focuses on that which is produced or enacted as a result of the speech act and its cultural history. As performatives, the cultural invention and practice of quantitative measurement and statistics are discursive practices that affect the respondent and the phenomena of interest while simultaneously enabling the conditions for their discursive response.

The Butlerian theory of performativity is helpful yet limited. As was discussed in chapter 1, although Butler attempts to account for the historicity of nature she still makes the same postmodern move of an always-already inaccessible nature due to the obscuring lens of culture (Barad 2007; Kirby 2011). More specifically, she does not account for the ways in which matter *matters*, the entanglement of nature and culture, and the intra-acting processes of these entanglements. Barad's posthumanist reconceptualizing of performativity accounts for the discursivity of both human and more-than-human ontologies. She writes:

> This account refuses the representationalist fixation on words and things and the problematic of the nature of their relationship, advocating instead a *relationality between specific material (re)configurings of the world through which boundaries, properties, and meanings are differentially enacted* (i.e., discursive practices, in my posthumanist sense) *and specific material phenomena* (i.e., differentiating patterns of mattering). (139)

This posthumanist reconceptualizing of performativity accounts for the performativities of matter as well as the measuring apparatuses of the quantitative.

For Barad, measuring apparatuses are specific material and discursive practices that have histories and ontologically (re)configure the world given their intra-actions with/in the world. Apparatuses are not objective instruments that are separate from and outside of the phenomena of inquiry; they are not prosthetic instruments; nor are they mere instruments, practices, or mediums for ideology or culture. Apparatuses are inseparable and part of the phenomena of inquiry and include the researchers, the instrumentation, the context and conditions of observation, the material arrangement of the context, and all of the practices within the context of measurement. Measuring apparatuses are boundary-making practices that produce, through their intra-active (re)configurings of the world, separations within phenomena that designate determinate boundaries of what matters and is excluded, of what's possible and impossible, and of what's intelligible and unintelligible. Apparatuses *are the material conditions of possibility and impossibility of mattering; they enact what matters and what is excluded from mattering*" (148). As iterative intra-active practices, apparatuses determine what matters and what is excluded, the discursive practices of apparatuses create determinate boundaries and properties of "entities" within phenomena, what Barad refers to as agential cuts. As agential cuts, the produced boundaries and properties enact a "resolution" of an "entity" within phenomena of ontic and semantic indeterminacy. Thus, the researcher, the measuring instrument, the material arrangement of the context of measurement, the discursive practices of measurement, the sampled respondents, the produced and enacted numerical "estimates," and the phenomena of interest are each ontological entanglements that are (re)configured via their intra-acting performativities. The performative question(s) or task(s) of a measuring apparatus enact agential cuts that produce determinate boundaries and properties within a phenomenon of interest. As Barad argues, measurement is about the intelligibility of the world to itself, and the apparatuses of measurement constitute the material conditions of what is possible and impossible.

The enacted and produced numerical "estimates" of measuring apparatuses are material–discursive phenomena. As Barad describes it, "*phenomena are differential patterns of mattering* . . . produced through complex agential intra-actions of multiple material–discursive practices or apparatuses of odily production" (140). As material–discursive phenomena, numbers, measurements, or quantitative data are a product of a myriad of forces; they are indeterminately ontic and semantic, produced and producing, intra-acting agencies. Thus, the question is not whether they "capture" or "validly estimate" that which they are purported to measure but rather, as an intra-acting agency, what might condition the producing and enacting of these material–discursive phenomena? And how might these intra-acting agencies enact, produce, or come to *matter*? This line of questioning moves away from representationalist concerns of meaning and validity toward that which is performatively enacted, produced, or *matters* from the intra-acting agencies of the statistic.

In light of a posthumanist performativity of quantitative measurement and statistics, the example of the black male statistical mean discussed above needs to be reconceived. The performative act of naming the statistical mean also has a history and does not occur independently. In order to estimate this measure of central tendency there had to be a research interest in knowing something about those bodies that are discursively produced as black and male. Thus, data was produced employing a measuring apparatus that performatively asked respondents about their racial identification, gender identification, and SAT scores. Whether using open- or closed-ended questions, the performative of the question is already situated in a historicity that enacts agential cuts of boundary-making categories of identity. As such, the measurement makes intelligible the material and discursive bodies who had been interpellated as black and as male and enacted as a result of the performative act and event of measurement between the bodies of the researcher, the measuring apparatus, and the sampled respondents. Furthermore, the performative act and event measured three variables—race, gender, and the measured construct of interest (e.g., SAT scores)—and while there is variation in the discursive enactment of these categories with/in the phenomenon, the estimated statistical mean re-enacts another performative by seemingly appearing to be singular when, in fact, it is a multiplicity. Again, myriad forces intra-act with the material–discursive practices of the measuring apparatus that produces the material–discursive phenomena of statistical estimates.

Thinking about measurement from the lens of performativity provides some theoretical possibility to move beyond the logics of representationalism toward the producing, enacting, and becoming of numerical ontologies. That is, if we think about the survey or measurement questions and their item responses as intra-acting performativities then this would make the practice of measurement an ontological entanglement with that which it seeks to observe. Understanding measurement from a lens of performativity would suggest that measurement is always-already entangled with and part of the phenomena of inquiry. In other words, the positivist claims of "objective" measurement, which is assumed because of its spatial separation from the object of inquiry, are put into question by the distributed agency of posthumanist performativity, whereby intra-acting acts seek intelligibility in phenomena of which the intra-actions are an entangled part. Furthermore, the iterative intra-acting process of measurement can then be understood to produce material–discursive phenomena that are measured traces and enfoldings of the phenomenon of interest.

These measured traces and enfoldings are employed and used in the quantitative methods that produce the numerical multiplicities of statistics. The performative production of statistics is always based, in part, on the relation and connection of practices and other ontologies in timespace. For instance, the statistical mean of black males produces a performative act and enouncement: "Black males had an average SAT score of 1000." If another element (i.e., variable) were added then it would alter and complicate the performative act (e.g., "Black males in poverty performed, on average, 100 points lower on the SAT than black males from median income families"). Even the ontology of the phenomenon of race would have temporal, spatial, and material implications on the measurement of it. For instance, prior to 9/11 some members of the Muslim American community did not perceive their bodies to be racialized; post 9/11 the shifted panoptic apparatuses of the State performatively racialized their bodies. What's important to note is that (1) the material–discursive phenomena of statistics takes on a history and ontology and (2) it (en)acts on others while others simultaneously (en)act on it through their own situated interpretations and deployments/employments. Thus, the intra-active performativities of statistics produce material–discursive phenomena that *matters.*

The numerical multiplicities of statistical estimation produce material and discursive phenomena that carry the hegemonic burden of being produced through a myriad of forces. Nonetheless, the multiplicities inherent in the numerical estimates are not readily accessible. Thus, rather than focusing on the meaning of the statistical estimates I argue for a focus on the produced differences via a diffractive reading/analysis. Before moving to a discussion on diffractive methodology I'd like to first discuss what counts and the data of quantification.

What Counts? The World of Data and Bodily Responses of Affect

Since the Enlightenment, quantitatively measured data have been understood to be abstract and objective extractions from the natural world. They're said to be value free and with the application of rigorous and systematic analyses can provide information about the "truths" of the world. This view of data has not only been deconstructed by Derrida's (1967) poststructuralist aphorism "there is no outside of the text"; Kirby's new materialist aphorism "there is no outside of nature" and Barad's posthumanist apparatus and performativity provide a framing to reconceptualize the ontology of data, in a posthumanist sense. That is to say, if mathematics are discursive practices of nature and intra-acting performativities are practices of the world trying to become intelligible to itself, then data are *potentially* everywhere, everything, and ubiquitous. As Barad states:

> Things don't preexist; they are agentially enacted and become determinately bounded and propertied within phenomena. Outside of particular agential intra-actions, "words" and "things" are indeterminate. Matter is therefore not to be understood as a property of things but, like discursive practices, must be understood in more dynamic and productive terms—in terms of intra-activity. (2007, 150)

Hence, as the world is intra-acting and phenomena are reconfiguring, every "thing" has the potential to be agentially enacted. Although data may be agentially enacted in phenomena that are always-already nature, it is not the "nature" of Enlightenment. New materialist data are understood to be vibrant and intra-acting agencies of the world. Data are material–discursive phenomena that are enacted from the specific practices of apparatuses that produce determinate boundaries within phenomena. Prior to the specific practices of apparatuses, data does not exist and remains indeterminate. It is the boundary-making practices of apparatuses within phenomena that produce data with determinate resolution.

Data, thus, exist in relation to other ontologies. They are not inert productions but rather lively intra-acting ontologies that are in relation and connection with all bodies beyond them. Data are both materially and discursively produced from the multiplicity of forces that include human and more-than-human ontologies. Although imbued with sociopolitical relations of asymmetric distributions of power and "difference," the assemblages of data are produced in events, acts, and situations and not based on inherent human characteristics. This has direct implications for the interpretation of statistical estimates of "difference." Data are better understood not by an interpretation of their supposed content but rather what they do in relation to other ontologies; how they act, enact, and intra-act with other composite bodies, things, words, or phenomena.

Thus, the question of "what counts" is less about what is data and more about what phenomena are intelligible or what knowledge can be produced with determinate resolution. While data are not just structured (i.e., numerical) and are potentially everywhere, everything, and ubiquitous, I contend that there are theoretical phenomena that are beyond the possibility of enacting agential cuts that produce determinate boundaries of resolution. These are constructs of metaphysics such as intelligence, cognition, perceptions, beliefs, and feelings; constructs of often psychic processes that have a history in psychometrics and the developments of latent variable modeling via factor analytic methods.

In the early 1900s, Charles Spearman developed what became known as factor analysis. As a method that rests on correlations, factor analysis models the correlation (or covariance) structure of three or more observed/manifest behaviors, relying on the assumption that what underlies this covariance structure of behavior is a latent construct or variable. It is assumed that the observed behaviors are causal behavioral expressions of the underlying latent construct. Latent variable modeling further developed into modeling methods such as confirmatory factor analytic models, item response theory, the Rasch model, latent class models, and latent profile analysis, among others. Latent variable models are among the most widely developed measurement tools in psychometric theory. The latent variable model accommodates both person and item parameters, specifies a relationship between the latent variable and the observed behavior, and is not limited to a population model. Thus, the models allow for flexibility in inferences to be made about each item, the test, and the estimation of the latent variable. Measurement error is specified for each item, as well as the test.

As observed in Figure 1, the latent construct is assumed to be associated with and materialized in the observed behavioral responses. In fact, based on the estimated model the conditional probability of an observed response is a function of the test-taker's theta (i.e., latent score or ability). Latent variable models also evaluate the fit of the model to the data. Thus, a hypothesized model is specified, data is collected, then the hypothesized model is evaluated based on its fit to the empirical data. The earlier latent variable models were evaluated on the basis of the traditional positivist framework for hypothesis testing, but later models (e.g., structural equation models or item response models) adopted the Popperian postpositivist lens of falsifiability. Under either lens of hypothesis testing, a realist interpretation of mental events is required in order to assume that there is a "true" model and, as such, a "true" construct.

A mental realist perspective assumes that the latent variable is supposed to refer to a real mental entity. In addition, given that the interpretation of measurement error for latent variables is analogous to true scores there is a trace of the assumption of a fixed and stable unobserved "true" construct.

This (post-) positivist understanding of the relation of the latent variable to the observables as well as the realist interpretation of the latent variable are profoundly haunted by metaphysical assumptions. As an assumption, metaphysics privileges the presence of the observable over the absent presence of the unobservable mental processes, assuming that the present observable fully and purely signifies the meaning, intentionality, or consciousness of the unobserved internal processes, or mental constructs. Thus, the presence of the observable is assumed to be pure whereas the absent presence of the unobserved mental processes is assumed to be impure and imperfectly signified by the mental construct. What this assumption overlooks is the residue, the trace of prior experience in the present observable that renders it also contaminated and impure (Derrida 1982). That is to say, the present observable is always signifying something beyond itself, not quite specified. As such, the exact referent of the observed behavior is always "to come." Educational and psychological measurement is essentially an act of discursive formations of mental processes onto observed processes and behaviors in the world. Even when we think we have captured the meaning of those mental processes they are always ambiguous, shifting, and slipping away. There is no possibility of accessing

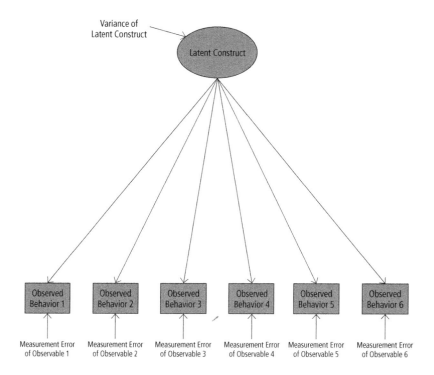

Figure 1. Classical Factor Analytic Model

the meaning, intentionality, and consciousness of inner mental processes via the signifiers of observable behaviors.

Although this deconstruction of the measurement of constructs of metaphysics might seem quasi-nihilistic we do know that affect *matters* and the new materialist focus on the mattering matter of bodies provides a reframed window of possibility. Affect, as Massumi (2002) conceptualizes it, is not action but the capacity to be activated. For Massumi, affect is beyond conscious perception and occurs more in terms of preconscious "visceral perception" that is materialized in human bodily responses. That is, the conscious experience of affect registers past experiences and situations in the physiology of the body that are "conserved and autonomically repeated" preconscious reactivations of bodily affect (30). Hence, while affects are often understood to be constructs of metaphysics the new materialist focus on affect as a reactivated process of preconscious bodily response opens up new opportunities for its measurement.

With the focus on preconscious bodily responses of reactivated affect, apparatuses are able to produce material–discursive phenomena of resolution. This is not an account of presocial affect or affect based on a fully conscious experience. Rather, this is a focus on the observed bodily responses to affective events, situations, or inquiries. By employing affect-specific boundary-making practices in an apparatus of measurement that will produce a variability of bodily responses, agential cuts can be enacted on what bodily responses are possible and what bodily responses are excluded. This may be the coded observation of the variability of embodied responses to an event. This may also include the bodily responses to open-ended or closed-ended survey questions on attitude toward or beliefs in something. Given the rapid technological developments in the apparatuses of biomarker measurement, it may be possible to measure physiological responses to social events, situations, or spaces. The focus here is not on an assumed construct of metaphysics, but rather the corporeal reactions to events, situations, or inquiries that are understood to be preconscious bodily responses of reactivated affect.

This world of data ontologies necessitates a reading and analysis that will illuminate their multiplicities. Thus I argue for a shift in focus on the produced differences that make a difference via a diffractive reading and analysis of the world of data.

Diffraction and a Diffractive Method with Quantitative Inquiry

Empiricism, more broadly, and the quantitative, in particular, have long been based on representationalist thinking and logics. Representationalism assumes that words, concepts, and ideas mirror that which they refer to. Critical scholars have long pushed for reflexive practices of social inquiry as a way to account for the researcher's subjective influence on knowledge production by radically questioning our assumptions about the phenomena of inquiry. While reflexivity has been widely accepted in qualitative research, quantitative social science research has lagged far behind because of the specters of the positivist claims to objectivity via the logic of mathematical reasoning. However, as deconstructed above, the assumption of the logic of mathematics as the language of natural phenomena is undermined by the Rotman and Kirby postulations of mathematics as a cultural invention with nonfixed pre-scriptions in time and space. Despite the stance of quantitative exceptionalism, practices of reflexivity have also been the focus of critical interrogation. As Barad argues,

> Reflexivity, like reflection, still holds the world at a distance. It cannot provide a way across the social constructivist's allegedly unbridgeable epistemological gap between knower and known, for reflexivity is nothing more than iterative mimesis: even in its attempts to put the investigative subject back into the picture, reflexivity does nothing more than mirror mirroring. Representation raised to the nth power does not disrupt the geometry that holds object and subject at a distance as the very condition for knowledge's possibility. Mirrors upon mirrors, reflexivity entails the same old geometrical optics of reflections. (2007, 87–88)

Reflexivity is like the optics of reflection. Reflexive practices seek to reflect on the representations of reality from a distance, maintaining the interest in and possibility for objectivity. Barad suggests that reflexivity simply mirrors the mirroring logic of representationalism; thus, an optics toward sameness and not difference. I want to move quantification away from such representationalist logics and beyond reflexive practices. Here, I lean on Barad's notion of diffraction in order to develop a diffractive method for/with quantitative inquiry.

In contradistinction to the optics of homology, diffraction is interested in the produced differences that matter. Diffraction is an idea out of theoretical physics that refers to the way in which wave patterns overlap and how waves bend and spread when they encounter an interfering structure. The classic example Barad gives is when waves from the ocean encounter an obstruction of land with a gap or hole in it. The waves bend and spread as they pass through the gap. The obstruction of land with a gap is a diffraction apparatus and the wave pattern is diffracted. Thus, diffraction is not about the reflective search for sameness but the focus on differences that make a difference. In other words, diffraction focuses on the nature or effect of relational and connected differences.

A diffractive methodology, as articulated by Barad, is a transdisciplinary approach that puts the theories of different disciplines in conversation.

By considering one disciplinary theory through another she seeks to pay particular attention to the boundary-making processes of each disciplinary theory and the ways in which one might rescue, recover, recuperate, or illuminate the other; making visible that which was excluded by the boundary-making practices of the disciplinary theory. My interest is to extend the diffractive methodology to have a particular focus on the methods of knowledge production. Like disciplinary theories, methods also entail boundary-making practices that produce overlapping yet different patterns of knowledge. For instance, quantitative methods produce knowledge about "how much" or "to what extent," yet the multiplicity of particularities of "how" and "why" that produce the "how much" and "to what extent" are less readily accessible. Thus I posit the importance of using multiple methods and a diffractive reading/analysis between/ through each method. This research process necessitates the employment of multiple and varied methods and con/text in order to diffractively read through multiple forms of data for social understanding.

A diffractive methodology does not mean mixed methods, where qualitative and quantitative methods are combined. While the triangulation of mixed methods focuses on the corroborating data between methods, a diffractive methodology is more concerned with the tensions, contradictions, and differences between the data that make a difference. Moreover, a diffractive analysis reads the differential data patterns of the methods through one another so as to illuminate differential patterns of mattering. As Taguchi (2012) states, a diffractive analysis seeks to make matter intelligible in new ways and to imagine other possible realities for the data. And, with its detailed attention to relational ontologies it critically accounts for the "movement of bodies" by analyzing the ways in which the various bodily assemblages are intra-acting and becoming and the ways in which my ontology, as a researcher, is affected by my intra-action with the data (Mazzei 2013). This allows for me as researcher to account for my practices of knowing in being, what Barad (2007) calls onto-epistemology. As a research process of intra-acting ontologies it doesn't fall prey to the standardizing logic of a method.

My articulation of a diffractive methodology suggests the use of multiple and varied text and methods in order to read the produced knowledges through one another with particular attention to their methodological boundaries and what's beyond; that is, no method or text is privileged over another. Analogous to Jasbir Puar's (2007) queer methodological philosophy, it is in the existing disjunctures and tensions between multiple and varied methods and text that potentially rich intra-acting data can produce more enhanced and complex social understanding. Multiple texts might include quantitative data, ethnographic data, sources from interviews, newspaper articles, legal documents, biographies and other written text, the Internet, documentaries, plays, or forms of film media. Multiple methods might consist of participant-observation ethnography, participatory-action research, visual ethnography, virtual ethnography, media ethnography, survey research methods, public opinion surveys, quantitative methods more broadly, literary criticism, narrative analysis, discourse analysis, and more. Each method and text has its strengths and limitations and, more importantly, produces different forms of knowledge. Some methods and text are more amenable and advantageous to the study of particular phenomena but the diffractive reading of the data from each method through the other methods can allow that which would have been missed otherwise to emerge and complicate/enrich the social understanding of any particular phenomena.

In the diffractive analysis of methods the focus is less on the complementarities of methods (though important) and more on how one method goes beyond or contradicts another or how there may be disjunctures or tensions between varied sorts of data. We see this with the example of Ayodeji Ogunniyi in chapter 1. If he was included in the sample for a survey examining social reproduction in educational attainment, the myriad of forces that produce his life trajectory would be part of the assemblage of the statistical estimate. When the statistical estimate is then read through his interview data, what emerges is a more complicated and diffracted difference that comes to matter. These methodological and con/textual interstices, I argue, are where the rich, complicated, and elusive forms of ontology and epistemology exist.

While quantitative methods are not a necessity for a diffractive methodology, this process provides a much richer resource for the numerical multiplicities of statistics. Quantitative measurement and statistics have methodological utility and like other methods can substantially contribute to enhancing social understanding via the diffractive reading of their knowledge products through the data of other methods. With statistics understood from the lens of intra-acting performativities, they then become ontological forms of produced knowledge and the diffractive analysis of multiple and varied methods and text can broaden the possibilities for new materialist analyses and deconstruction. It is in the messy and slippery interstices of methods and via the diffractive process that the impossible possibility of the quantitative for critical social inquiry can be found. The next two chapters of *Inheriting Possibility* are instantiations of these quantitative possibilities for cultural studies.

3

Parenting Performativities

Assemblages of "Difference" and the Material–Discursive Practices of Parenting

SOCIAL REPRODUCTION IS INHERENTLY a material–discursive process. Much of social science theory on social reproduction has rested on the Cartesian split between nature and culture and, as such, has undertaken limited analysis of structural relations. These theoretical perspectives have either understated the structuring forces of the discursive, assuming a deterministic influence of a fixed, immutable corporeal substance; or, they have overlooked the *doing* and *mattering* of "natural" phenomena. Inheritance and social reproduction are the product of the myriad material–discursive forces that are producing and produced by timespace; imbued in these forces is always an assemblage of structural relations of "difference." This new materialist reworking of inheritance and social reproduction also has implications for social inquiry. As I argued in chapter 2, the assumptions of the Cartesian split are also what upheld social science empiricism, particularly for quantitative methods. New materialisms assume that social inquiry is not the study of phenomena from a disconnected outside, but rather from a profoundly inseparable within. As such, the inquiry of social reproduction in education can no longer assume distance from phenomena, nor will the mirroring optics of reflexivity secure any hopes of objective observations. A diffractive reading and analysis that is concerned with the produced differences from the data of multiple methods is necessary, not for objectivity but in order to move beyond the logics of representationalism. This is particularly relevant for the quantitative inquiry into social reproduction in education.

In this chapter I analyze the assemblages of "difference" in the material–discursive practices of parenting, a phenomenon that has been substantially examined in social reproduction studies. Although the influence of parental involvement on achievement outcomes has recently been challenged (Robinson and Harris 2014), parenting enrichment practices have consistently been found to be associated with child development (Duncan and Brooks-Gunn 1997) and academic achievement (Dixon-Román 2013; Duncan and Brooks-Gunn 1997; Phillips et al. 1998), among other outcomes. In fact, parenting practices have also been found to be strongly associated with family socioeconomic background (Dixon-Román 2013; Duncan and Brooks-Gunn 1997; Lareau 2003; Phillips et al. 1998; Robinson and Harris 2014). Despite these findings, research on parenting practices has also been a contentious area of work given that the analysis of race and class differences in parenting practices easily slips into narratives of pathology and deficiency. In other words, it becomes how we can make the practices of parents of color and poverty more like those of white middle-class parents. In this chapter, I demonstrate how a new materialist analysis of "difference" in parenting practices opens up new possibilities for thinking, analyzing, and interpreting social reproduction.

Quantitative studies on social reproduction in education have often focused on variables of "difference" such as race, gender, and class. However, the analysis and interpretation of "difference" in social reproduction studies in education has been contentious ground; scholars have challenged the use and interpretation of variables such as race in social statistics (Leonardo 2013; Zuberi 2001; Zuberi and Bonilla-Silva 2008). Despite the commonsense knowledge of race as a social construct that is a byproduct of the social system and the process of racism, in much of the social sciences the statistical estimates of race continue to be interpreted as a causal effect; that is, race becomes understood as the cause of the differential estimation of an outcome. Consequently, this line of interpretation construes the effect as something that is inherent to race, such as biological, cultural, or social deficiencies. The same can be said about gender, class, sexuality, or disability; what I refer to more broadly as "difference." In this chapter, I demonstrate how the assemblages of inheritance and a diffractive analysis open up new possibilities for analyzing and interpreting data on "difference" in social reproduction studies, without falling into the trap of anthropocentric limitations.

Thus, I examine the following research questions: To what extent are differences in parenting practices contingent on the child's race and gender? To what extent are parenting practices endogenous to parental bodily expressed responses to gender roles and norms in parenting? How much of the group differences in parenting practices is accounted for by parental bodily expressed responses to gender roles and norms? To what extent do the parents' and grandparents' socioeconomic resources account for the variability in parenting practices? How do dominant scripts of masculinity (re)configure parental intra-actions and practices with the child? In what ways does parental social mobility affect parenting practices? And in what ways does child sexual identification (re)configure parental intra-actions and practices with the child? Using structural equation modeling and data from the Child Development Supplement of the Panel Study of Income Dynamics, I chart the associations of parents' and grandparents' socioeconomic resources with the parents' material–discursive practices of parenting, with a particular focus on the raced, gendered, and classed assemblages, and the ways in which parental bodily responses to questions on gender roles and norms matter. Interwoven into the same analytic fabric, I also diffractively read through data from the literary analysis of Anne Lamott's *Operating Instructions* and *A Journal of My Son's First Son,* Alfred Lubrano's *Limbo,* and rapper Common's memoir *One Day It'll All Make Sense,* as well as drawing from sources of film media such as the independent film *Pariah* and "How Not to React When Your Child Tells You That He's Gay," a YouTube video that went viral. By situating these multiple forms of data in the historicity of the assemblages of structural relations of "difference," understanding the material–discursive performativities of parenting as boundary-making practices, and diffractively reading through the data, I demonstrate how parenting practices are a result of myriad forces that cannot be reduced to pathology or deficiency but rather convey the inheritance of constraining, disenabling, and even violent sociocultural and historical conditions.

Research Literature on "Difference" and Parenting Practices

Parenting practices are among the most widely studied phenomena of social reproduction in human learning and development. They have been studied in association with cognitive development (Duncan and Brooks-Gunn 1997), social and emotional development (McLoyd 2008), achievement (Dixon-Román 2013; Duncan and Brooks-Gunn 1997; Phillips et al. 1998; Robinson and Harris 2014), and college attendance (Charles, Roscigno, and Torres 2007). The cultural logic has gone like this: the social problems of inequality in child development, achievement, college attendance, youth delinquency, and deviance all stem from a lack of parental involvement and poor parenting. A substantial amount of scholarly work has challenged this cultural logic by considering the material conditions and resources that may constrain the options of parenting (Phillips et al. 1998; Robinson and Harris 2014), and other work has interrogated the ideological system that produces "difference" (Dixon-Román 2013; Ridgeway 2011). Here, I want to review some of the seminal work in this literature to uncover how "difference" has been treated in social reproduction studies on parenting practices, in order to clearly delineate not just the limitations of this literature but also my point of departure.

Gender is a social category that has long been studied in parenting practices. In recent works, Ridgeway examines how the cultural meanings associated with gender frame every dimension of social life:

> The everyday use of sex/gender as a basic cultural tool for organizing social relations accounts . . . for why cultural meanings associated with gender do not stay within the bounds of contexts associated with sex and reproduction. Instead, the use of gender as a framing device spreads gendered meaning, including assumptions about inequality embedded in those meanings, to all spheres of social life that are carried out through social relationships. (7)

Parents' beliefs, behaviors, and practices inform children's gender socialization. While there is little to no evidence of actual biological differences in girls' and boys' "innate brain wiring" (Eliot 2010), parents begin to treat their sons and daughters differently at an early age, reinforcing and reproducing differences in abilities and preferences between male and female children. For sons, parents tend to emphasize the importance of independence, competition, and education, whereas for daughters parents stress the importance of manners, nurturing habits, and social relationships (Hill and Sprague 1999). In a meta-analysis of over 170 studies regarding parents' sex-differentiated treatment of children, Lytton and Romney (1991) found similarities in the amount of warmth and time that parents shared with their sons and daughters and few differences in parents' communication styles, disciplinary actions, and encouragement of math achievement based on the sex of their child. However, their analysis also revealed significant differences in parents' support of conventionally differentiated sex-typed activities, such as encouraging boys to play with trucks and blocks, and providing toys such as dolls for girls.

In *Unequal Childhoods* (2003), Annette Lareau makes an argument for the importance of social class with respect to parenting styles—making the argument that both white and black middle-class families employ what she refers to as "concerted cultivation" while working-class and poor families, also regardless of race, practice what she terms "the accomplishment of natural growth." Concerted cultivation involves constantly assessing and encouraging children's talents, opinions, and skills—scheduling children for extracurricular activities, reasoning with them, and monitoring and intervening in their interactions with outside institutions. Following the logic of the accomplishment of natural growth, the focus is on providing children with basic supports such as comfort, food, and shelter. Here children's development is viewed as something which will occur on its own, and thus these children spend a majority of their time in or near the home engaging in informal play with peers, siblings, and other relatives.

Throughout her book, Lareau focuses on the differences in childrearing practices between classes, making an argument that these differences often overshadow variations that may arise as a result of a family's race (which we will see below has also been empirically challenged). A theme that is ever present though rarely discussed, however, results from her choice to highlight the lives of both girls and boys in each economic class and each racial category. Although this study focuses on parenting at the intersection of race and class, Lareau also notes parents' reinforcement of gender-differentiated activities:

> We found gender a very powerful force in shaping the organization of daily life. Despite some active moments, girls are more sedentary, play closer to home, and have their physical bodies more actively scrutinized and shaped by others than do boys. (68)

For example:

> Much of her [Katie's] play is more sedentary than the active movements of boys, with a stress on femininity. In the house, she enjoys her Barbies (she has fifteen). With a neighborhood girl, she will have long periods of practicing the development of herself as a

beauty object (something that was never observed with the boys in the study). Katie also watches television and plays Nintendo. (86)

For nearly every child throughout the book some meaningful mention of gender occurs, whether referring to the different style of play the girls engage in, the tighter restrictions on girls' movements, how parents are concerned about developing sons' masculinity, or the gendered division of parenting labor.

Similarly, Lareau notes that working-class fathers tended to demonstrate an aggressive form of affection toward their sons, such as when a working-class black father hugged his son from behind while mocking him for watching an action movie. However, because this theme is never fully articulated, instances where gender differences may be at play also go unnamed. For instance, the mother of a middle-class black girl intervened in a situation where her daughter may have been dealing with a racist bus driver. This interventionist approach appeared to be in contrast to how the parents of a middle-class black boy dealt with potentially racist situations when their son was around—being more reluctant to read race into a situation and therefore ignoring it. However, the theme of gender differences, even in parental racial socialization, is never fully articulated or analyzed.

As described by Lareau, parenting reinforced difference through parents' acceptance and encouragement of specific activities. Hofferth and Sandberg (2001) found that the amount of time spent on reading and in organized programs increased faster with age for girls than for boys, whereas boys' time with sports increased faster than for girls. Overall, students of color spent less time in free play than their white counterparts, and girls' play time decreased faster with age than boys'. Lytton and Romney (1991) note that though other forces, such as peer influence, shape children's disposition to certain activities, parents play an important role in exacerbating differences, particularly through choices regarding clothing, activities, toys, and environment, and disapproval of "gender-inappropriate" behavior.

As demonstrated by Peters's (1994) study of adolescent home behaviors, similar sex-differentiated parenting practices emerged around activities and discipline that continue for children through their adolescence. By examining both adolescents' and parents' perceptions, Peters found that sons frequently completed outdoor chores (e.g., mowing the lawn, taking out the trash), whereas girls were more likely responsible for indoor chores (e.g., dusting, cleaning dishes). While daughters reported having stricter curfews, sons had more frequent parental permission to leave the house and use the family car. In a more recent study, Demo and Cox (2000) also found that daughters performed more housework than sons did, and the tasks they were assigned reflected gender stereotyped appropriate behavior. Ridgeway describes household division of labor as a "dynamic battleground" that is "strikingly unequal" and a basis for gender socialization (2011, 128).

Because parents raise boys and girls in very distinct psychological learning contexts, it is thought that this differential treatment influences their long-term outcomes in areas of behavior, personality, and achievement (Block 1983; Eliot 2010). Block found that parents encourage boys to be more independent, curious, and competitive by allowing them more freedom to play and do work outside of the home; conversely, girls had less experience with the outside world and tended to need more help with problem-solving activities because parents restricted them through more structured activities, emphasis on propriety, and concentration on supervision. As Eliot notes, "Simply put, girls spend more time talking, drawing, and role-playing in relational ways, whereas boys spend more time moving, targeting, building, and role-playing as heroes" (34). The implications of these early types of play and interactions with parents manifest in children's skills and abilities academically.

Other works informed by Bourdieu's theory of social reproduction have focused more specifically on social class variability in parental practices. For instance, Dumais (2006) examined the effect of cultural capital and parental habitus in early childhood on teacher's perceptions. Bourdieu (1977) postulated that while there are later social structurings where cultural capital continues to accumulate, the inculcation of habitus is most durable during primary socialization, suggesting that cultural capital and parental habitus should have a larger effect at younger ages than older ages. Using the Early Childhood Longitudinal Study, Kindergarten Class of 1998–1999 data, Dumais measured parental habitus and cultural capital and modeled their effect on teacher's perceptions, controlling for kindergarten math test score, gender, and minority status. Although the main effect of parental cultural activities was not meaningful, there was consistently a meaningful interaction between parental cultural activities and socioeconomic status. Moreover, the parents' college expectations and desire for their children to have drawing skills had meaningful effects on teachers' perceptions, suggesting an association with parental habitus. In a study informed by Bourdieu's forms of capital (Dixon-Román 2013), I examined to what extent parental uses of social and cultural capital mediated the effect of family economic capital on the growth of math and reading achievement in black males. I not only found that parenting practices were substantially associated with and constrained by family economic capital (as measured by family income and wealth) but that parenting practices in the use of social and cultural capital substantially mediated the effect of family economic capital on their sons' level of performance. Both of these studies underscore the social class variability of parenting and its material effects on the children's educational prospects.

In more recent work, Robinson and Harris (2014) comprehensively analyzed a whole host of measures of parental involvement and their association with parental social class and race. Consistent with the previous literature, they found that regardless of parental involvement at home or at school, high-social-class parents have greater rates of parental involvement than less educationally and economically resourced parents. In contradistinction to the narrative of Latinx and black parents valuing education less than their white and Asian counterparts, Robinson and Harris found little to no difference by race/ethnicity in the value placed on schooling and the educational involvement of parents. Although they found little association of parental involvement measures (as distinct from parental enrichment practices) with achievement, Robinson and Harris still emphasize the importance of parental involvement with other child development outcomes.

While there have been some really important contributions from this line of work, many of the studies are theoretically silent on "difference"; thus the interpretation of their differential results is often problematic, and all of them suffer from the limits of anthropocentrism. While some of the work that I discuss here does engage critical social theory, an overwhelming amount lacks a critical social theory of parenting practices, let alone "difference." With two exceptions (Dixon-Román 2013; Ridgeway 2011), "difference" remains theoretically unaddressed in much of this work; thus even where there is a social theoretical framing on the analysis of parenting practices, "difference" by race or gender is treated as a "natural" given. Unfortunately, this has led toward interpretive narratives of pathology, deficiency, or depravity, without any acknowledgment of the cultural construction of race and gender or the ideological systems they are by-products of. Moreover, all of this work privileges the human organism, not accounting for the more-than-human ontologies that intra-actively reconfigure power relations. Thus, this chapter seeks to provide not only a new materialist theory of "difference" and parenting practices but also a way to interpret "difference" in studies on social reproduction without falling into the modernist homogenizing and essentialist trap.

"Difference" and Social Statistics

Studies on social reproduction are inherently about the examination of "difference." With federal policies such as No Child Left Behind and the Every Student Succeeds Act, the national educational research agenda in the United States has been on estimated "differences" in standardized test performance by race, gender, class, and linguistic diversity. This has produced a mountain of work that has examined estimated "differences" in parenting practices and child achievement, much of which focuses on heterogeneity by race and class. As I argued earlier, the positivist paradigm has produced atheoretical or theoretically unsophisticated work on social reproduction. This has especially been the case for social categories of "difference" such as race and gender. The investigations are often framed by previous empirical findings, ideology, or modernist social theories that essentialize groups and seek to homogenize "difference," and the interpretations tend to render narratives of pathology, deficiency, or depravity. Structural critiques are seldom leveled and the implications are often about how to make the marginalized "normal." Given the longstanding use of statistical approaches to the examination of "difference," several scholars have produced work in tension with the interpretation of "race effects" in social statistics. Thus, I will discuss the literature on race in social statistics as a window into the broader issue of interpretation of the statistical estimation of "difference," including gender, class, sexuality, and dis/ability among other "naturalized" social categories. As a way to enter this conversation, it is important to theoretically situate race. Thus, I begin by taking a detour into the recent trends in critical studies on race, to consider how they have informed the critical scholarship on race and social statistics.

In critical theories on race, race is understood to be a byproduct invention of a social system, process, and ideology of racism (Bonilla-Silva 1997; Jackson 2008; Leonardo 2013; Mills 1997; Omi and Winant 2014; Perry 2011; Roberts 2011; Zuberi 2001). This is an ideology that permeates the actions and interactions of everyday life. There is no outside of race (Leonardo 2013). Even in the silence and seeming absence of racism in language or daily life, its specters rear up in mysterious and often misrecognized ways. While the sociopolitical system of racism has gone through various re(con)figurings, the two most relevant for our purposes here are that of the post–civil rights era and the more recent "post-race" era, following the 2008 election of President Barak Obama.

One of the major historical junctures and legal shifts with substantial impact (for better and for worse) on processes of racism was the civil rights movement and the various legislations that came as a result. Prior to civil rights legislation, overt racist policies of discrimination and segregation were not only legal but rampant throughout the United States. During the era of the civil rights movement many laws were overturned and legislations enacted that not only sought to racially desegregate the United States but to also enable and protect the rights and lives of people of color (as well as other marginalized groups). The institution of these legal and policy shifts materially and discursively reconfigured race relations. The former more overt discursive acts of racism or discrimination (that were inscripted and included in law) began to diminish (although not disappear) due to their legal consequences. In addition, the mood of the nation was such that racist language and behaviors became increasingly understood as socially unacceptable and politically incorrect, socially censoring such discourse. This historical and legal process had substantial influence on how processes of racism materialized in everyday life (Bonilla-Silva 1997; Jackson 2008). As argued by Judith Butler (1997) and John Jackson, the censorship of the "politically incorrect" inadvertently forecloses the possibilities for the critical dialogue necessary for contesting and challenging pejorative ideologies of "difference." It's not that racism or the racialization of bodies disappeared, but that racism cleverly escapes the panoptic purview of the State via ideology and its materialization in the practices of policies, institutions, and everyday intra-actions that maintain the hauntings of racial formations. Thus, not only is racism difficult to pinpoint, it is the very inability to point it out that makes what Bonilla-Silva calls "colorblind racism" so powerful.

The symbolic election of Barack Obama in 2008 also set in motion what many have characterized as a post-racial society. It is said that the election of Obama to the most powerful political position in the United States is the "sign" that race is no longer the major determinant that structures people's lives. But, as we have seen from public opinion data, that is far from social reality (Pew Research Center 2015). What haunts the "sign" is exactly that which it is said to move beyond, the insidious ideology of racism. As a critical turn against the dominant understandings of "post-racial," Leonardo argues that post-race is not about moving beyond racism or being blind to race, but indeed quite the opposite. Post-race, Leonardo states, "is the *politics of being anti-race,* or the dispreference for the continuation of a racially organized society" (148). It necessitates race-consciousness in the interests of contesting and challenging racial formations, moving toward a horizon of possibility. Post-race analysis interrogates the limits of race theory; it is an ambivalence toward race that challenges both white supremacy as well as the meaningful solidarities of raced identities. Post-race analysis is a necessary theoretical lens that interrogates the ongoing existence of white supremacy while seeking to push critical social inquiry on race in new and promising directions of hope and possibility.

Although a post-race lens has not been taken up in the scholarship on race and social statistics, its implications may not be that different. As a challenge to quantitative social science scholarship on race, scholars have argued against the use and interpretation of variables of "difference" such as race and gender as causal. The arguments take more than one form. Engaging theories of causation, statistician Paul Holland (2003) argues that a causal variable must be manipulable. Thus, as a socially constructed phenotypic property someone is born with, race cannot be a causal variable. He points toward the ontological impossibility of a counterfactual for race and suggests that the "race effect" reflects differential experiences in society while a statistical interaction between race and a causal variable estimates the degree of discrimination in the causal variable. Sociologists and demographers of race argue that if, in fact, it is understood that race is a social construction that is a byproduct of the social process of racism, then to interpret the "race effect" as causal is theoretically problematic (Zuberi 2001; Zuberi and Bonilla-Silva 2008). Zuberi discusses how, from eugenics to contemporary scholarship, the social sciences have had a history of treating race as a causal variable, producing theoretically problematic interpretations about race. He, like others (Holland; Zuberi and Bonilla-Silva), suggests that race should be included as a variable but appropriately interpreted as a social construction that is a byproduct of the social process of racism. A post-race studies lens would theoretically agree with the critical perspectives that have informed the work on race and social statistics, with a particular focus on critiquing both the ideological system of racism along with the byproduct of racial identity and reproducing identity politics.

While critical theories on race that have helped inform the scholarship on race and social statistics have been extremely helpful in challenging modernist analyses and interpretations of "difference," they are still human-centric. The centering of the human in critical race scholarship is quite understandable, especially since there is a history of raced bodies being dehumanized or constituted as only part human (Weheliye 2014). Thus, this becomes a theoretical move to affirm the humanity of those who have not been recognized by the State. Unfortunately the artificially constructed identity and "difference" of the human-centric arguments upholds the dualism not just between human and nonhuman but also between culture and nature and mind and body. The rejection of the liveliness of bodily matter overlooks and misses the vibrant and consequential materiality of interpellations of "difference." As Hames-García states, "The biological body is not inert matter in the face of racial ideologies" (2008, 326). Racialized interpellations do intra-act with the body, as empirically demonstrated, for instance, in the social psychological research on stereotype threat and the resultant increase of anxiety (Steele and Aronson 1995). The ontology of power relations do not just exist in the discursive but are very much entangled in the biopolitics of the complex and intra-active corporeal matter of the body.

As a project that seeks to push back against the popular Western academic employment of Foucault's biopolitics and Agamben's bare life, in his 2008 work *Habeas Viscus* ("you shall have the flesh"), Weheliye seeks to insert the theoretical work from black feminist literary studies in order to more adequately account for the processes of power and racializations of the body/flesh. For Weheliye, racialization is not to be reduced to race or racism but is the very process of differentiation and hierarchization that produces the entanglement of race, gender, class, sexuality, and dis/ability among other structural relations of "difference." He argues that posthumanist and antihumanist theories assume that everyone equally occupies the space of humanity, without accounting for the ongoing historicity of sociopolitical relations and the ways in which political violence has been constitutive of the hierarchy of humanity. In particular, he puts to work Sylvia Wynter's sociogenic principle and Hortense Spiller's theory of the flesh so as to develop a theory of racializations that accounts for the ways in which sociopolitical relations and violence mark the flesh and discipline the ontologies of humanity into full humans, not-quite-humans, and nonhumans.

As a way of developing a theory of racializations that is situated in sociopolitical assemblages and accounts for the anchoring of difference in the ontogenic flesh, Weheliye leans on Wynter's (2001) sociogenic principle. By incorporating theoretical work in neurobiology, Wynter rejects cultural and biological explanations of race while still accounting for the ways in which the fabrications of race, as sociogenic, become ontogenic via the flesh. Neurobiology, for Wynter, provides a theoretical route to explain how racializations become part of the ontologies of the body via neurochemical processes that reconfigure the experience of the self. Thus, the always-already ontologies of the anatomy of the body are positioned in intra-action with the sociogenics of race. As a product of sociopolitical forces, race is then not inherent to anatomical ontologies but rather those ontologies become racialized assemblages through their encounters of racialized events, situations, or acts. Weheliye further states:

> Consequently, racialization figures as a master code within the genre of the human represented by Western Man, because its law-like operations are yoked to species-sustaining physiological mechanisms in the form of a global color line—instituted by cultural laws so as to register in human neural networks—that clearly distinguishes the good/life/fully-human from the bad/death/not-quite-human. (27)

The master code that Weheliye posits of racializations, I argue, are not just enacted via human cultural laws and neural networks but also inherited in the mattering matter of food, clothes, odors, and taste. This is evidenced in the racial interpellations that go beyond that which is seen. The historicity of the sociopolitical forces of racializations has materially and discursively produced racial formations beyond the visual sense. As Smith (2006) has delineated, while the visual sense of the flesh may have been the inaugurating sense, colonialists began to associate their other senses with that which they observed of the flesh (e.g., "I smell nigger"). Thus, the ontologies of odors or tastes, for instance, become racialized assemblages.

As a way of drawing a distinction between the legal constitution of the body and the social designations of the flesh, Weheliye also calls upon Spillers (2003) theorizing of the flesh. As Spillers insightfully states "before the 'body' there is 'flesh,' that zero degree of social conceptualization that does not escape concealment under the brush of discourse or the reflexes of iconography" (as quoted by Weheliye, 39). Prior to the legal constitution of the body is the formation of the flesh, a formation that is bound by the markings or traces of political violence designating a hierarchy of humanity. The traces of political violence in the flesh are what Spillers refers to as "hieroglyphics of the flesh" that are produced from the instruments or acts of violence such as whips, police brutality, mass shootings, or more subtly through unspoken acts or complicit silence in speech. Spillers argues that the "hieroglyphics of the flesh" are transmitted to future generations and are concealed in the narrative of pathological or biological explanations of hierarchies of "difference." "Racializing assemblages translate the lacerations left on the captive body by apparatuses of political violence to a domain rooted in the visual truth-value accorded to quasi-biological distinctions between different human groupings" (Weheliye, 40). It is the political violence and disciplining of the flesh that designates bodies as full humans, not-quite-humans, and nonhumans; rendering certain bodies as exceptional and the outside of exceptional as disposable. Applying the new materialists' lens of assemblages provides a way of accounting for the quantum anthropologies of "difference" in reconfiguring power relations.

Assemblages and the Quantitative Inquiry of Re(con)figuring Structural Relations

As discussed in chapter 1, assemblages are systems made up of the organization, arrangement, relations, and connections among actualities, objects, or organisms that seemingly appear as a functioning whole. Assemblages acknowledge the ontologies of the more-than-human bodies that intra-act within and with/out the human body. Moreover, assemblages understand social categories such as race, gender, and class as situated in events, acts, and situations rather than characteristics of human subjects. Thus, as a theory that critiques both the structural relations of "difference" and identity politics and accounts for more-than-human ontologies, assemblage theory is not just post-race, it is also posthumanist. Here, I want to consider how a lens of assemblage might have critical promise for approaching the quantitative analysis of "difference" in social reproduction studies.

While much of the work on social reproduction has either been atheoretical or situated in social theory, it has not adequately accounted for the assemblages of "difference." As I have argued, any analysis of reproducing power relations must account for the intra-activity of both more-than-human and human, nature and culture, and material and sociocultural forces. These often overlooked more-than-human performatives are often critical features to the (re)configuring of power relations. For instance, the 1973 U.S. legalization of the female right to surgically remove the matter of the fetus and placenta from the womb (re)configured gendered structural relations in material conditions and discursive control of the body, including the legal constitution of the fetal organism as a separate being. Thus, any analysis that does not account for more-than-human, "natural," or material intra-acting ontologies is missing important dynamics to the (re)configuring of power relations.

In each generation of shifting historicities, structures such as race, gender, and class (among others) undergo material and sociocultural re(con)figurings. Race, gender, and class are structural relations that are part of the (re)configuring entanglements of space, time, and matter. In other words, race, gender, and class are more-than-human interpellations and are part of the more-than-human ontologies of material resources and conditions entangled with the discursive formations and limits of lived experiences. This implies that their historicities are complex, shifting, differentiating, and multiplicative. In any given social situation, we cannot think of their assemblage as a simple additive contribution but rather as a nonfixed convergence and operation of each one working through the other.

This is also the case over the life course and through the (re)configurings from one generation to the next. This sense of structural relations as complex, differentiated, and working through one another—as assemblages—creates space for the particularities of, for instance, a parent's own childhood to show up in their practices of parenting despite the parent's adult material and sociocultural resources and conditions. In other words, the structural relations of the grandparents when the parents were growing up may mark the structural relations in the parenting practices of the parents (in)dependent of the parents' adult structural conditions. Thus, like institutions (Mare 2011), the assemblages of (re)configuring structural relations outlive people, too.

The assemblages of reconfiguring structural relations are important for the analysis of multigenerational effects of inequality in research on social reproduction. As a signifying practice that constitutes bodies and the limits of social life, changes in law and policy are known to take as much as thirty years before their effects materialize in changes in social conditions and cultural practices (Mezey 2001). As an example, the 1968 Fair Housing Act outlawing discrimination in housing practices discursively and materially reconfigured the structural relations of race, gender, and class, in that those who were more ready to benefit from this regulatory measure were middle-class people of color and women (Sharkey 2013). Although this policy was legislated in 1968 it was weakly designed and poorly enforced. In fact, the Reagan administration was able to reverse many of the policies that Housing and Urban Development adopted under the Fair Housing Act, to the point that not one fair housing case was initiated during the first year of the Reagan administration despite the rise in the number of complaints (Massey and Denton 1993). As a result, a middle-class mother's adult socioeconomic conditions may not reflect the conditions she grew up in, where the wealth-accumulating practice of home purchasing was much more difficult, particularly in more resourced neighborhoods with better quality schools. Furthermore, her adult material and discursive practices would likely have enfolded traces of the condition(ing)s that she grew up in, reconfiguring the structural relations of her parenting practices. Other examples of policy and political economic shifts include the Civil Rights Act of 1964, *Roe v. Wade* in 1973, deindustrialization beginning in the 1960s, mass incarceration in the mid-1970s, the growth of neoliberal policies and female labor in the workforce in the 1980s, globalization, and rapidly increasing income and wealth inequality beginning in the late 1970s. Each of these intra-acting policies and political economic shifts has seen a delayed materialization in conditions and practices. Although the children growing up in the 1960s and 1970s, for instance, did not spend their formative years under the growing material and discursive constraints of economic inequality from the 1980s onward, they likely did live them as adults. The major legal and political economic shifts of the 1960s and 1970s have likely (re)configured the assemblages of structural relations not just of that generation's children but also of the experiences of learning and development of those children's offspring.

Assemblages of reconfiguring structural relations are critical for the quantitative analysis of "difference" in social reproduction studies. They provide a lens that moves away from the essentialism of identity politics by understanding the multiple categories of "difference" as situated in the intra-acting performativities of the events and situations of the measurement encounter. The theory of assemblage is in accordance with the notion of statistical estimates of "difference" as multiplicities (discussed in chapter 2) as well as situating the emergence of the estimate as a product of a myriad of forces including the assemblages of "difference." Theoretically, assemblage also includes the more-than-human intra-acting ontologies among the forces. Thus, statistical estimates of "difference" are materially and discursively produced and producing, and need to be more critically interpreted as intra-actively enacted from the relation and connections of the sociocultural and historical conditions of the structural relations of measurement. The current chapter seeks to quantitatively examine the multigenerational materiality of the assemblages of race, gender, and class structural relations in parenting performativities.

Assemblages of Parenting Performativities

As alluded to in the previous section, parenting practices are material–discursive practices. They are embodiments that are situated in timespace and mediums for reconfiguring structural relations. The structural relations that materialize in performativities of parenting are most readily understood from the lens of assemblages. Here, I will use the example of gender performativities in parenting for pedagogical simplicity, though I assume these gendered parenting performativities to be converging and operating through the structural relations of race, class, sexuality, and dis/ability among other social categories of "difference."

With her theory of gender performativity, Judith Butler interrogates the cultural belief in "natural genders" and their assumed inherent ties to sexuality. According to Butler (1990), gender is not an internal organizing principle of the body that causes individuals to have particular characteristics and act in particular ways in line with their anatomical sex. Rather, gender identity is "a personal/cultural history of received meanings subject to a set of imitative practices which refer laterally to other imitations and which, jointly, construct the illusion of a primary and interior gendered self" (138). Over time, the "sedimentation" of gender norms for an individual and for society as a whole has produced a belief in dichotomous "natural sexes." The performance of gender has become normative to life to such an extent that what are actually stylized repetitions of acts seem inborn and uneventful. The mundane nature that gendered acts have taken on creates the illusion of their fixed, "innate" presence. While I think Butler has it right regarding the sedimenting process of gender norms, I do part with her conception of matter as that which is enacted only from the materialization of discursive acts. Instead, I incorporate Karen Barad's (2007) posthumanist theory of performativity. For Barad, materiality is discursive and discursive practices are always-already material. Matter is not assumed to be a fixed, immutable corporeal substance but rather a substance that has mutable, intellective, and communicative ontologies. Thus, the sedimentation of gender performativity is a result of the entanglement of material and discursive intra-actions.

The performativity of gender materializes in parents' beliefs and ideas of parenting and gendered roles in parenting as well as practices. Parents both reproduce and resocialize beliefs about what males can and should do and what females can and should do. This includes who can and should be the breadwinner and who can and should be the nurturer. These beliefs are also already materialized in the everyday practices that parents engage in with their child. Depending on the parents' gender ideologies, these already materialized everyday parenting practices may also be gendered. Parents' practices in intra-action with their children—the cultural knowledge, sensibilities, and practices transmitted by the family as well as the social relationships and networks—are often boundary-making practices that enact differently for their sons than for their daughters (as seen in the research literature discussed previously). The gendered ontology of these practices may include washing dishes or laundry as chores for girls and outdoor work or garbage removal for boys. Parents may also be more inclined to cook with their daughters and build something with their sons. In addition, parents may be more apt to show emotional warmth to their daughters than their sons in order to inculcate dominant masculinity.

As we have seen, parenting performativities are not simply or even neatly gendered. Parenting performativities are assemblages of structural relations of "difference" such as race, gender, class, sexuality, and dis/ability. The intersectional lens misses the much more complicated, messy, and nuanced dynamics of the inherited events and situations. Assemblages account for the ways in which the gendered parenting performativities are both complicated and queered by the explicit and implicit social categories and experiences of social situations. I contend that in order to study the assemblages of performative processes it is necessary to diffractively read and analyze through the data of multiple sources and methods.

Diffractive Analysis of the Assemblages of Parenting Performativities

A diffractive analysis is a reading of multiple sources of data through one another. Given the focus on difference rather than sameness (e.g., reflexive practices), diffractive analyses are particularly interested in the tensions and differences in the data in order for the multiplicities of the phenomena to emerge. This is particularly relevant for the analysis of the assemblages of "difference" in parenting practices so as to affirm heterogeneity and not fall into the trap of narratives of pathology, deficiency, or depravity. Here, I employ the analysis of structural equation models of parenting practices, close readings of memoirs, and analysis of film media sources.

For the quantitative analysis I use data from the Child Development Supplement (CDS) of the Panel Study of Income Dynamics (PSID) (Hill 1991). The PSID is a nationally representative longitudinal data set containing information about families and each of the individuals in those families collected through interviews every year starting in 1968 and every other year starting in 1999. These interviews collected information such as detailed income sources, employment, education, family composition, and residential location. The CDS collected behavioral, psychological, and achievement data from 2,394 families of the PSID with 3,563 children aged twelve and under in 1997. The longitudinal family economic and child development data makes the PSID one of the richest datasets to study intergenerational and multigenerational processes of social reproduction. (For further details of the quantitative methods and results, please see Appendix A.)

Given my interest in multigenerational processes of social reproduction, I chose to analyze memoirs that had some degree of multigenerational structure in the narrative. In rapper Common's memoir *One Day It'll All Make Sense,* his mother provides commentary throughout and Common speaks of and to his daughter at various points. In *Limbo,* Alfred Lubrano discusses what it was like growing up in working-class homes, and then, as a college-educated adult, the challenges of raising a middle-class child. Anne Lamott's *Operating Instructions* and its sequel, *A Journal of My Son's First Son,* have the virtue of being multigenerational between

the two books. Each depicts different variations of multigenerational social processes and assemblages of parenting practices.

I also employ the analysis of two sources of film media. The first is a
YouTube video of a Southern gay male coming out to his family. This video
went viral and provides a glimpse into what it is like coming out to a homophobic family. The other source of film media is an independent film about
an urban black female's experience of exploring her sexuality and ultimately coming out to her family. Both sources of film media, diffractively read
through other data sources, produce differences that make a difference.

It's a Boy! Posthumanist Performativity and Bodily Responses to Ideals of Parental Gender Roles

Parenting practices are always-already an assemblage of a myriad of material and discursive forces. Parenting is something no one knows everything
about but everyone has an opinion about. Parenting is a rather mysterious
social phenomenon because the desire for universal proscriptions tends to
conflict with the individual particularities of child development. Arguably,
the purpose and goal of the pedagogical practices and behaviors of parenting are to teach, develop, socialize, and discipline the body of the offspring
within and for the world they inherit. These practices begin early, even before the traumatic arrival of one's progeny, and as medical technology has
advanced it has enabled earlier disciplining of the body to further mitigate
the enfolding assemblages to come.

In her best-selling book *Operating Instructions*, Anne Lamott (1993)
candidly shares her thoughts, feelings, and experiences, as a first-time
single parent, of late pregnancy and her son's first year. Among the many
experiences she talks about, Lamott describes in detail what it was like
when she learned her son's sex.

> I lay there on the little table at the hospital with my stomach sticking
> out, Manning [a friend] near my head holding my hands, a nurse by
> my feet patting me from time to time, one doctor running the ultra-
> sound device around and around the surface of my tummy, the other
> doctor taking notes until it was his turn with the needles.
>
> The ultrasound doctor was showing me the first pictures of my
> baby, who was at that point a four-month-old fetus. He was saying,
> "Ah, there's the head now . . . there's the leg . . . there's its bottom,"

and I was watching it all on the screen, nodding, even though it was all just underwater photography, all quite ethereal and murky. Manning said it was like watching those first men on the moon. . . . [The doctor] pointed out the vertebrae, a sweet curved strand of pearls, and then the heart, beating as visibly as a pulsar, and that was when I started to cry. (5–6)

Two weeks later she received a call from the nurse about her amniocentesis test. The nurse "talked about the findings for a while, although I did not hear a word, and then she said, 'Do you want to know its sex?' And I said yes I did. . . . It is a boy" (7). Notice she had to wait two weeks for the tests to come back for the nurse to make particular enouncements about the fetus. By 2009, when her son was having his first child, Lamott (2012) states that her son's girlfriend "had an elaborate space-age ultrasound at four months, which indicated that the fetus was a boy: the technician printed out Jax's picture for us" (5–6). Twenty years later, medical technology had advanced enough to be able to make credible, instantaneous enouncement that even includes 2-D, 3-D, and motion-picture imaging.

The gender interpellation by the technoscientific medical apparatus is one of the classic examples that Butler, Barad, and others have pointed to as that which initiates the iterative process of becoming gendered. Furthermore, it is the iterability of gender interpellations that produces the sedimented embodiment of gender performativity that is seemingly naturalized and taken for granted. The performative acts of this medical apparatus do not just constitute the gender of the fetus but also, via the amniocentesis test, the "normally abled" fetus as well as the economic and racialized interpellations from the ultrasound. As Barad states,

Ultrasound technology designates specific material-discursive practices, constraining and enabling what is seen and produced in accordance with its iteratively intra-active technoscientific, medical, economic, political, biological, and cultural development as an ever-changing phenomenon, and by its related and particular usages as a material-discursive apparatus of bodily production in intra-action with other historically and culturally specific apparatuses. (2007, 212)

When situated within specific cultural and historical intra-actions, the political, economic, and racialized forces of ultrasound technology become further illuminated. As Barad discusses, the "epidemic of infertility" that is narrativized to disproportionately affect white, affluent, highly educated women is, in fact, a social problem that affects nonwhite and poorly educated women disproportionately more. The false narrative resulted in the development of reproductive technologies that enabled the further reproduction of white babies while overlooking the environmental racism (e.g., ecological toxins) that is understood to be a major influence on infertility.

These iterative intra-actions that begin prior to the child's arrival in the world initiate the reiterative process of gendered assemblages both in parenting practices and parental gender roles. Lamott (1993) laments, "I wish I had a husband. I wish Sam had a dad. I hope God sends him one someday. It is a huge thing not to have" (21). In order to underline what she sees as the significance of this absence, she then states, "I got sad because Sam wasn't going to have some Alan Alda/Hugh Beaumont dad hanging around, throwing him up into the air and teaching him how to do manly things, like how to pee standing up and how to fix the toaster oven" (21). Lamott expresses a belief in the importance of the male parental figure in order to corporeally discipline material and discursive practices of masculinity. She is not unique in this regard. Paternal involvement is believed to be important for many parents, especially those of white males and females (see Figure 2).

The heteronormative and patriarchal belief in the importance of male parental figure involvement is not surprising but it is important to take note that it is not equally shared. The estimated differences in parental bodily expressed responses to questions on paternal involvement are substantial between the parents of white males and the parents of black males and females. Parents of white male children, on average, expressed the importance of paternal involvement at 63 percent of a standard deviation greater than parents of black males and 78 percent of a standard deviation greater than parents of black females. When one considers the structural focus of social welfare policies on poor single mothers and the mass incarceration of black and Latino males since the 1970s, the sociocultural and historical conditions that likely contribute to these racialized and gendered differences become illuminating. Interestingly, in the predominantly black church that Lamott (1993, 28) attended when she was pregnant with Sam, "Only one (white) man in the whole congregation asked [her] who the father was."

Despite what could be understood from Figure 2 regarding black par-

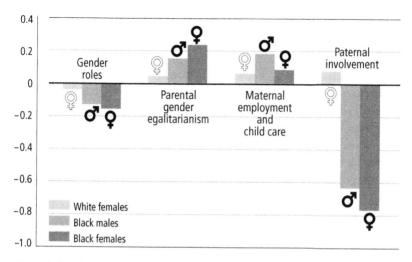

Figure 2. Standardized differences by child race and gender in parental embodied expressed responses to questions on gender norms and roles in parenting. (White males are the reference group.) Source: Child Development Supplement to the Panel Study of Income Dynamics.

ents' beliefs in paternal involvement, rap artist and actor Common's mom talks about her perspective on the importance of Common's father in his life despite her disagreements with him. In Common's memoir, *One Day It'll All Make Sense,* his mom says, "No matter what went on between Lonnie [Common's father] and me, it had nothing to do with Rashid [Common]. He didn't choose his father; I did. He should not have to pay because his parents' relationship didn't work. A son needs his father, and Lonnie always loved Rashid" (26). By reading this narrative through the data in Figure 2, the multiplicity of the statistical estimated difference begins to emerge— what can also be understood as differences that make a difference.

Interestingly, as a parent himself, Common also gives us a glimpse into his own struggles with the need for greater balance between his professional and personal life. Addressing his daughter, Common writes in a letter:

I fight with myself because I know that sometimes I just have to stop and be. Be there for you. Be there with my time and attention. I think one of the hardest things I have experienced is finding a way to balance my dreams with yours. I know I can be selfish because my dreams mean so much to me. I figure that once I attain my goals,

I can take care of all my loved ones. But, of course, there's no end, there's no stopping place. That's why I have to find the balance. (258)

As a first-time parent to a now almost three-year-old, I can identify with Common's struggle for greater balance and the desire to spend more time with my son. Although Common was not asked about how he viewed the importance of paternal involvement, his above statement was not couched in gendered terms (e.g., "father") but rather the importance of his involvement as a parent. He speaks to the material and discursive limits of pursuing one's (professional) dreams while raising a child, what would appear to seem like a trade-off or sacrifice for one over the other. As an affluent black male parent to a daughter who likely would discursively identify with being black, he implicitly reveals yet another multiplicity: the assemblages of race, gender, and class in parenting practices.

Assemblages of Race, Gender, and Class

Parenting practices are not just performativities but assemblages of structural relations of "difference" such as race, gender, and class. These structural relations affect everything from what parents do with their children to where they choose to live to the extent to which and how they intra-act with people from other groups or social spaces. Common talks about what his experiences with race relations were like growing up within the racially homogenous and economically disadvantaged timespace of Chicago's South Side:

Growing up on the South Side of Chicago, you have very few opportunities to interact with someone who isn't black. Yeah, you might buy an ice-cream cone from a white store clerk or see Latinos or Asians when you went downtown, but in most of the places where you spent your time, you really didn't cross paths with other types of folk. That shapes you. It wasn't until I started high school that I had any significant contact with people who weren't black.

Think about it: in my community, the richest person and the poorest person were black. You had black bankers and lawyers and businesspeople, but you also had black bums and hustlers and junkies. You had my mother, who was a teacher, a businesswoman, and later a principal. And you had my uncle who was struggling with addiction. The point is, never in my life did I think that being black would help or hinder me in a way that I couldn't address with hard work. It just was. (26–27)

Common's lack of perceived material–discursive constraint is likely a product of his mother's social and economic position in the community as a principal with a PhD and later his own economic success as an entertainer. Additionally, the material place of the South Side of Chicago was a racialized assemblage that "shapes you." The iterative intra-actions of the racialized assemblage of place (re)configures what is possible. Common's narrative is also an example of not just the iterative production of racialized visions of the world but also differentially formed practices of parenting as a result of the particularities of timespace.

Parenting performativities are always-already formed and shaped by the timespace in which they emerge. Common's ontologically particular timespace of where and when he grew up is, in part, what materially reconfigured differential practices of parenting. What parents learn to do, know to do, and have the resources to do is always a product of the assemblages of intra-action in timespace. We can see these assemblages materialized in the racialized and gendered pattern of responses to survey questions and observations pertaining to parenting practices.

For all four areas of parenting practices (i.e., cultural practices, social relationship practices, expressed affect toward parenting, and emotional and cognitive stimulation) there are very clear racialized differences and less pronounced differences by child gender, where the biggest difference was in parental emotional and cognitive stimulation. While Common's above narrative points toward the ontologies of multiplicity as situated in timespace, the racialized and gendered statistical estimates of difference in Figure 3 suggest the extent to which the racialized and gendered material–discursive conditions of timespace enact assemblages of parenting performativities.

In order to further unpack these racialized, gendered parenting performativities, I examine to what extent they are endogenous to parental bodily expressed responses to questions on gender norms and roles in parenting. Figure 4 presents the standardized raced and gendered statistical estimates of difference in parenting practices after accounting for parental bodily expressed responses to questions on gender norms and roles in parenting.

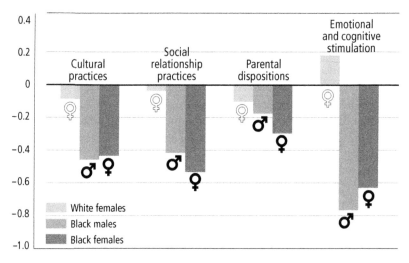

Figure 3. Multiple group analysis of parenting practices. (White males are the reference group.) Source: Child Development Supplement to the Panel Study of Income Dynamics.

In each area of parenting practices, the standardized statistical estimates of racialized gendered difference were reduced substantially, as much as 50 percent of a standard deviation for some parenting practices. Each estimated difference is now less than 10 percent of a standard deviation with the exception of cultural practices between white males and black females, and expressed affect toward parenting between white males and both black males and females. In fact, the estimated difference in expressed affect toward parenting between white males and black males increased by 10 percent of a standard deviation. This latter estimate could be a result of the absence of presence of parental bodily expressed responses to questions on racialized norms in parenting or the classed dimensions of timespace. Racialized assemblages in parenting practices are not just shaped in timespace but also by material–discursive forces of ontologies of race. For instance, it is ever more clear now that parents of children of color have to teach their children how to behave in the presence of policing authorities as a protective measure against their autonomic, preconscious bodily response being perceived as a threat. This is a racialized assemblage of affective bodily responses of constraint that goes beyond that which has been conceptualized as a classed dynamic, regardless of race (Lareau 2003).

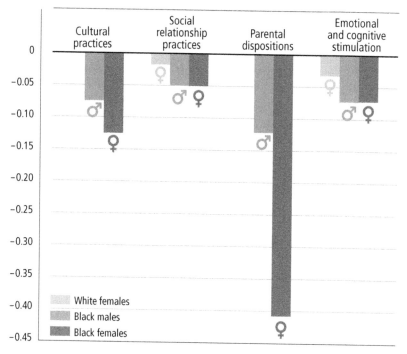

Figure 4. Multiple group analysis of parenting practices accounted for by parental embodied expressed responses to questions on gender norms and roles in parenting. (White males are the reference group.) Source: Child Development Supplement to the Panel Study of Income Dynamics.

Multigenerational Assemblages of Parenting Performativities

Although racialized assemblages in parenting practices can be clearly understood under the apparatus of racialized practices of State surveillance, the assemblages of parenting performativities are also enacted as a result of multigenerational material–discursive forces. In *Limbo*, Alfred Lubrano eloquently captures his life story alongside other people who grew up in working-class homes and who now, via higher education, are living middle- to upper-middle-class lives. These are people he refers to as straddlers. Lubrano talks about how their class differences as a result of social mobility materialize as enfolding historialities of differential patterns of childrearing practices. He states that many of the straddlers considered it to be bad parenting to simply hand things over to their children, including education.

Leticia Vega and her straddler husband had a fight about it before they even got married. At the time, the children were hypothetical, but Leticia's feelings were quite real. "My husband-to-be said over dinner once he wanted to send any kids he would have to Harvard or MIT, and he'd pay for it. I told him, 'That's the most stupid thing I ever heard. If you give kids something, they'll never value or appreciate it.' It was a big blowout." (186)

In a related discussion Leticia and her husband also disagreed about passing down land to their children. Leticia stated: "I'm not going to protect assets just to pass them on. You can't instill values in kids if you just give them things. The things I most cherish are things I worked for. And so many times, inheritance leaves kids at each other's throats" (186). Leticia's concerns were seemingly about the discursive act of giving and the formed and shaped affect, but what is easily missed in this discourse are the always-already intra-acting ontologies of the body and the ways in which the accumulated material assets will intra-actively effect/affect their offspring, materially reconfiguring their offspring's determinate boundaries of possibilities.

Lubrano discusses another straddler, Gillian, who expressed her belief that in the working class a child is supposed to be independent by the age of eighteen.

"By then, you've done your job as a parent," she says. But her husband says that your kids never grow up and you're always working for them. When it came time for her son, Joe, to pick a college, Gillian harkened back to her own upbringing. She had no car; there was no money. The University of Buffalo was down the street. So that's where she went. And that's where her son should go, she told her husband. But he disagreed, saying the boy deserves to go where he wants. "To me, his going away to school was a waste of money," Gillian says. "What is this 'deserves' stuff?" Gillian's husband has a sense of entitlement he's passed on to Joe, Gillian says. And it's evident throughout their neighborhood, an upper-middle-class enclave. "It drives me insane the way people here raise their kids, acting like the world revolves around their little darlings." (182)

In both Gillian's and Leticia's examples there is a sense of appreciation for the work ethic that was produced from working-class upbringings and a disdain for the corporeally shaped affect of entitlement that is the norm in the material–discursive conditions of their middle- to upper-middle-class neighborhood assemblages. Gillian's expressed reaction is, in part, a re-activation of affect from prior experiences that autonomically materializes in the body.

Both of these examples also provide insight into the enfolding matter of sociocultural processes of social mobility that, in part, enable multigenerational effects. Multigenerational effects are enabled in many ways. One such example is what Thomas Shapiro (2005) calls transformative assets, "meaning resources that can put a family on an economic and social path beyond the means of their salaries" (62). These might include asset transfers and gifts from parents to their adult offspring to pay for college, down-payment assistance for a home that is more expensive than the offspring would be able to afford with their salary, or helping to pay the tuition for grandchildren's quality early childhood education or private K–12 schooling. Each of these forms of transformative assets would not only materially reconfigure the determinate boundaries of possibility for their offspring but also what pedagogically matters and is excluded from mattering for their grandchild's learning and development.

In discussing data on racial inequality in inheritance, Shapiro states:

> What the low level of inheritance from grandparents corroborates is that the legacy of grandparents of black baby boomers, who lived and toiled under harsh discrimination and glaringly different conditions, did not include financial resources. We see a glimpse of the racial reality of two generations ago continuing to impose and structure differences onto the present generation of young adults and a generation of children still coming up. (72)

The enfolded historicities of wealth in the United States have been a force of racialized assemblages. The racializing assemblage of material wealth is a matter composed of sedimented historialities with differing and deferring trajectories of possibility. This has been enabled both by policy apparatuses that privilege the accumulation of existing wealth and the racializing assemblages that have designated the humanity and proprietorship of particular material bodies. Wealth *matters* and its mattering reconfigures material possibilities by differentiating and hierarchizing bodies—all of which can shape and influence the practices of parenting and their child's development.

In order to examine the extent to which class structural relations have multigenerational effects on parenting practices, I examine the associations of parents' and grandparents' socioeconomic resources such as family income, educational attainment, occupational prestige, liquid assets, and family structure variables with parenting practices. Here, I am interested in examining the amount of variability in parenting practices that is uniquely accounted for by parental bodily expressed response to gender norms and roles, parent socioeconomic resources, and grandparent socioeconomic resources. Figures 5, 6, 7, and 8 present data for each measured domain of parenting practice.

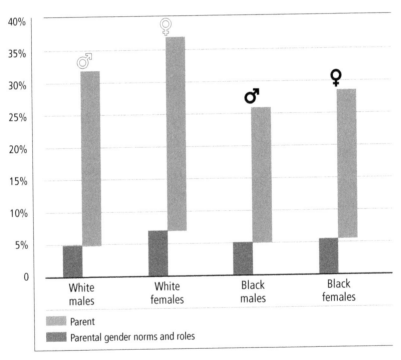

Figure 5. Percent of variability in cultural practices accounted for by parental gender norms and roles, parent socioeconomic resources, and grandparent socioeconomic resources. Source: Child Development Supplement to the Panel Study of Income Dynamics.

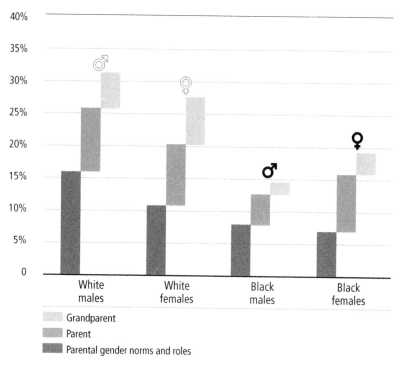

Figure 6. Percent of variability in social relationship practices accounted for by parental gender norms and roles, parent socioeconomic resources, and grandparent socioeconomic resources. Source: Child Development Supplement to the Panel Study of Income Dynamics.

As can be seen in the figures, grandparent socioeconomic resources do not account for any of the variability in parenting cultural practices. The parents' socioeconomic resources appear to account for a large proportion of the variability. In contrast, parental social relationship practices are clearly endogenous to multigenerational social forces. In fact, for white males, grandparent effects account for almost as much as parent effects. While there are multigenerational effects on parental expressed affect toward parenting, this is only the case for white males and females. In fact, all of the accounted-for variability in parental expressed affect toward parenting for black males and females was through parental bodily expressed responses to questions on gender norms and roles in parenting. This is not ignorable since parental expressed affect toward parenting is positively

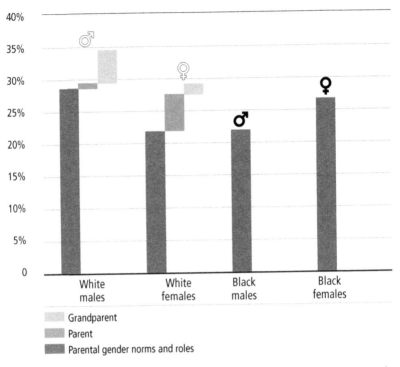

Figure 7. Percent of variability in parental expressed affect toward parenting accounted for by parental gender norms and roles, parent socioeconomic resources, and grandparent socioeconomic resources. Source: Child Development Supplement to the Panel Study of Income Dynamics.

correlated with parental practices of emotional and cognitive stimulation. Finally, while there were multigenerational effects on parenting practices of emotional and cognitive stimulation, parent socioeconomic resources seem to account for the majority of the variability. Thus, multigenerational class structural relations matter more for some parenting practices, less for others, and they do vary by child race and gender. The iterative intra-actions of enfolding multigenerational class structural relations contribute to producing determinate bodily material boundaries of racializing assemblages of parenting performativities.

When diffractively read through the memoirs, the above statistical estimates are both corroborated and fractured. For instance, the affect of entitlement, as a practice of parenting, that is talked about by Lubrano's strad-

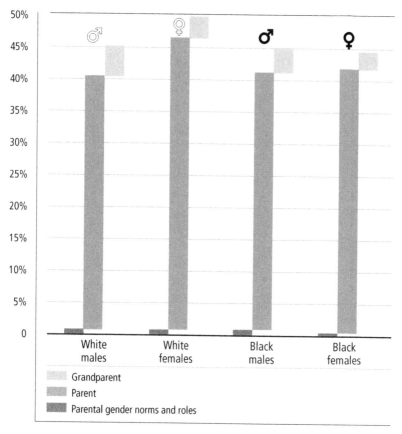

Figure 8. Percent of variability in parental emotional and cognitive stimulation accounted for by parental gender norms and roles, parent socioeconomic resources, and grandparent socioeconomic resources. Source: Child Development Supplement to the Panel Study of Income Dynamics.

dlers appears to be more complicated than the non-multigenerational effect of the statistical estimates. For many straddler parents there is a concern for materially shaping affects of entitlement based on their practices of parenting such as buying their child a car, paying for them to go away to college, or giving them an inheritance of property. This is complicated not just by differential perspectives between straddler parents but more so between a straddler parent with a partner who grew up in privilege.

Straddlers with partners who grew up middle class or affluent often experience differences and tensions not just between them and their partner but also between them and the experience of their offspring. Straddler Rebecca speaks to what parenting is like with a partner who grew up middle class and the inheritance of childrearing:

> The children and their father (and now Rebecca) have philosophical discussions about Sartre over the potatoes. [Their father], a downtown attorney with educated parents, takes pains to explain everything. A word will come up that stumps the kids and he'll suggest they go to the dictionary. He will suspend dinner to have his children look up a place they never heard of in the atlas. Rebecca cannot imagine a working-class family interrupting mealtime to ascertain the latitude and longitude of the Marshall Islands. "He quizzes them in the shower about foreign countries. It's amazing to me. I find myself jealous of their childhood." (190)

Such seemingly ubiquitous pedagogical experiences of book-based knowledge replicate not only what these kids will learn about in school but also what they will be assessed on in standardized tests (e.g., the SAT). The home-situated, conversational form of these pedagogical experiences is what makes them tacit and taken-for-granted forms of knowledge. These seem universal because they are situated in at-home everyday conversations and give the appearance of being common sense. (I will return to tacit knowledge and what is preconsciously experienced as familiar in chapter 4 with the SAT.) Diffractively reading through the statistical estimates of parenting practices also illuminates how the combination of both parents' material and discursive resources intra-act to substantially materialize in their corporeally different practices as well as the sorts of tensions that are among the myriad forces that haunt the quantitative estimates.

Rebecca expresses jealousy of these privileged forms of childhood experience. This could also be interpreted as a re-activation of prior experiences from her working-class origins that produce a preconscious bodily response of jealousy. While conversations on Jean Paul Sartre may be less likely among the working class, the other educative practices are plausible. What materially separates the working class from the middle class is the latter's materially reconfiguring greater financial resources, as well as particular forms of performative practices that tend to be more closely aligned to those privileged by society's dominant institutions. For instance, a more well-resourced family will have the possibility of actually traveling to some of the countries discussed or will be more likely to use some of the dictionary-based words in their professional occupations. In the documentary *Born Rich*, Josiah Hornblower explains that once when he was asked what the capital of Chile was he knew the answer not because he had memorized it but because it re-enacted a bodily affect from when his father took him there to go fishing when he was growing up. This kind of intimate and embodied experience with the mattering matter of place is not just invaluable, it becomes a taken-for-granted specter in school achievement and test scores.

The Absence of Presence of Sexuality

Although we are able to analyze the raced, gendered, and classed assemblages of parenting performativities, the markings of sexuality haunt the above narrative and statistical estimates. The absence of presence of sexual difference is a result of the heteronormative lens of most preexisting normal probability social science surveys, including the Panel Study of Income Dynamics. While I think it is important that these surveys begin to include quality measures of gender and sexual variability, I want to diffractively read the above data through two sources of film media as a way of producing diffractive patterns that would not have otherwise emerged to haunt the data. Again, with an understanding of statistical estimates such as number and multiplicity, diffractive readings produce and focus on differences within that make a difference.

In a 2014 YouTube video that went viral, "How Not to React When Your Child Tells You That He's Gay," we get a glimpse into what happens when a young gay male from Georgia comes out to his homophobic family. After a brief debate on theological versus scientific perspectives on whether homosexuality is a choice, a female family figure states the following:

> I'm going to tell you . . . that you have chosen that path, we will not support you any longer. You will need to move out and find wherever you can to live and do what you want to because I will not let people believe that I condone what you do.

From there, it very quickly escalates as we hear his family members verbally and, it sounds like, physically attacking him. The boy asks his family,

"What is wrong with you people?" and we hear a male figure (presumably his father) say, "No, what's wrong with you? . . . You are a disgrace. . . . Unfortunately, I'm sorry to say it but you are." The video ends on this somber tone.

His family members in this video, who include more than just his mother and father, make it clear that they understand his "choice" of homosexuality as unacceptable and will not be associated with him as such. There appears to be a history of discourse on whether homosexuality is a choice or not, which seems to culminate to this traumatic and violent event. Informed by theological ideology, their response is so vehemently visceral that they not only physically attack him but disown him and force him to move out of the house. To justify their decision to disown Daniel, the family's decision is lodged in a theology of free will, of Daniel's choice of who and what kind of gendered body to desire or love. The theo-logic goes like this: God gave us free will in order to demonstrate our obedience and love to "him"; and, homosexuality is a morally corrupt behavior in the eyes of God; thus, those who "choose" to desire those of the same gender are being disobedient and not demonstrating their love for God. Of course, this is incompatible with the corresponding theological belief in predestination, that God is an omniscient, omnipotent, and omnipresent being. To counter this theo-logic Daniel leans on scientific theories of personality formation during the first six months of life whereby he interprets his sexual orientation not as a choice but as a "natural" phenomenon.

Both of these arguments rest on logics of a fixed nature that is irreducibly different from culture. Not only is the theology of homosexuality illogical, Daniel's scientific logic assumes a biopsychology that "naturalizes" discursive formations of the body and that doesn't take up the always-already ontologies of the body. This is one contemporary instantiation of the violent acts that continue to manifest as a result of the taken-for-granted divisions of nature and culture and the ways in which they inform even parenting performativities. The abjection and racialized assemblage of his family's performative acts didn't just disown Daniel but also produced a spacing between them and him, rendering the alterity of his body as not-quite-human. Diffractively reading Daniel's story through the above data illuminates the differential patterns that haunt the multiplicity of the statistical estimates of parenting practices for white males. It's not a matter of whether the estimates "represent" the parenting practices of Daniel's white (gay) male experience, it's a question of how the parenthetical as read through this video might produce differential patterns in relation to the statistical multiplicities of parenting practices with white males.

The video of this very materially and discursively violent familial dialogue, shared via the Internet, enabled topological relations that dramatically reconfigured the power relations of its "private" discourse that went "publicly" viral. The potential power of these "private" performative intra-actions are both the psychological and physiological traumas that can be experienced and processed in the vulnerable state of solitude and loneliness and (in)dependent of others who are empathetically supportive. While the shame and dereliction of being "a disgrace" to those who gave one life most certainly would affect one emotionally and physiologically, the performative act of "coming out" has also been found to be associated in later life with reduced risks of psychopathologies of anxiety and depression and neurohormonal cortisol levels that control stress (Juster et al. 2013). To be clear, these are not assumed to be fixed, immutable psychophysiological and neurohormonal processes but rather vibrantly intra-acting ontologies with the materialities and discursivities of being openly gay. The "private" boundaries of the intra-activity between both material and discursive processes became dramatically reconfigured by the topological relations of the viral Internet video.

Uploading this video to the digital architecture of social media enabled the more-than-human ontologies of computational algorithms to do what Luciana Parisi (2013) calls "soft thinking" (i.e., algorithmic modes of thought, decision making, and mentality) that transgressed the boundaries of the "public" and "private," the neighborhood, and even the State, further facilitating the conditions of its viral-ability. The sociocultural norms of this "publicly" reconfigured and contaminated timespace within the porous boundaries of the "private" enabled voluminous support (and, to be sure, homophobic ridicule). His supportive friends created a GoFundMe site that seemed to produce enough financial support since Daniel, the nineteen-year-old gay male in the video, asked that further financial donations be made to Lost-n-Found Youth, an organization that supports homeless LGBTQ youth. The topological relations enabled not just a reconfiguring of the "public"/"private" spatial boundaries but also of the sociocultural and material conditions of that space.

It's important to note that this instantiation cannot be generalized beyond the time/space/matter of this situation. Daniel was lucky that his YouTube video was intra-actively selected by the algorithms to go viral and that it received the response that it did, because most instances would not necessarily receive such a response—let alone be recorded in the first place. The power of the "private" more often than not prevails. It's also important to mention that to be sure, there are also the warm endearing examples of parenting responses to their child's sexual becoming. In a *Huffington Post* article on March 15, 2013 (Sieczkowski 2013), we get a glimpse into such an example. A father who apparently overheard his son planning on "coming out" to his parents preemptively left his son a note saying, "I overheard your phone conversation with Mike last night. . . . The only thing I need you to plan is to bring home OJ and bread after class. . . . I've known you were gay since you were six, and I've loved you since you were born." Thus, not only is the tactic of making "public" the homophobic parental response to "coming out" very much situated in the time, space, and algorithmic practices of the digital, the digital also allows the "publication" of alternative parental responses to their offspring's sexual becoming.

Another instantiation can be seen in Dee Rees's 2011 independent film *Pariah*. Alike is an adolescent black female in Brooklyn New York who is exploring her sexuality. Her mother, played by Kim Wayans, is deeply religious and her father is a detective in the New York City police department who maintains a complicated and estranged marriage, with a mistress on the side. Her mother, in particular, is concerned with Alike's "tomboy" bodily behavior and dress style as well as her association with her friend Laura. Alike's mother implores her father to talk to her. In a late-night conversation, he reluctantly asks her: "Say, uh . . . there's this new women's club, over there by the liquor store. . . . Do you . . . have you . . . you haven't heard anything about it, right? Called the 'Kitty Litter' or 'Cat Box' or something like that." Alike responds, "Na, I never even heard of it," knowing she has been there on more than one occasion. Her father responds, "Good. 'Cause it's uh . . . that's a rough neighborhood. You know that right, I had a case over there. You want to be careful, stay away from that *element*, in case it ever comes up" (italics mine).

Alike's friend Laura is an out lesbian who plays a mentoring role for Alike. Laura lives with her sister because she was kicked out of her mother's home (we are left to believe it is because of her being a lesbian). In the one scene where we meet Laura's mother, her mother doesn't say a word. She doesn't even let her in the house. Laura simply wanted to tell her mother that she had officially passed her GED test. Once Laura began to share the good news, her mother shut the front door.

In a later scene where Alike's parents are fighting and her mom is criticizing her father for not being around and more involved, Alike comes out as lesbian to her parents. In one instant, Alike confirms her mother's suspicions and what her father refused to believe. The second she states, "I'm a lesbian. Yeah, I'm a dyke," her mother physically attacks her and has to be pulled off by her father before she will stop, not unlike the scene in the YouTube video with Daniel. The emotional rage of her mother's attack leaves us to wonder how much of that anger was about Alike's sexuality and how much was her mother's displaced anger toward Alike's father, as she yells at him, "Get off me! You cheater, you get off me!" The power dynamics of the material–discursive situation were deeply made up of the sticky assemblage of masculinity, homophobia, religious moral respectability, the economizing of the body, and the social disabling of the body. Alike was literally and figuratively beaten back to a fetal position. As a racializing assemblage, the parenting performativities toward both Alike and Laura produce "hieroglyphics of the flesh" that intra-actively reverberate through the neurobiological ontologies of their bodies. The next scene we see Alike still in fetal position being comforted by Laura, staying with her, never to return home. While we see her father eventually come to visit her and embrace her, her mother's bodily response remains restrained and imprisoned by religious ideology. To this life/bodily-rupturing moment, Alike states in a poem, "I am broken, I am broken open, breaking is freeing, broken is freedom."

Alike's social situation and, in particular, her parents' intra-active performative acts, diffractively read through the quantitative estimates of parenting practices with black females, highlights the complex and differentiated ontologies of the assemblages of parenting performativities. The statistically estimated relational differences between white males and black females was greater than 40 percent of a standard deviation for both parenting cultural practices and parenting social relationship practices and greater than 60 percent of a standard deviation for parental emotional and cognitive stimulation. These comparative estimates tend to be interpretively reduced to essentialized ontologies of radically separate and different groups. Diffractively reading Alike's black (lesbian) female narrative through this data illuminates the enacted agential cuts between the measured groups within the phenomenon of parenting performativities. The intra-activity between parents and the assemblages of their child's ontologies are haunted by the parenthetical, producing differences that profoundly queer the received meanings of the statistical estimates of parenting practices with black females. The produced differences go beyond the multiplicities of parenting practices of emotional and cognitive stimulation to performatively enacting a cut of alterity, "deviance," and radical difference in the ontologies of the children.

These and other assemblages of parenting performativities enact differentiating cuts based on the raced, gendered, classed, and sexualized ontology of the child. The phenomenon of parenting we also see is partially endogenous to the parental bodily expressed responses to questions on gender norms and roles in parenting and multigenerational socioeconomic forces. As assemblages, parenting performativities enact and produce differences as modes of disciplining, socializing, and shaping the ontologies of their offspring so as to enhance or maintain the social legacy of their family.

Conclusions

In his 2005 work *The Hidden Cost of Being African American*, Thomas Shapiro has this to say about inheritance:

> American society is of two minds about inheritance and we seem to want it both ways. We take pride in our accomplishments, often marking them in monetary terms, and see nothing wrong in passing on what we earned to our children. Indeed, part of the motivation for working hard and acquiring things includes bettering our family and our children for future generations. This notion, however, collides with the equally strongly held notion of meritocracy because inheritances are unearned, represent a different playing field entirely, and have precious little to do with merit, achievements, or accomplishments. We live with this duality, partly because we deny what inheritances represent, partly because we see it in individual and family terms, and partly because the current political balance heavily favors those with advantages and privileges. (85)

In this passage Shapiro sharply and poignantly captures the pulse of parenting and inheritance as well as the inherent ideological contradictions between their aims and the ideals of meritocracy. The data presented in this chapter indicate that there are multigenerational forces on parenting performativities. The assemblages of parenting performativities are produced by a myriad of forces, some of which include the parents' adult material–discursive conditions as well as the conditions they grew up in, all of which contribute to producing determinate bodily material boundaries of racialized assemblages. We also learn about some of the complicated and contingent ways that parenting performativities produce determinate bodily material boundaries of racialized assemblages. Parenting is an assemblage of performative intra-actions that enact agential cuts in the offspring's body that seek to enhance or maintain the social legacy of the family. Wealth *matters* and its mattering reconfigures the material enfolding possibilities for children and grandchildren. The enacted cuts may be by way of socializing how to be "male" or "female"; "black" or "white"; or "lesbian," "gay," or "heterosexual." The enacted cuts are sometimes even in the violently ruptured space of disowning, so as to disassociate a family from the "chosen deviance" of its offspring. The statistical estimates of the complicated, messy, and contradictory performativities of parenting are often haunted, such that the statistical often produces singular narratives of that which is already a multiplicity.

The study of parenting performativities must analyze the assemblages of structural relations of "difference" via diffractive readings through multiple data sources. Inherently, the study of social reproduction is the study of "difference." Thus, the examination of social reproduction is a comparative analysis of difference. Such comparative analysis often falls into the colonialist trap of narratives of pathology, deficiency, and depravity, especially with phenomena such as parenting practices. Assemblage shifts the analytic lens away from identity toward the relations and connections among the social events, actions, and situations of parenting. Thus, it inherently points to the structural conditions that relationally enact, produce, and shape the performativities of parenting. While every method produces data with a parallax view that is within and part of phenomena, the diffraction of multiple data sources brings into sight the differences within phenomena that complicate and mess up the neat and simplified narratives that are often produced from one data source; this is especially the case with the statistical. Thus, reading the data of one method through another enables the emergence of multiplicities that would otherwise haunt the singularity of method. For parenting performativities, the stakes are too high to not diffractively read for the assemblages of structural relations of "difference."

Assemblages of parenting are just one of many performative forces that enact social reproduction in education. As one of the primary influences of teaching, socializing, and shaping the body, parenting performativities constitute one of the most substantial forms of inheritance. Although falling short of determining it, parents (and grandparents) do what they can to enhance or maintain the social legacy of the family. The more they have and the more they are privy to, the more they are able to pass on to their offspring. Thus, the "hard work" of privileged offspring is already advantaged by the taken-for-granted sociocultural and historical legacy they were born into. The materiality of these taken-for-granteds permeate all dimensions of life, including parenting and SAT scores.

4

Inheriting Merit

The SAT as an Institutionalized Measuring
Apparatus for Social Mobility

Let me pause a moment to examine the phrase "social mobility," for this is the heart of my argument. A high degree of social mobility is the essence of the American ideal of a classless society. If large numbers of young people can develop their own capacities irrespective of the economic status of their parents, then social mobility is high. If, on the other hand, the future of a young man or woman is determined almost entirely by inherited privilege or the lack of it, social mobility is nonexistent.

—James Bryant Conant, "Education for a Classless Society"

IN THIS ESSAY, published in *The Atlantic Monthly* in May of 1940, former Harvard University president James Bryant Conant calls for a move away from the existing system of aristocratic selection of the nation's leaders based on inherited wealth and toward a system of meritocratic selection based on demonstrated and measured intellectual capacity. Inspired by Thomas Jefferson, Conant was a leading proponent for an ideology and definition of meritocracy based on academic merit, a radical idea at the time. He hoped to enable a socially mobile society (regardless of social inequality) via a focus on "equality of opportunity" for education. Conant's famous essay became, arguably, the written preamble and manifesto for the ideology of meritocracy based on intellectual merit as it has come to be understood today.

One of the main instruments developed for the "objective" measurement of intellectual merit was standardized tests such as the SAT. In fact, most of the applicants admitted to Ivy League institutions prior to the SAT were white Anglo-Saxon Protestant (WASP) males from a particular pool of elite prep schools in the Northeast region of the United States (Karabel 2005; Lemann 1999). The student bodies were racially and economically homogeneous, and there were concerns about the level of academic performance at these institutions. James Bryant Conant and his protégé Henry Chauncey imagined and developed a plan to reorganize the structure of opportunity in the United States via a meritocratic model of admissions to the nation's elite institutions of higher education (Lemann 1999). With the collaboration of Princeton University psychometrician C. C. Brigham, the then newly developed and popular instruments of intelligence testing were appropriated in order to develop a standardized college admissions test: the Scholastic Aptitude Test, now known as the SAT. This test would serve as a mechanism for measuring and selecting students based on intellectual "merit," not social pedigree. Today, standardized tests such as the SAT have become and continue to be one of the more highly weighted measures of selection for admission to most colleges and universities in the United States.

Although seemingly well intentioned, the fatal assumption of the ideology of meritocracy—as I will both theoretically and empirically demonstrate—is that "equality of opportunity" is possible regardless of inequality. The main argument of this chapter is that the ideological aims of meritocracy for fluid social mobility regardless of social inequality are an impossibility; inequality of condition will always compromise the goals of equality of opportunity without policy interventions that regulate the possibilities for equitable treatment.

As the quintessential institutionalized measure of merit, the SAT has become both a taken-for-granted socially legitimating apparatus and material–discursive force of society, both implicitly (by taking or not taking the test) and explicitly (based on performance) aiding in the distributing of bodies and the selecting of the political and economic elite. Karabel (2005) argues that the definition of meritocracy has always been aligned with the political and economic elite, paralleling the case of the intra-active performativities of the SAT. As we will see, this has also had the virtue of reconfiguring new possibilities for the intellectual elite (i.e., the sons and daughters of academics). Thus, as an institutionalized measuring apparatus of selection the SAT has contributed to processes of social reproduction while enabling the possibility of limited social mobility for an elite few. More concerning, meritocracy has become the ideological and systemic legitimation for the neoconservative political interest in rugged individualism and is complicit in the persistent reproduction of social inequality since the 1970s. The fatal assumption of "equality of opportunity" regardless of social inequality has enabled the evolution of a new system of social reproduction legitimated by taken-for-granted instruments like the SAT.

In this chapter I diffractively analyze the material–discursive forces of the SAT. I treat the ideology of meritocracy as involving entangled material and discursive phenomena that produce the intra-acting measuring apparatus of the SAT. I understand the SAT to be not a preexisting or prefixed passive instrument but rather an inseparable constitution of particular practices that continue to be reworked and re(con)figured through intra-actions with other phenomena. As Barad writes, *"Apparatuses are themselves material-discursive phenomena, materializing in intra-action with other material-discursive apparatuses"* (2007 203). Apparatuses enact agential cuts that create resolution between what matters and what is excluded from mattering. Thus, I analyze not just SAT scores but the ontology of the SAT and its entangled becoming with society, test-takers, and myself as researcher. I examine (1) the extent to which the intra-acting apparatus of the SAT has produced a distribution on the material–discursive significance of the SAT and, as a result, preparation for it; and (2) the degree to which the material–discursive forces of social inequality over multiple generations materialize as enfolded historicities in the social distribution of SAT scores. In other words, to what extent is merit, as measured by the SAT, a complex and differentiated inheritance of enfoldings of sedimented historialities? And, how enduring is the reconfiguring of inheritance enfolded with/in timespace? The analyses of this chapter are based on data from the television series *Gossip Girl*, biographic narratives from *Limbo* and *Privilege*, the quantitative analysis of SAT scores from the National Longitudinal Survey of Youth, and public-figure SAT scores from the Internet. Following the development of the SAT as an apparatus, I begin by discussing the materiality and discursivity of the ideology of meritocracy and how despite its aims for social mobility it has created a new system of reproduced constraints and possibilities for social inheritance and multigenerational inequality.

SAT as an Apparatus

Well-established and institutionalized instruments of measurement such as the SAT are assumed to be "objective" instruments of intellectual ability and predictive of future academic performance. The SAT is said to provide nonsubjective and noncontingent "valid" information that can be used in complement with other college application materials to make a fair admissions decision. As an equated measure with multiple forms, it promises to measure the same constructs for each cohort, regardless of administration, and over time. The instrument is understood to be made up of an arrangement of items that are administered in a controlled and timed setting (with exceptions made for persons with learning disabilities). The material arrangement of the contexts and conditions of administration, the bodily responses to the testing event, the neighborhood conditions of growth, the equality of educational opportunities via school and community resources, ecological influences on neurobiological and physiological development, and the political economy are all understood to be independent of the instrument of measurement. While this positivist account of measurement has been the dominant orientation to the SAT, as will be discussed later in this chapter, it has provided limited and inadequate accounts of the formation, ontologies, effects, and affects of the apparatus of the SAT.

According to Barad (2007), apparatuses are specific material and discursive practices that have histories and ontologically (re)configure the world given their intra-actions with/in the world. They are not objective instruments that are spatially separate from and outside of the phenomena of inquiry. They are also not prosthetic instruments that simply function to enhance human capacities. In addition, apparatuses are not the Althusserian instruments, practices, or mediums of ideology. Apparatuses are inseparable and part of the phenomena of inquiry and include the researchers, the instrumentation, the context and conditions of observation, the material arrangement of the context, and all of the practices within the context of measurement. Measuring apparatuses are boundary-making practices that produce, through their intra-active (re)configurings of the world, separations within phenomena that designate determinate boundaries of what matters and is excluded, of what's possible and impossible, and of what's intelligible and unintelligible. Apparatuses "*are the material conditions of possibility and impossibility of mattering*; they enact what matters and what is excluded from mattering" (148). As iterative intra-acting practices, apparatuses create determinate boundaries and properties of "entities" within phenomena, what Barad refers to as agential cuts. As agential cuts, the produced boundaries and properties enact a "resolution" of an "entity" within phenomena of ontic and semantic indeterminacy.

As intra-acting agencies, apparatuses are open-ended practices that enact agential cuts that reconfigure the world, while also being reconfigured by the world. Through their reconfiguring with the world, apparatuses have sedimenting histories that are ingrained through their iterative intra-activity. Thus, the researcher, the measuring instrument, the material arrangement of the context of measurement, the discursive practices of measurement, the respondents, the produced and enacted numerical "estimates," the phenomena of interest and its sedimented historiality, policies, and political economic forces are each ontological entanglements that make up the intra-acting performatives of the apparatus. The performative question(s) or task(s) of a measuring apparatus enact agential cuts that produce determinate boundaries and properties within a phenomenon of interest. As Barad argues, measurement is about the intelligibility of the world to itself, and the apparatuses of measurement constitute the material conditions of what is possible and impossible.

With this posthumanist conceptualization, the SAT is an apparatus that continues to enact and reconfigure what is possible and what is excluded from mattering for ability, merit, and college admissions. As will be discussed below, the apparatus of the SAT emerges out of two ideological movements in science and social policy: eugenics and meritocracy. As an apparatus it consists of reconfiguring boundary-making practices that include the following: an arrangement of items that are administered via paper-format during specific dates and times and at specific locations; test-takers who sit at tables often in large spaces with many other test-takers; a highly competitive context and practice with known high stakes; a large and thriving market of test-preparation companies and courses; colleges and universities that require SAT scores for their applications and admissions considerations; a sedimented historiality of material practices and sociocultural imaginaries of the SAT; (in)equality of educational opportunities via schooling and neighborhood resources; context and practices of education and social policies; the political economy; and test-item content that registers autonomic, preconscious bodily responses due to varying degrees of familiarity not just with the knowledge of the items but with the mattering substance of the items (such as Josiah's experience of Santiago). The latter is also the case when a test-taker is primed about their group identity and negative group stereotype prior to taking the test (i.e., stereotype threat) and, more generally, with the intra-acting material of the paper and No. 2 pencil of the test and the material arrangement of the

timed testing conditions that preconsciously reactivate anxious bodily experiences because of the test's high stakes. All of this, and more, intra-act
to become the boundary-making practices of the apparatus of the SAT.
Thus, the estimated SAT scores are a product of myriad forces. Scores are
intra-acting agencies that are determinately ontic and semantic and produced and producing. Thus, as an apparatus that intra-actively produces
what's intellectually and socially possible, the SAT reconfigures enfolding
future possibilities.

Meritocracy, the Ontology of the SAT, and Why It Matters

Since the beginning of the U.S. republic there has existed a social ethic
and ideology that suggests that as long as a person works hard they should
be able to obtain a piece of the "American dream." The empty signifier of
the "American dream" has meant something different to many different
people and communities, but for most it meant the freedom to become
who you want to be (i.e., "the pursuit of happiness"). Implied in this ideology is that everyone has unbridled "equality of opportunity" and chances
at life; assumed is that the same input of hard work produces the same
outcomes for everyone, regardless of social position. In the twentieth
century, with the advent of intelligence testing and standardized testing,
"hard work" became increasingly associated with "merit," among other
factors (e.g., wealth). But, what is "merit"? How does a society evaluate it?
And in what ways have the iterations of definition been enabling for some
and constraining for others? The answers to these questions have not been
consistent, and often, in contradiction to the ideal of equality of opportunity, have served the interests of the political and economic elite.

In higher education, the concept of merit has changed over time to
serve as the proverbial measuring stick for institutions to determine admission. Before the ubiquity of entrance applications with page-long
checklists, selective institutions would judge candidates on simple measures of their intelligence and academic abilities as evaluated by the "college boards," an essay style exam used by Ivy League institutions. Implicit
in this metric, however, was the availability of secondary education, since
high-school completion is largely a phenomenon of the twentieth century. The desire to exclude waves of immigrants in the early 1900s brought
selective institutions to redefine their measures of merit through character and other intangibles in order to weed out students they found to be

"disagreeable," in particular Jewish and black students (Coe and Davidson 2011; Karabel 2005). Thus, in addition to admissions policies that targeted athletes and the sons and daughters of alumni, they excluded applicants who did not convey white Anglo-Saxon Protestant culture. Indeed, good character, wealth, and WASP culture were oftentimes synonymous.

Despite his own privileged social history James Bryant Conant became increasingly concerned with the lack of intellectual rigor at Harvard and the legacy of wealthy aristocrats. He saw Harvard as the training ground for the nation's political and economic elites, and recognized the institution's enabling of those who inherited the social status of their family. Relatedly, as a centrist, he was troubled by the increasing threat of the Cold War. For Conant, social inequality in society was okay and to be expected, but rigidity in social mobility would produce social classes and, ultimately, class consciousness. Inspired by Thomas Jefferson, he believed the only way to maintain fluid social mobility was to enable "equality of opportunity" via education. As the demand for higher education increased in the early twentieth century (and especially after World War II with the GI Bill), merit came to be perceived by the larger public as "equality of opportunity" such that "unlike the class-bound societies of Europe, achievement rather than the prerogatives of birth would determine one's fate in life" (Karabel 2005, 3). Conant and Chauncey saw the development of the Scholastic Aptitude Test as a way of "objectively" measuring intellectual merit while at the same time restructuring society to enable greater opportunity for the intellectually talented and more fluidity in social mobility.

Initially used as a measure to identify National Merit Scholars, the SAT eventually was adopted in admissions policies for selective institutions and gradually the majority of colleges and universities across the country. The SAT helped shape the concept of merit, as the seemingly objective test results were also "for a variety of reasons, not always attributable to intelligence" (xiv). The constructs of quantitative and verbal reasoning were defined based on the cultural knowledge of the dominant group and institutions. Thus, like the ideology of meritocracy, the cultural capital of the SAT became increasingly more aligned with the intellectual and economic elite. The sons and daughters of academics were growing up with the habits of mind and exposure to the cultural practices and resources the SAT measured. For instance, reading was not enough; one would have to have the cultural tastes for the text that the SAT would reference. In addition, the vocabulary used on the SAT required a knowledge of the particular definition of a word according to how it was deployed in the context of the test item. This point came under examination when researchers noted that greater degrees of item performance differences between African American and white American test-takers existed on the easier SAT verbal items than the harder items (Freedle 2003; Santelices and Wilson 2010). Freedle theoretically argued this to be a product of cultural familiarity, with the everyday words on the easier items having far more variability than the school- or textbook-based words of the hard items; what I argue to be pre-consciously experienced forms of the familiar. As Karabel documents,

> In 1956, the sons of business executives (22 percent of all fresh-men) outnumbered the sons of professors (5 percent) by a ratio of more than 4 to 1; in 1976, the sons of professors—who constituted perhaps one-half of one percent of the American labor force—made up more than 12 percent of Harvard freshmen, compared to 14 percent for the sons of business executives. (539–40)

In sum, given that the nation's academics were predominantly white and privileged, this meant that the high performers on the SAT were also predominantly white and privileged.

With the efforts of civil rights legislation, the increased weight placed on the SAT in admission to selective institutions, as well as the fast-rising average SAT scores at these institutions, the economic elite began to turn to test preparation in order to ensure their child's admission and economic future. While Stanley Kaplan targeted the students of Brooklyn's public schools, especially those of Jewish background, John Katzman, the rich alumnus of Princeton University who founded the Princeton Review test-preparation service, focused on the private-school students of Manhattan. As Lemann describes, in response to the "objective" measure of college admissions, the privileged "were hiring SAT tutors at prices running up to the hundreds of dollars an hour—if not "advisors" who'd "help" kids write their personal, deeply felt applications essays for fees in the thousands. . . . They were having doctors certify their children as learning-disabled, be-cause that way ETS would let them take untimed SATs" (1999, 229).

With the privileged increasingly anxious over their test performances, Katzman saw an opportunity in this market. Test-preparation courses not only became big business but a taken-for-granted practice of the upper middle class. The Educational Testing Service (ETS) and the College

Board came under increasing societal and legal pressures when public figures such as Ralph Nader questioned their validity and successfully led
the passing of the Admissions Testing Law that required testing companies to release the already administered versions of their standardized test.
This not only aided the test-preparation companies but it also affected the
measuring apparatuses as testing companies like ETS then had to develop
better methods of test security and increase the item production for their
measures. Some would say the "truth in testing" law was a victory for test-
taking consumers; others would say that it was only a victory for the
test-preparation companies. Now, SAT preparation courses are found in
most private secondary schools as well as many privileged public secondary schools. And this says nothing of the upwards of $40,000 that parents
will pay for college coaches and $8,000 for two-week academic summer
camps that include SAT preparation. The rules and logic of the apparatus
of competitive college admissions may have shifted but the power relations were merely reinscribed under new discursive terms and material
conditions. As Bourdieu (1986) has argued, even when well-intentioned
policy mechanisms are implemented to enable greater fairness and equity
of opportunity, the privileged develop more socially clandestine practices
and institutions to ensure their social legacy.

While the SAT was implemented as a mechanism to enable greater
"equality of opportunity," the discursive assumptions about what is preconsciously experienced as familiar and the material constraints of the
development of test preparation for the elite have produced a new system
of social reproduction. The children and grandchildren of academics and
the affluent, the beneficiaries of the material–discursive knowledge assessed on the SAT, have and will continue to have an advantage going into
the SAT. These forms of both implicit and explicit preparation have become both socially distributed and unquestioned ritualized practices for
college-bound high-school seniors across the country.

The Social Distribution of SAT Significance and Preparation

In season one, episode fifteen of the TV series *Gossip Girl*, the episode
opens with the following commentary:

> There are three things we do alone. We are born. We die. And, for a
> high-school junior headed for college, we take the SATs. And while

the test is said to measure our best traits, preparing for it inevitably brings out the worst. Humility becomes self-doubt, striving becomes obsession; some are driven to self-medication, while others cling to the security of being part of a group. And anyone who is used to bending the rules will find themselves breaking them.

Preparation for taking the SAT has become a ritualized practice for the majority of college-bound high-school students. With the increasing importance accorded the SAT, test-preparation companies have further developed their courses, test-preparatory technology has kept pace with the rapid IT advancements, and the performative preparatory practices of youth have reconfigured with/in timespace. As the quote above suggests, the stakes are high for everyone and students will do anything they can to obtain a score that will reflect favorably and competitively on their "best traits" of intellectual ability. It has also long been the case that both explicit and implicit forms of preparation have not been equally distributed or part of everyone's everyday life. While findings on coaching or test preparation have been mixed (Briggs 2009; Powers 1993), what this literature has not accounted for is the extent to which there is a social distribution to the significance given to the SAT—and correspondingly, the ways in which such significance materializes in practices of test preparation as well as the material–discursive training of everyday practices of enrichment opportunities. I critically examine both of these questions using data from the CWTV series *Gossip Girl* as well as analysis of survey responses on enrichment opportunities (which is later found to substantially matter for SAT performance), and biographical narratives from Lubrano's *Limbo* and Khan's *Privilege*. Each of these forms of data provides a different angle and lens of insight into the process and phenomena of preparation for the SAT, and I diffractively read these data sources with and through one another in order to illuminate the multiplicities that would not emerge from each on its own.

The CW television series *Gossip Girl* ran for six-seasons and chronicled the social lives of elite private-school youth from the Upper East Side of New York City. Based on the novel series written by Cecily von Ziegesar that captures her experiences of attending the Nightingale-Bamford School in Manhattan, the narrative of the TV series centers around a social media website, called Gossip Girl, which airs the rumored personal and private affairs of five youth, in particular. All of these youth come from elite families of multiple generations of wealth and privilege, with the exception of one middle-class male who resides in the socially stigmatized outer borough of Brooklyn. He struggles to gain acceptance and even when he begins dating one of the popular elite youth he is still socially labeled and treated as an outsider. Thus built into the series are the ontological realities of the social divisions that exist within these elite private schools. Due to private-school efforts to increase diversity, these processes of youth social relations in elite schools have captured the attention of recent works including Shamus Rahman Khan's 2011 ethnographic investigation of St. Paul's School as well as the 2013 documentary *American Promise.* While this section will use an episode from *Gossip Girl* as a window into the intra-acting apparatus, discursive ritual, and significance of SAT preparation for private-school youth, I will also lean on other material–discursive phenomena to discuss more broadly the distribution of patterns of mattering preparation.

The episode opens with each of the youth studying vigorously either individually, in a group, or with their nanny; stressing and obsessing at levels occasioned by no other test; and getting an energy boost from drinking coffee for presumably long study hours. These are just a few of the emotions and practices that become part of the SAT preparation experience. The youth (mis)recognize the test as having substantial significance not so much with respect to what their score might materialize about their self-worth but rather how it might have a determination on their future possibilities and social legacy. We see this with Blair Waldorf's determined desire to go to Yale by any means. She sees attending Yale as necessary for being faithful to her own inheritance, and as directly contingent on her SAT performance. Others, like Dan Humphries, see the significance of their SAT performance as potentially reconfiguring and enabling future possibilities of social mobility from their middle-class life. And, while some youth may see it as "just a test" or not their "family's way," others don't even fathom an alternative option. Middle-class homeschooled character Vanessa, and Nate Archibald, an elite private-school youth, share these socially distant sensibilities with each other:

NATE: Eh, tell me something, why do you do SAT practice tests if you are not planning on taking the exam?

VANESSA: To help Dan study. I'm a film maker. The best education for me is making films.

NATE: I never met anyone who thought that college was an option.
VANESSA: My parents are artists. My sister's a musician. Just like
    going to an Ivy is your family's way, not going to college is mine.

With SAT preparation as the conversation point, Nate's statement of never
having met "anyone who thought that college was an option" points toward the inherited ontology of unquestioningly attending college among
the privileged, the assumed vital significance of the SAT, and the social
distance from those who do not possess such an orientation. Vanessa
makes clear that her inherited "family's way" is as artists who do not take
the SAT, let alone go to college. Vanessa and Nate provide instantiations
of the enacted differential patterns of mattering the apparatus of the SAT
enacts. The material–discursive forces of one's inheritance will form and
shape whether one understands intra-acting with the apparatus as unquestionable or as not necessary. Thus, not only does the institutionalized
apparatus produce determinate boundaries of significance but also an inherited distribution of its significance.

Even beyond the world of elite private-school youth, the significance of
the SAT substantially shapes how one approaches preparation for it. As a
child from a working-class home who did go to college, Finn shares in an
interview with Alfred Lubrano (2005) how what his parents did to aid in
his preparation was not common practice in his community.

> In high school, my parents got me a tutor for the math part of the
> SATs, to bolster a lackluster PSAT score. That sort of thing happens
> all the time in middle-class neighborhoods. But we were setting
> precedent among our kind. Most kids I knew from the community
> were not taking the SATs, let alone worrying about their scores. If
> you're from the middle class, you do not feel out of place preparing
> for college. Parents and peers help groom you, encourage you, and
> delight in your progress. (56)

Finn's reflections corroborates with what was expressed by Vanessa above.
The working class do not all accord the same significance to the test and,
as a result, approach preparing for it differently. Finn's parents apparently
understood the SAT's importance for the application process and saw the
stakes as high enough that they were willing to invest in a tutor to help him

prepare for the exam—a practice that was certainly less common for the working class than the affluent, where it has become the norm.

However, it is also the case that not all affluent youth necessarily agree with the significance of the SAT and in many ways buck against the social legacy that they were born into. In the conversation between Vanessa and Nate referenced above Vanessa explains her family's occupational history as artists, reminding us of how narrow the SAT is in what it purports to measure. As we see here, the privileged constructs of measurement have the unfortunate virtue of materially marginalizing and deterring participation for youth who are not interested in a life and career of numbers, analytical reasoning, or literary and linguistic engagement. This is the case not just for poor, working-class, or middle-class youth, but for all youth. Steven Amory, one of the youth who attended the elite private St. Paul's School interviewed in Shamus Khan's (2011) *Privilege,* was an artist who played the guitar, wrote poetry, performed in plays, and featured his paintings in the school's art shows. In a conversation with other students regarding their preparations for an upcoming assignment and the SATs, Steven makes very clear his understanding of the test's material significance.

> I just can't do that kind of stuff. I'm not bad at it. But what does it get you? Yeah, maybe into Harvard. But then what? Law school? . . . And then you're working like crazy. Like my dad. He doesn't even know how to live. Or he forgets what it's like to be a normal person. A person at all. I'm not going there. I'm finding what I like, not doing whatever it takes for me to be "successful"—whatever that means. (146)

In one discursive move, Steven happens to put into question the material significance of the SAT, higher education, hard work, and what is materially constituted as "successful." He dismisses preparing for the SAT by questioning to what end. He queries the associated higher education because he believes that it will lead to a life of working beyond what he sees as reasonable and being "a normal person," while referring to his father as an example. Not only is Steven acknowledging the materially reconfiguring boundaries of possibility that are agentially cut by the apparatus of the SAT but he's also questioning the worth of how the materially reconfigured intra-actively enacts a particular work ethic he's not interested in.

For Steven, that form of "success" was associated with the SAT and he was determined to be faithfully unfaithful to his inheritance in order to not fall into that trap.

In stark contrast, the elite youth of *Gossip Girl* (mis)recognized the material significance of the SAT and prepared by having SAT tutors, several SAT preparation books, Princeton Review handhelds for SAT preparation, and taking multiple SAT preparatory courses. Their middle-class peer Dan Humphries only had flash cards and the several SAT preparatory books that Nate gave to him. But as a student at an elite private school Dan was also privileged, given that there are working-class youth who may not even be aware of the test. In Lubrano's *Limbo*, Renny Christopher, for instance, hadn't even heard of the test until her guidance counselor told her that it would be a good idea for her to take it, at the last minute. Unlike Finn or the elite youth of *Gossip Girl*, Renny had very little understanding of the SAT's material significance going into taking the test, let alone the opportunity to prepare for it.

Other working-class youth who may have understood the significance of the SAT (or similar college admissions tests) still may not have participated in any form of test preparation due to both limited family resources and the institutional practices of their high school. Ayodeji Ogunniyi, the first-generation Nigerian immigrant who became a public school teacher, is one such youth. I first heard his story on NPR's *Weekend Edition Sunday*, and later followed up with Ayodeji to learn how he understood the SAT and whether he prepared for the test. He said that he did take the test seriously but did not participate in any forms of test preparation. Ayodeji explained:

> You would think that educators would push their students to score toward a 36 [the top score on the ACT], but we were given score goals in the high teens or lower twenties. So after-school test prep was usually advertised to students that were expected to perform poorly. In addition the focus was also taken from the ACT and placed heavily on the PSAE test [Prairie State Achievement Examination], which was used to measure the school's academic performance. So when I say "it was assumed that I was doing my best" it's because as honor students we would either meet or exceed the low expectation of scoring in the high teen or low twenties. We understood (teachers and counselors would tell us this) that coming

from a low-income area and being a minority, we would get favored treatment from universities.

Referring to the focus on the PSAE test, Ayodeji implicitly speaks to the federal policy of accountability testing, then known as No Child Left Behind (NCLB).[1] Under NCLB, schools were consistently under the looming threat of school closure and takeover. Thus, many schools did what they could to meet adequate yearly progress targets, including cheating (Fausset and Blinder 2015) and focusing their pedagogical resources on certain areas at the cost of others. Ayodeji seems to understand his school's practices as a function of the latter. That is to say, Ayodeji understood the school's test-preparation pedagogical practices as focusing on not just the state exam, the PSAE, but the "students that were expected to perform poorly." This is not unrelated to how he understood the school's rationale of test performance and college admissions. The school's teachers and counselors, Ayodeji explained, seemed to inculcate the idea that students from low-income schools and students of minority status were given preference in college admissions—although at the time affirmative action policies had been waning since the 2003 *Grutter v. Bollinger* Supreme Court case (539 U.S. 306), and legacy admissions maintained as much as a 45 percent admissions advantage for privileged applicants (Hurwitz 2011). The apparatus and racialized assemblage of college admissions produced determinate boundaries of schools and student *bodies* that materially and discursively *mattered* in shaping schooling practices in college admissions and test preparation. Thus, college admissions test preparation is also intra-actively reconfigured by the federal policy context, the school's collective understanding of the social dynamics of admissions testing, and the school test-preparation pedagogical practices.

In addition to policy forces and school institutional practices, others have spoken to linguistic norms and cultural familiarity and their implications on test performance. As Finn argues, working-class everyday language likely does not aid in high performance.

A child from a working-class home is at a huge disadvantage . . . because he's used to a narrower world of expression and a smaller vocabulary of thought. It's little wonder that kids from working-class homes have lower reading scores and do less well on SATs than middle-class kids. (Lubrano 2006, 56)

Although Finn's argument pejoratively assumes the working class to be linguistically deficient, his statement could be reinterpreted via inheritance and Freedle's cultural familiarity hypothesis, which suggests that test-item performance differences are a function of the variable cultural understanding of everyday language. The political economy of timespace and the material–discursive forces of inheritance produce multiplicity in everyday practices and their effects. More important, Freedle's cultural familiarity can be better understood not as conscious experiences of the familiar but of preconscious reactivations of bodily affect. As a result, the discursive norms and assumptions of the SAT will produce variability in responses.

Everyday practices have also been found to substantially vary by family social and economic background (Dixon-Román 2013; Lareau 2003; Roksa and Potter 2011). Using the NLSY of 1997, I examined the social variability of the number of enrichment opportunities such as having a home computer, home dictionary, or taking extra classes or lessons (see Appendix B for a description of the methods and results). The ordered polytomous logistic regression results indicate that, on average, affluent youth (as measured by parents' illiquid assets, which include assets that are not easily liquidated such as total value of home, land, business partnership/professional practice, any other real estate, and vehicles) were more likely to have higher rates of enrichment opportunities than their nonaffluent counterparts with no illiquid assets (see Figure 9).

For instance, affluent youth were 17 percent more likely to have three enrichment opportunities in contrast to their nonaffluent counterparts, and, nonaffluent children were 11 percent more likely to have no enrichment opportunities in contrast to their affluent counterparts. The model also indicated that youth who had fathers with a graduate-level education were more likely to have greater rates of enrichment opportunities than their peers who had fathers with a high-school level education (see Figure 10).

More specifically, children of graduate-level fathers were twice as likely to have three enrichment opportunities and 12 percent less likely to have one enrichment opportunity than their peers with high-school educated fathers.

Lastly, the NLSY97 measured the level of risk in the family's physical home and neighborhood environment, including items such as whether the home had electricity and heat when the youth needed it or the frequency of gun shots in their neighborhood (see Appendix B for measure). This is an important measure given that a family is less likely to have a computer

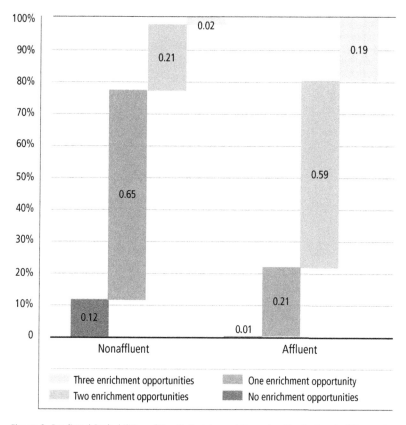

Figure 9. Predicted Probabilities of Youth Enrichment Opportunities by Level of Parents' Affluence. Source: National Longitudinal Study of Youth 1997.

in the home, for instance, if they are struggling to maintain the heat and electricity. Or, the degree of neighborhood gun violence may topologically reconfigure the spatial boundaries of the neighborhood, deterring youth from participating in extra classes or lessons, as is the case in some Chicago neighborhoods where youth have to use caution in going to places like public libraries that are in gang territory. Recent research has even found that exposure to a local homicide within a week prior to a reading assessment substantially reduced the performance of African American children in Chicago (Sharkey 2010). These empirical results further instantiate the enduring material effect of performative acts like local homicides on affective bodily responses in alternative domains with/in timespace. To say

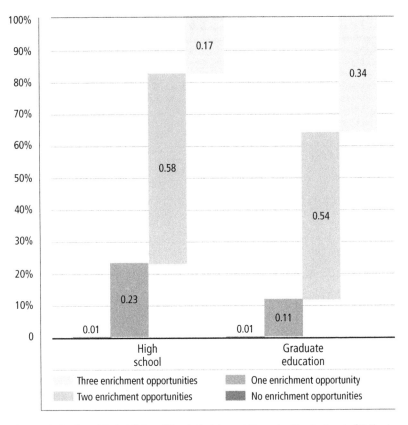

Figure 10. Predicted Probabilities of Youth Enrichment Opportunities by Level of Father's Education. Source: National Longitudinal Study of Youth 1997.

nothing of the urban political economy of neighborhood resources and enrichment opportunities, what I have referred to elsewhere as the political economy of comprehensively conceived education (Dixon-Román 2012). The material–discursive forces of these home and neighborhood conditions have meaningful intra-actions in youth lives.

The results of the analyses indicate that the greater the risk in the youth's physical environment, the less likely they were to have enrichment opportunities. To be more specific, the youth in high-risk environments were twice as likely to have one enrichment opportunity while their peers in low-risk environments were more than twice as likely to have three enrichment opportunities (see Figure 11).

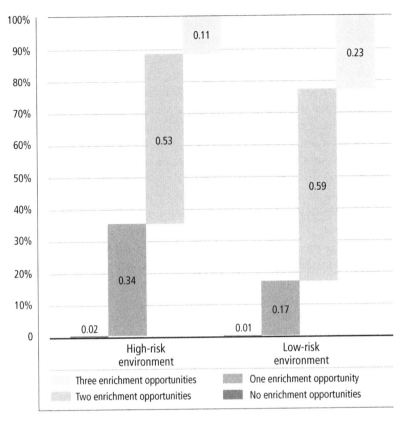

Figure 11. Predicted Probabilities of Youth Enrichment Opportunities by Level of Neighborhood Risk. Source: National Longitudinal Study of Youth, 1997.

This data on youth enrichment opportunities is telling when diffractively read through the data of the bio/graphical film media and written text. The socially predictive youth enrichment opportunities would be indicative of Nate's greater enrichment opportunities than Vanessa's and even Dan's lack of preparatory resources in contrast to Blair's spa study group. The statistical models provide circumscribed and provisional estimates of the extent to which these practices intra-act with other materially and discursively constituted phenomena, but are the more easily seen. What haunts the estimates of the measuring apparatus are material–discursive practices such as Nate giving test-preparatory books to Dan, an act that Dan's middle-class counterparts at public schools would likely not

have had the benefit of. And, more important in Dan's case, the material–
discursive practices that he developed from the privileged timespace of
elite private schooling advantages him in contrast to his public school
middle-class counterparts in ways that maintain an absence of presence in
the statistical models. Steven's affect toward the SAT, how it materially reconfigures possibilities, and his desire not to participate are specters in the
quantified data even though he would likely have relatively more enrichment opportunities, particularly as a private-school student. What continues to haunt these predicted probabilities is the significance placed on
the material–discursive force of the SAT apparatus and the intra-actions
of schools, parents, and test-takers as a result, such as working-class Finn's
parents acquiring a tutor to help with test preparation. The apparatus of
the SAT *matters* not in predictive or deterministic ways but rather in materially reconfiguring the determinate boundaries of future possibilities
and what's precluded from mattering. A diffractive reading here begins to
illuminate the differences between the methods that describe differential
patterns of mattering in SAT test preparation.

In becoming with the data on SAT preparation, how am I intra-actively
produced by the product and phenomena of the SAT? In what ways am I
mutually constituted by the analysis? As I read the data on the distribution
and significance of the SAT and test preparation I was reminded of how
I conceived of and understood the SAT. Despite conceptual shifts and
the growing test-preparation industry in the 1990s, the discourses that I
recall—as a youth growing up with the assemblages of being black, Puerto
Rican, working class, able-bodied, and in various parts of the East Coast—
contained both a burgeoning belief in the development of ability alongside the contradictory retaining of the vestiges of eugenics ideology where
the SAT was understood to measure innate, fixed ability. In fact, it was an
open secret that although it was believed that intelligence was something
that everyone could develop, it was also believed that the SAT was designed to measure one's innate aptitude and to be biased against people
of color, women, and the poor. These material–discursive formations led
toward the belief that it was not worth putting much effort into preparation as it was understood to be difficult (if not impossible) to change
your expected score. It was, in part, because of these (mis)conceptions or
(mis)recognitions that I did not invest much time in explicit forms of test
preparation outside of a few computer-based practice tests. This says nothing of the fact that test-preparatory courses were also beyond the finan-

cial means of my family. Obviously, these understandings have shifted substantially. Not only are the ideals of developed abilities much more prevalent in society but the accessibility and diversity of test-preparation products has increased substantially. I also have a more theoretical understanding of the apparatus and have even worked for the College Board and ETS. Thus, my understanding of the SAT has substantially shifted from the intra-acting vestiges of those historicities.

Beyond the intra-acting material and discursive forces of the SAT apparatus in my life, I want to reinsert myself into the intra-acting fabric of the data so as to speak more directly to how the data affected me. Despite the ontological shifts of the SAT away from the baggage of eugenics ideology (though not totally), it still retains the assemblage of understandings as being a significant determinant of college admission and as a measuring apparatus that produces agential cuts of relational and connected differences that determine boundaries of future possibilities. The affects of anxiety and uneasiness returned as I reconsidered the awkward act of sitting behind a cafeteria table with only a No. 2 pencil and calculator in order to respond to over one hundred critical reading and mathematics questions within the limited yet exhausting timespace of three hours. On the one hand, in thinking/imagining with Finn or Renny, I had a feeling of social loneliness and despair, especially with Renny. That sense of despair is relative to what Finn imagines his middle-class peers doing and, more profoundly, from learning at the last minute about the SAT as Renny did. On the other hand, I felt the anxiety, pressure, exhaustion, and focused desire to get into an Ivy League school of the elite youth of *Gossip Girl* and *Privilege.* In fact, the anxiety and pressure were what seemed to affect me most as I considered the possibilities of needing to either maintain my family's social legacy or to make my middle-class family's financial sacrifice of sending me to an elite private school worth the investment. The association of my home and neighborhood material–discursive conditions with enrichment opportunities also reaffirmed and shifted how I thought about the intra-acting matter of neighborhood violence and pedagogical constraints. This diffractive reading of the data, then, reveals multiple forms of knowledge on the ways in which the SAT measuring apparatus intra-actively affects and is affected by society, youth, and myself, as well as the power relations embedded in these processes.

Interestingly, while the SAT was developed to measure the intellectual ability of applicants, the intra-active becoming of the SAT with the youth

test-takers has also produced preparatory practices that are studying, re-
searching, and measuring the material–discursive product of the SAT; in
other words, the world trying to become intelligible to itself. Thus, the apparatus of the SAT has produced a mutually constitutive and entangled
measuring that discursively renders only one of those measurements to
materially matter in the end analysis—the score itself. As we see here, the
entangled material and discursive conditions of preparation are more enabling and less constraining for elite youth. In other words, the substantial material distribution of youth enrichment opportunities is nothing to
sneeze at for more than one reason. Enrichment opportunities have been
found to be associated with outcomes of learning and development including achievement measures (Dixon-Román 2013; Phillips et al. 1998). They
also provide urban marginalized youth, in particular, with alternatives for
out-of-school time beyond the often limited and narrow options of sports.
Moreover, as we will see in the next section, everyday material–discursive
enrichment practices—the more implicit forms of test preparation that
are materially distributed—matter substantially for SAT performance.

Multigenerational Inequality and SAT Performance

Social distribution in preparation for the SAT has been less examined than
how family background correlates with SAT performance. In the 1960s
especially, when elite institutions like Harvard, Princeton, and Yale were
feeling the pressures of new legislation such as the Civil Rights Act of 1964
and the socially volatile mood of the nation as many urban centers began
to see race riots, the SAT increasingly came under the public's microscope
(Karabel 2005; Lemann 1999). The test was charged with being biased
and falsely objective. And, although many of these earlier charges were refuted by ETS and the College Board on empirical grounds, various jour-
nalists, scholars, and politicians have argued that the test advantages the
affluent (see, for example, Crouse and Trusheim 1988; Elert 1992; Guinier
and Torres 2002; National Association for College Admission Counseling
2008). As an institutionalized mechanism of access to higher education
and, in theory, social mobility, these charges against the SAT were most
certainly in contradiction to its stated aims and promises to enable "equality of opportunity." The claims against the SAT led to several investigations
into the association of SAT performance with family background factors

such as race, gender, family income, and parents' education. Although the findings were pretty consistent, the interpretations most certainly were not.

Family Background and SAT Performance

Several studies have investigated the relationship between family socio-economic background and performance on the SAT, and all have consistently found a positive association. Even the College Board regularly reports the average SAT scores by test-taker race/ethnicity, gender, and family income (among other social categories). The College Board has also conducted investigations examining the relationship between parental income and education on SAT performance, finding results very similar to those of other studies (Camara and Schmidt 1999). However, Camara and Schmidt argued that while parental income and education have a strong relationship to SAT performance, (1) parental income and education are related to most other predictors and outcomes of academic performance, such as high-school GPA and rank; and (2) Hispanic/Latinx and African American students from comparable socioeconomic backgrounds still scored lower than their Asian American and white peers. Zwick (2004) also argued that the SAT is a "wealth test" only in the sense that every other measure of educational achievement is a wealth test. In other words, the socioeconomic and racial/ethnic performance differences are not an issue of the test but of society.

While the logic of this argument makes much sense on its face, especially on empirical grounds, it makes a strong epistemological assumption about both the test and society. That is to say, these arguments assume that the test is developed in a vacuum and completely unrelated to the material and discursive processes of society. The choosing of any particular object(s) of measurement is not just culturally constructed but also a political decision in and of itself. The cultural construct of measurement determines what processes of achievement are important and what constitutes what is "merit-able," as Vanessa and Steven reminded us above. In addition, even after determining particular construct(s) of merit, the development of the measure then includes a sample of observed behaviors that theoretically capture the variability of expressed behaviors in the construct(s) of interest, which has the consequence of excluding alternative behaviors and ways of knowing, particularly those of marginalized group members. Moreover, as a diffractive measuring apparatus, the SAT inherently produces overlapping, intra-acting differences. Cronbach (1988) and Messick (1988) remind us of this in their conceptualization of the use and interpretation of test scores as having social consequences; for instance, who is and is not accepted to the most selective institutions in the country. Those social consequences are also associated with labor-market outcomes such as adult income and wealth holdings as well as access to public office. As we saw above, the children of privileged families are more likely to receive the implicit and explicit preparation that is culturally aligned with the SAT. Thus, not only is the test a product of society, it is also simultaneously producing and reproducing a legitimated social hierarchy.

This social hierarchy is not unrelated to Camara and Schmidt's (1999) second point. Not only do Camara and Schmidt not account for all relevant family socioeconomic variables (e.g., family wealth or multigenerational resources), they also fail to account for other theoretically relevant processes such as stereotype threat or cultural familiarity. Thus, while their implied argument of social inequality as the issue of differential performance on the SAT is relevant, Camara and Schmidt miss vitally important processes that might put into question the testing practices and validity of the diffractive measuring apparatus of the SAT. The Journal of Blacks in Higher Education Foundation (1998) published an article showing that family income differences do not explain the differences in total SAT scores by race/ethnicity. The article, however, additionally reported that black students from families with incomes between $80,000 and $100,000 perform 141 points lower on the SAT than their white counterparts, a substantially smaller difference than for those in poverty. Even after accounting for the associations of parental education and high-school achievement, the associations of family income on SAT scores are substantial, nonlinear, and nearly twice as large for the self-identified black students (Dixon-Román, Everson, and McArdle 2013). Thus, there is much more to the black–white SAT performance differences than what is captured by the parents' socioeconomic position.

In order to further understand the social and schooling dynamics of SAT performance differences, Everson and Millsap (2004) examined both individual and school-level effects on SAT performance to evaluate the extent to which the variability of schooling matters. The statistical models employed enabled them to account for the variation in individual test-taker characteristics and the variation in school-related characteristics. Their results indicated that not only do the characteristics of the school matter but that after accounting for the school and individual variation, the SAT performance gaps were reduced on average by a half of a standard deviation, approximately 110 points on the total SAT scale. These findings suggest dramatic differences in the distribution of resources between schools, which are also closely tied to a family's race and socioeconomic status (Massey and Denton 1994) and their effects on SAT score differences.

Each of these studies included only parental education and family income as measures of family socioeconomic background. More recent work focused on measures of family wealth as stronger indicators of both social and racial stratification. Using data from the National Longitudinal Survey of Youth 1997, Dixon-Román and Kim (forthcoming) found that family total assets and total illiquid assets are substantially associated with SAT performance over and above family income, parents' education, test-taker's high-school achievement, and several other relevant variables. In addition, the family wealth association was more than twice the size for the SAT-mathematics than for the SAT-verbal. Thus, previous research on the SAT had been masking a substantial amount of covarying stratification associated with family wealth. Moreover, because family wealth is accumulated over a lifetime and generations, this finding also points toward the potential importance of multigenerational inequality and its effects on SAT performance.

The existing research on family socioeconomic background and SAT performance has shed light on the importance and limitations of family income, family wealth, and parents' education in accounting for the variations in SAT performance. However, these studies have not examined the extent to which there might be a multigenerational effect on SAT performance.

Multigenerational Inequality and Academic Achievement

Although no studies to date have examined multigenerational effects on SAT performance, other investigations have considered the cumulative or lagged effect of multiple generations of inequality on processes of child development and achievement (Dixon-Román forthcoming; Kalil et al. 2004; Mandara et al. 2009; Phillips et al. 1998; Roksa and Potter 2011; Sharkey and Elwert 2011; Yeung and Pfeiffer 2009). This line of research suggests that the influence of the parents' resources on their child's development may be further aided by the resources of the grandparents; or, more important, that the parents' adult resources may not capture the residual variation of the conditions the parents grew up in. For instance, Phillips et al. reported that "maternal grandparents' educational attainment . . . affect[s] their grandchildren's [Peabody Picture Vocabulary] test scores even after controlling parents' educational attainment" (126).

Despite these plausible explanations, other studies using broader measures of achievement do find the grandparent effects to be accounted for by the parents. Using ordinary least squares regression to examine the standardized fifth-grade California Achievement Test, Kalil et al. (2004) found that the effect of grandparent education operates via parent education and accounts for relatively little of the test score differences. Mandara and colleagues (2009) fit a structural equation model to data from the National Longitudinal Survey of Youth in order to examine differences in adolescent achievement. The model indicates that the maternal grandparents' socioeconomic status (SES) had an indirect effect on adolescent achievement via the mother's achievement, parent's socioeconomic status, and parenting practices, but no direct effect. Similarly, using the PSID, Yeung and Pfeiffer (2009) sought to examine the effect of early childhood home environment on the magnitude and increase of racial differences in achievement scores. They fit three different grade cohorts to regression models predicting achievement in 1997 and 2003, and found that while paternal grandparent education had a meaningful direct effect on applied problems in particular, this effect was completely mediated by parent socioeconomic factors and early childhood home environment. These studies suggest that grandparent education and socioeconomic status do not influence the grandchild directly but indirectly via the parent's resources, supporting the idea of a simple linear Markovian inheritance process.

In spite of these results, two recent studies have accounted for multigenerational processes via other mechanisms of social stratification, such as the parents' conditions of growth and neighborhood conditions net of the parents' adult neighborhood conditions where the child is growing up. In an investigation using the Panel Study of Income Dynamics, Roksa and Potter (2011) examined parents' social background, cultural capital, parenting practices, and child achievement. Parents' social background was operationalized as four categories of class mobility (i.e., stable middle, stable working, new middle, and new working) based on the parents' current level of education and the grandparents' level of education when the parents were growing up. Their results indicate that there is substantial variation between these four categories of social background and both parenting practices and achievement. Similarly, Sharkey and Elwert (2011) used the PSID, but treated neighborhood conditions as a socially stratifying mechanism and examined multigenerational neighborhood effects on both math and reading achievement. They found not only that the neighborhood conditions the parents grew up in have a direct effect on the grandchild's math and reading achievement, but that the effect is larger than the effect of the parents' adult neighborhood conditions where the grandchild is growing up. Lastly, Dixon-Román (forthcoming) also used the PSID to examine multigenerational effects on the growth of reading skills. The grandparents' total value of stocks and mutual funds and permanent income had positive associations with the rate of growth in reading achievement, controlling for the parents' socioeconomic resources as well as whether the child was born low birth weight, attended daycare, or attended private school. Each of these studies provides meaningful evidence of multigenerational effects by accounting for the social position or conditions the parent grew up in. Moreover, they all indicate that not accounting for multiple generations of inequality underestimates the persistence of inequality in grandchild achievement.

There are good reasons for multigenerational effects on child achievement. As Mare (2011) suggests, when considering multigenerational effects it is important to conduct institutional analyses because institutions and their practices are longer lasting than individuals. For instance, affluent parents who come from affluent families likely have more resources to invest in their child's development and future, in contrast to affluent parents who come from poor families. They may also have the benefit of greater institutional social networks to aid and support their child's growth. Like Ivy League schools, private schools also have legacy policies for admission, which means that a grandchild may benefit from the affluence and privilege their grandparents allotted to the parents. Or, due to having grown up in the cultural practices and sensibilities of affluence, the parents' dispositions and practices may be more closely aligned with the norms and rules of dominant institutions. Alternatively, as discussed in chapter 3, in each generation of shifting historicities there are material and sociocultural re(con)figurings of structures such as race, gender, and class. Race, gender, and class are structural relations that are part of the (re)configuring entanglements of space, time, and matter. In other words, race, gender, and class

are more-than-human identities and are part of the more-than-human ontologies of material resources and conditions entangled with the discursive
formations and limits of lived experiences. This implies that historicities are
complex, shifting, differentiating, and multiplicative. As assemblages that
work through one another, complex and differentiated structural relations
over the life course and across generations enable the possibility for the particularities of when a parent was growing up to manifest in their offspring
despite the parent's adult material and sociocultural resources and conditions. In other words, the structural relations of the grandparents when the
parents were growing up produce markings of the structural relations in
the grandchild (in)dependent of the parents' adult structural conditions.
For instance, the major legal and political economic shifts of the 1960s and
1970s have likely (re)configured the structural relations not just of that
generation's children but of the experiences of learning and development
of those children's offspring too. Thus, the reconfiguring of structural relations is important for the analysis of multigenerational effects of inequality, as the ontologies of structural relations do outlive people too. Each of
these plausible explanations suggests that the simple, linear Markovian inheritance process in fact does not capture the full variation of familial social
history and its effect on child achievement.

This is particularly important when considering multigenerational effects on SAT performance. To trace one example, the SAT has been the
primary institutionalized mechanism for college admissions for several
decades now. Taking the SAT has not only become a ritualized practice
for college-bound high-school juniors, a whole industry has developed
around preparation for it. This test-preparation industry, as was illustrated
above, has substantially benefited the affluent more than the poor. In addition, the postulated complex enfolding of residual pasts via inheritance
also suggests that the sons and daughters of "limbo" parents, those who
have moved to a more highly educated social class, would not have the
same experiences as their counterparts coming from multiple generations
of educated forbears. Thus, the grandsons and granddaughters of the highly educated are more likely to be exposed to the implicit forms of preparation, such as cultural practices and language that are assessed on the SAT,
than their counterparts who are sons and daughters of "limbo" parents.
As I discussed earlier, the grandchildren of academics and the affluent are
more likely to be the beneficiaries of the cultural knowledge assessed on
the SAT and, as a result, have an advantage going into the test. It is for

these theoretical reasons that I examine the effects of grandparents' educa-tion and parents' wealth (as a multigenerational measure) on youth SAT performance over and above parents' education, permanent income, and several other theoretically relevant variables.

Multigenerational Analyses of Youth SAT Performance

In order to examine for multigenerational effects on youth SAT perfor-mance I quantitatively analyzed data from the National Longitudinal Sur-vey of Youth 1997. By using a statistical method known as structural equa-tion modeling, I was able to examine the processes that in theory have a direct association with SAT performance as well as those processes that have an association with SAT performance via other variables. Thus, for example, theoretically we might believe that family wealth would be di-rectly associated with youth SAT performance, and we may also believe that family wealth is associated with the number of enrichment opportu-nities, which may also in turn be associated with SAT performance. Thus, part of the family wealth association with SAT performance would be a result of its enabling greater enrichment opportunities that provide prepa-ration for the SAT. By using structural equation modeling to analyze the NLSY97 data, I was better able to examine some of the underlying pro-cesses of inheritance intra-acting with SAT performance.

With the aim of illuminating multigenerational effects, I examined the association of maternal and paternal grandparents' education with youth SAT performance. While the mother's level of education had a positive as-sociation with SAT performance, the paternal grandparents' level of edu-cation had a slightly larger positive association (see Figure 12).

These estimates indicate that the grandparents' education matters slightly more than the parents' education. They also indicate that even if the mother has a graduate-level education, the grandchild with high-school educated paternal grandparents will perform, on average, 62.4 total SAT score points lower than counterparts whose paternal grandparents have a graduate-level education. The estimated difference for first-generation college youth SAT performance and those youth from multiple genera-tions of paternal grandparent graduate-level education is larger than one-half of a standard deviation on the total SAT score scale. For Latinx/Hispanic youth, the estimated paternal grandparent effect is substantially larger, given that their median paternal grandparent education was at a

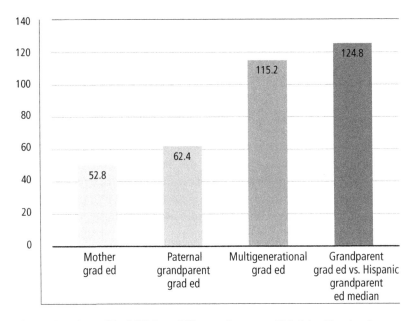

Figure 12. Estimated Total SAT Score Difference Between a High-School Level and Graduate/Professional School Education for Mothers and Paternal Grandparents. Source: National Longitudinal Study of Youth 1997.

fourth-grade level—plausibly a factor of the inherited transnational processes of immigration. This means that the SAT performance of Latinx/Hispanic youth who are first-generation college applicants was, on average, 177.6 points lower than that of their counterparts coming from multiple generations of graduate-level education. These estimated differences were certainly enough to determine admission to selective institutions. As an institutionalized measuring apparatus, these effects suggest that the more a family is formed and shaped by the discursive knowledge and materialized ways of knowing of graduate-level education, the more the grandchild is aligned with the apparatus of the SAT. These results also further underscore the enduring multigenerational effect that grandparents have in reconfiguring the material future possibilities of their grandchildren.

In addition to grandparents' education, I also examined the association of the parents' wealth (as a measure of both current and previous generation economic status) with youth SAT performance. In particular, parents' illiquid assets had a positive association with youth SAT performance. As shown in Figure 13, the estimated SAT performance difference between youth with $125,000 in family illiquid assets (the sample median) and those with no family illiquid assets was 141 points. This estimated difference is almost 75 percent of a standard deviation on the SAT scale and, again, certainly enough to determine admission to selective institutions of higher education. As discussed above, the economic elite are much more likely to have a greater number of enrichment opportunities and more SAT preparation and, as such, are more likely to be familiar(ized) with the material construction and timespace production of the intra-acting performative measuring apparatus and practice.

I also examined the effect of enrichment opportunities, as a measure of performative practices of implicit preparation, on SAT performance. The estimated association was substantial (see Figure 14). For every increase in enrichment opportunities there was a 42 point total SAT score increase. Thus, the social distribution of enrichment opportunities partially accounted for the social distribution in SAT scores. Furthermore, part of the parents' illiquid assets association with SAT performance and all of the father's level of education association with SAT performance is a product

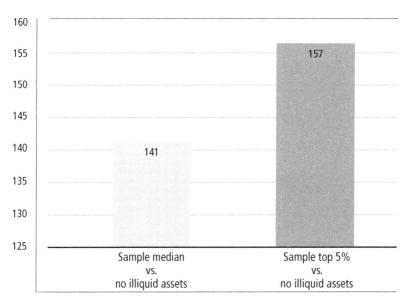

Figure 13. Estimated Total SAT Score Difference Between Youth from Affluent Families and Youth from Nonaffluent Families. Source: National Longitudinal Study of Youth 1997.

of the enabled enrichment opportunities as both increase. In contrast, we also learned above that as the risk in the home and neighborhood environment increased, the number of enrichment opportunities substantially decreased. While the home/neighborhood risk did not have a direct association with SAT performance, we learn here that much of the association between SAT performance and the material conditions of risk is a product of the disenabled or constrained number of enrichment opportunities.

School-related enrichment such as youth high-school achievement and whether they attended a public or private school each had meaningful associations with SAT performance. Youth high-school achievement was found to have a substantial positive association; that is, for every one unit increase on a 4.0 grade-point-average scale there was, on average, a 200 point increase in total SAT scores. In addition, youth who attended private schools scored 26 points higher than youth who attended public schools. These school effects are also a function of family socioeconomic resources. Both youth high-school achievement and private-school attendance were associated with the father's level of education, while the risk of the neighborhood environment was also associated with high-school

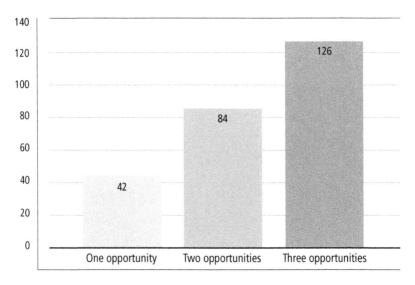

Figure 14. Estimated Total SAT Score Difference Between Youth Who Participated in Zero, One, Two, and Three Out-of-School Enrichment Opportunities. (Zero out-of-school enrichment opportunities are the reference group.) Source: National Longitudinal Study of Youth 1997.

achievement, and the parents' illiquid assets were associated with private-school attendance. In fact, youth from the sample median of total illiquid assets ($125,000) were 15.4 times more likely to attend a private school than their counterpart with no illiquid assets. Although the youth high-school achievement effect is substantial, the association is likely underestimated given the variability of the quality of schools with, as mentioned above, more privileged public schools now offering SAT preparation courses.

While we find that there is a substantial social distribution to SAT performance that is multigenerational and associated with increased enrichment opportunities, both school-related and out-of-school, these effects are most certainly not deterministic. There are always test-takers who defy the odds and score substantially higher than the average score for other test-takers with a similar family social history. For instance, the singer and songwriter Kesha grew up in a single-mother home in poverty yet scored a 1500 on the SAT; well above what the average test-taker of her family social background would have scored. As another example, singer and songwriter John Legend, who grew up in a working-class home, can be assumed to have performed well given that he was admitted to highly selective institutions such as Harvard University and the University of Pennsylvania. Indeed, the scores on the SAT are not completely socially determined and have enabled alternative possibilities for the few who have defied the odds.

It is important to convey that SAT scores are not completely socially determining. That is, SAT scores do not strongly or completely socially determine one's life chances or trajectory. As an example, former president Bill Clinton scored a 1030 on the SAT, good enough to be admitted to Georgetown University but not good enough to be admitted to more highly selective institutions. However, his score clearly did not constrain his opportunities to become a Rhodes Scholar, governor of Arkansas, or president of the United States. Another case in point would be rap artist Macklemore. In his single "Ten Thousand Hours" (with Ryan Lewis) he not only shares how he performed on the SAT but further questions the system of meritocracy at the same time:

No Child Left Behind, that's the American scheme
I make my living off of words
And do what I love for work
And got around 980 on my SATs.

In a play on Malcolm Gladwell's 2008 book *Outliers* where he posits that ten thousand hours of practice will lead to success, Macklemore questions the current apparatus of federal educational policy, the "American dream," and the system of meritocracy. He encourages youth to follow their passion rather than working behind the mundane desk of modernity. And, moreover, he states that he scored a 980 on the SAT but has achieved what the meritocratic system would not have predicted. Each of these social narratives illuminates the multiplicities of the above-presented graphemes of the statistical and the intra-acting ontologies with the apparatus of the SAT.

But how do we make sense of those intra-acting ontologies that haunt the institutionalized norming of the SAT? In what ways does the lens of inheritance help to further unpack the assemblage of these social narratives? And how might a diffractive analysis between the methods begin to highlight the multiplicities of the data? If we recall the model data in our reading of the social narratives, we can pinpoint that despite John Legend's or Kesha's social background they both stated that they did well academically in high school. In fact, John Legend was homeschooled on and off by his mother, which likely enabled him to be able to finish high school at the age of sixteen, and Kesha attended a music school in a suburb of Nashville that was ranked as one of the top public high schools in the country, and had an average combined SAT score of 1206. At a young age both also had the opportunity to participate in beyond-school enrichment opportunities that were related to singing, music literacy, and songwriting. In contrast, reading the quantitative via the lens of their social narratives lets slip the alternative social ontologies of the models. For instance, although we don't know the level of education of John Legend's grandparents we do know that his grandmother had a significant influence in his life, teaching him how to play the piano beginning at the age of three and encouraging him to sing in the church gospel choir. Kesha's mom was a singer and songwriter and had Kesha involved in her professional life from a very young age, including encouraging Kesha to sing and write. These early and longstanding enrichment opportunities along with multigenerational forces may have mattered substantially for these students' academic development. And, although Kesha's mom was living in poverty when Kesha was born she did secure a new publishing deal for her songwriting in Nashville, Tennessee. Thus, there is variation around the duration of lived poverty, what conditions her mom grew up in, or what Kesha's family's economic resources were as a youth; all of which would materially form and shape her development. While the model treats the material conditions of economic resources and social position as static, Kesha's narrative reminds us of the ways in which the models can mask these dynamic material vibrancies and shifts.

While the intra-acting models indicate that home/neighborhood risks do not have a direct association with SAT performance, Bill Clinton's biography may suggest otherwise. Clinton grew up in a home with a stepfather who was an alcoholic and abusive toward his mother and his stepbrother. There were even multiple occasions where young Bill had to step in with the threat of violence. While the family's resources may have constrained his enrichment opportunities, equally as plausible (and potentially the most constraining of all the intra-acting forces) are the social pressures and stressors of ongoing domestic violence. The affective weight of such social pressures and stressors could be impairing within the already anxiety-laden performative practice and timespace of the SAT.

The ready interpretation of such social narratives (including Bill Clinton and Macklemore) is to narrativize each of them as being unique, as having a hard work ethic, and as tending to affectively persevere or be "gritty." Policymakers and scholars such as Ralph Nader, Robert Sternberg, and Edmund W. Gordon have argued for the importance of affect in considering college admissions. It could even be argued that, although not explicitly, the SAT does implicitly capture a dimension of situational affect based on how the test-taker understands the tests, the significance they place on it, and how they are feeling in the timespace of administration. However, although measures of emotional intelligence have been developed they are yet to materialize in college admissions practices.

Others have gained recent attention for their work on the psychological measurement and study of what they call "grit" (Duckworth et al. 2007). Simply put, grit is a psychological theory of perseverance and passion. According to Duckworth and colleagues, it "entails working strenuously toward challenges, maintaining effort and interest over years despite failure, adversity, and plateaus in progress" (1087–88). This quality is purported to contribute to the success of individuals in their respective fields. It's plausible that the measurement of grit might be better able to account for the statistically constituted outliers. The problem is, theoretically speaking, what is grit? whose grit are we talking about? and grit for what, when, where, and how? My concern is that the "grit" we are talking about is that which is materially and discursively constituted by the privileged, particularly given its measurement in association with privileged constructs. As discussed earlier, intra-actively formed significance matters as to how one engages in performative acts. In other words, if youth even know about the SAT then how do they understand it and what kind of significance do they place on it for their future possibilities? This ultimately has direct implications for how (and if) they go about preparing for the SAT.

I raise this because the notion of "grit," as I understand it, is very much formed and shaped by material–discursive forces. That is to say, as an affect, grit is a preconscious "visceral perception" that is materialized in human bodily responses. Nor is grit a universal or core affective process that can be taught and then applied more broadly. Based on prior experience, people preconsciously place different meanings and significance on different things in life, and this is often informed by one's social position. Persevering and sustaining is also not unrelated to the resources one has with which to persevere and sustain. A runner's endurance in a race will always be enhanced or constrained by the amount of sleep they got the night before, the amount of water they have for hydration, and whether their body is familiar with running in the weather conditions and terrain of the day. Thus, the material and discursive resources matter for how "gritty" one can be. To privilege one person's "grit" that results in success in the job market over and against another's "grit" as a success on the streets (each of which not only takes a different orientation but uses a different affective process and cultural logic) simply privileges one over and against another while overlooking and missing the important particularities of the two.

Most important, in what ways are the "grit" of some-bodies materially and discursively responded to and intra-acted with differently? Here, I am thinking about the ways in which certain bodies are raced, gendered, classed, (dis)able-bodied, or sexualized in social events or situations, and how those interpellations are intra-acted with differently. While I do not question that each of the social outliers worked hard, I do question the implicit contrast that other youth do not and that all youth who worked hard were provided the same material–discursive resources and return. In fact, if "grit" was a personality characteristic that wasn't tied to a field or goal, existed irrespective of material–discursive resources, and transcended timespace (implied by the measurement), then one could ask why Bill Clinton and Macklemore did not do as well as John Legend and Kesha on the SAT. Clearly they were "gritty" enough to be successful politically and artistically, but why didn't they have the "grit" to do as well on the test? While affect is clearly important, I question its importance independent of the intra-acting material–discursive forces with/in the timespace of inheritance.

To further expound this argument I want to use the career-break narrative of John Legend. As an undergraduate student, he was at the University of Pennsylvania in Philadelphia at a time when neo-soul was vibrant and a number of new artists frequented the social spaces of the area. Artists such as Bilal, Jill Scott, Musiq Soulchild, the Roots, and Erykah Badu were regulars. His roommate in college just so happened to be the cousin of then newly emerging hip-hop artist Kanye West. He also had a good friend who told him about an artist he needed to connect with, and he eventually had the opportunity to meet her in a recording studio. That artist was Lauryn Hill and the album she was working on was her Grammy Award–winning *The Miseducation of Lauryn Hill*. Ms. Hill needed a piano player for a song she was putting together and invited John Legend to perform. This became Legend's first commercial song, "Everything Is Everything."

While the University of Pennsylvania provided a certain degree of material–discursive resources that were likely helpful for John Legend, this instantiation has more to do with what was enabled by the assemblage of his attending the elite institution. Here, we see the myriad forces that produce a seemingly serendipitous life event that enabled the intra-active agency: being in the city of Philadelphia at such an opportune moment, having a college roommate whose cousin was an artist who signed Legend to his first record label, and being able to meet Lauryn Hill at a moment when she needed a piano player for what was to be a Grammy Award–nominated song. As the place for neo-soul in the mid-90s, the assemblage of Philadelphia mattered in materially reconfiguring his future possibilities. The relations and connections of each of these events enabled John Rogers to become John Legend. It is clear from this narrative that John Legend's hard work and perseverance required the intra-acting myriad forces of the assemblage of these life events to reconfigure his material possibilities.

Thinking diffractively, I also want to consider the ways in which the intra-acting fabric of the data has affected and constituted my ontology. In looking at my own social biography, I was reminded that my Puerto Rico–born paternal grandmother was taken out of school in the fourth grade to help with the family farm and my Puerto Rico–born paternal grandfather had completed the eleventh grade. Although both of them studied for their GED years later while in New York, what the assemblages of the model suggest is that paternal grandparents' education during the timespace of the parents' childhood development matters slightly more than the parents' adult education level. Prior to this inquiry I hadn't thought about the ways in which my SAT performance may have been a partial, complex, and differentiated product of my father's parents' education level when he was growing up. I can begin to imagine how their linguistic and cultural familiarity could have been in conflict with the material–discursive apparatus of the SAT.

This is a theoretical point that though empirically demonstrated (Freedle 2003; Santelices and Wilson 2010) has been refuted by the Educational Testing Service (Dorans 2004; Dorans and Zeller 2004). I contend that linguistic or cultural multiplicity has never been examined in association with the SAT, it has merely materialized in the imperfect diffracted markings of other measured phenomena such as race and class. Moreover, I further assert that much of the social distribution on SAT performance would likely be accounted for by the multiplicity of material–discursive practices. In addition, I am also reminded that although both of my parents have owned homes at various points throughout my life, their total illiquid assets have always been generally low and neither of them owned a home while I was in high school. Given these factors, my average public high-school GPA and enrichment opportunities, and my mother's level of education, the SAT measure would seem to have done relatively well at estimating my family's social position of the moment but, as was the case for Clinton, it did not do well in predicting my academic or social potential. To state this more bluntly, this diffractive reading further affirmed my understanding of the SAT as being, to a substantial degree, a measure of social stratification that contributes to the institutionally legitimated rigidity in social mobility. Thus, for many socially and economically marginalized youth, the SAT helps to constrain their material–discursive possibilities for social mobility.

Concluding Considerations: Meritocracy, Social (Im)Mobility, and Accountability

In his 1940 article "Education for a Classless Society," James Bryant Conant posits:

> You are all familiar with the old American adage, "Three generations from shirt sleeves to shirt sleeves." This implies a high degree of social mobility, both up and down. It implies that sons and

daughters must and can seek their *own* level, obtain their *own* economic rewards, engage in any occupation irrespective of what their parents might have done.

The old American adage that Conant is referring to is exactly that, old and outdated. The adage assumes that wealth is merely passed down by family business and that hard work and intellect are necessary for the second and third generation to maintain or advance it. Implicitly it places complete faith in a market that will work these processes out in a fair and just way, and it doesn't account for the new forms of (virtually effortless) wealth management and growth in our contemporary moment of global neoliberal capitalism. Moreover, the adage naively assumes that the affluent won't do what they can to maintain their family's social legacy. But, there is another reading and interpretation that is more contemporary. The notion "from shirt sleeves to shirt sleeves" over multiple generations could also be understood as the rigidity of poverty and social mobility. And, although many ideologically still believe in the traditional interpretation of the adage the more contemporary latter interpretation is closer to the material–discursive realities analyzed in this chapter.

Research has indicated the persistence of intergenerational inequality, and the material–discursive consequences of multigenerational inequality have been empirically demonstrated. The data of this work points toward multiple understandings of intra-acting multigenerational forces with SAT performance. Whether it is the intra-acting effect of the paternal grandparents' education or the early and meaningful enrichment opportunities that a grandparent provides, multigenerational forces of inequality matter. The multigenerational forces of enfolded historialities also materialize in the markings of the intra-acting association of the parents' illiquid assets. As a phenomenon that captures a family's economic legacy and measures both current and past social and racial inequality, parental wealth is a complex and differentiated identity of origin. Moreover, the intra-acting test-preparation industry and the significance given to the SAT both are socially distributed based on their given material and discursive resources. These inherited multigenerational forces of inequality radically point toward the materially reconfigured (im)possibility of social mobility from the SAT apparatus with/in the material conditions of profound inequality. Thus, as the institutionalized measuring apparatus of meritocracy, the SAT has reconfigured new determinate boundaries of material possibilities for social mobility for a small number of those who historically were excluded from the mattering elite institutions of higher education, but it has substantially contributed to that which Conant feared: a more rigid society in terms of social mobility.

The Conant–Jeffersonian ideal of meritocracy—involving concern for a socially mobile society from generation to generation, regardless of social inequality in society; as well as a call for "equality of opportunity" (not material condition) for education in order to enable those aims—may have provided the enumerated underpinnings for the ideological legitimation of the neoconservative political interest in rugged individualism. Even though Conant would not have agreed with the persistent reproduction of social inequality (what he characterized as social class divisions), he seemed to overlook the vibrant, dynamic, and formative matter of material conditions. The ideology of meritocracy that he was a proponent for—a system of selection based on the measurement of the most talented in society, who would go on to lead the nation—has in turn provided the ideological and systematic legitimation for the existing system of reproducing and increasing inequality.

Although an enumerating measure of legitimation, the measuring apparatus of the SAT is not passive but rather has an intra-acting ontology. The ontology of the SAT has shifted with the various iterations of merit(ocracy) and each shift has been followed by re-nuanced performative practices by the elite in order to maintain and ensure their family's social legacy. The SAT is not a pre-fixed or passive apparatus that is separable from the testing industry (subjects) and the test-takers (the objects of observation) but rather a measure that has been constituted through iterative reworkings and re(con)figurings of practices given its intra-action with other phenomena such as the evolving constitution of "merit," the shifts in society, and the changing nature of the testing industry and preparation companies. The ontology of the SAT discussed in this chapter alongside the social biographies underscores how the SAT does not simply produce a cartography of intellectual ability for college admissions but also maps the social, cultural, racialized, and economic boundaries of the test-taker *bodies*. On the one hand, the material–discursive conditions of the test-takers constrain and enable their possibilities for preparation and, relatedly, performance on the measuring apparatus; on the other hand, the measuring apparatus produces material–discursive phenomena (test scores) that *re*work and *re*configure the test-takers' material possibilities.

The measuring apparatus of the SAT diffracts a distribution of scores that intra-actively produces determinate boundaries of the intellectual ability, social and economic position, race, gender, and (dis)ability of each test-taker. These diffracted differences—or relational and connected differences that make a difference—do have material consequences in peoples' lives. Given the high stakes of the SAT and how it is tied to college admission, the quality of the college to which a student is admitted, or the possibility of earning an academic scholarship, these diffracted differences can have consequences on the test-taker's social future and the possibilities for social mobility or immobility. Thus, given that the SAT does not stand alone but is an apparatus inseparable from and intra-active with other material–discursive phenomena of the world, the ethical question of responsibility must be considered. Although the intra-active lens of a quantum anthropology would suggest that responsibility lies with all intra-acting agents, the questions of accountability require more attentiveness to the consequences of asymmetrical power relations. In what ways is the testing industry accountable for intra-actively producing a measuring apparatus that is materially and discursively constituted by the privileged? How is the test-preparation industry accountable for further enabling and preparing the affluent substantially more than the poor? To what extent are neoliberal and punitive federal social policies accountable for the increasing and unconscionable wealth inequality? And in what ways are the admissions policies and practices of colleges and universities, which both enable the taken-for-granted practices of the testing industry and use those test scores as a primary measure for admission decisions, contributing to less diverse and more privileged student *bodies* at elite institutions? These are the intra-acting agencies that have the power to *re*work and *re*(con)figure the materializations of merit and the apparatus of the SAT as well as the intra-active practices of college admissions.

Enfolding Possibilities

N EW MATERIALIST INTERVENTIONS into theories of social reproduction and quantitative inquiry in education open up new and exciting possibilities for the materialist analysis and deconstruction of force
and power relations in education. In this concluding chapter, I begin by
critically considering how social policies of social mobility have enacted
agential cuts of both possibility and impossibility. As an intervention into
critical policy studies, I demonstrate the import of diffraction as an analytical approach to reading and analyzing that which is said to regulate
and enable justice: the law and policy. A diffractive analysis of more-than-
human ontologies can go beyond theoretical perspectives and the data of
critical social inquiry to include the analysis of policy. Multiple policies are
often designed to address different proximal interests while having similar
distal aims. There are many social policies targeting social mobility. I will
focus here on the example of first-generation college admissions and diffractively analyze it through admissions practices with legacy applicants.
Through this diffractive analysis I seek to highlight how the two seemingly
contradictory policies need each other and are doing very similar discursive and psychic work.

I then put myself into the larger intra-acting fabric of this book project. Rather than "reflecting," as if I were a distant observer, I discuss more
broadly how this work has ontologically affected my thought and understanding of questions on social reproduction and social inquiry. I discuss
what I learned both from theoretical interventions as well as empirical
results. With the new materialist focus on process over position and the
body over cultural constructions, I argue, alongside Puar (2007), that
perhaps the focus on social reproduction needs to shift toward regenerative capacities. I also consider two important critiques of new materialisms. The first pertains to what seems to be a silence in the philosophical work on the human and more-than-human ontologies of indigenous
studies and black literary scholarship. The second criticism is related to

the specters of positivism in new materialisms. That is, new materialisms could be questioned for being another iteration of appropriations of the "natural" sciences for the developments of the "social" sciences. What is the same? What is different? And, how do those similarities and differences function for our contemporary moment? My lessons learned most certainly point toward new lines of potential and exciting inquiry.

Finally, I will provide some remarks on the enfolding possibilities of where I think critical inquiry *must* go. The ubiquity of the digital and the ways in which the ontologies of algorithms are reconfiguring timespace as well as reshaping material and discursive realities has made quantification ever more relevant. While there was warrant to question the Enlightenment idea of the grand book of the universe being written in the logic of mathematics, there is no question that what underlies the ubiquity of digital ontologies is the myriad of algorithms of computation. Not only does this make critical inquiry's hermeneutics of suspicion toward quantification foolhardy (or problematic) but I will argue that it also runs the risk of rendering critical inquiry irrelevant. Furthermore, I will contend that the critical theoretical and cultural studies interests of deconstruction and new materialist analyses of power relations are at stake and must work from within in order to implode the regenerative capacities of power and structural relations.

A Diffractive Analysis of Social Mobility Policy

In the essay "Force of Law," Jacques Derrida has this to say about the law and the possibility of justice:

> Law is not justice. Law is the element of calculation, and it is just that there be law, but justice is incalculable, it demands that one calculate with the incalculable; and aporetic experiences are the experiences, as improbable as they are necessary, of justice, that is to say of moments in which the *decision* between just and unjust is never insured by a rule. (2002, 257)

According to Derrida, the law is not justice because the law is the calculable, finite, universal, and singular of coded rules; whereas justice is the incalculable, infinite, particular, multiple, impassable, and impossible. Justice is the experience of aporia. Aporetic experiences are the experiences of the impassable and impossible. Derrida speaks to three aporetic experiences of justice. The first aporia is that every decision rests on preexisting law which is also based on the repression and deferral of justice from the violence of its instituting foundation. Each case is different and requires the singular interpretation that an instituted rule or regulation is not able to guarantee. The second aporia is that every decision is undecidable. The decision to calculate through the law enacts cuts and divisions that amount to the learning and interpretation of the pretended universality of the rule for the singularity of the other (i.e., the particularity of each instantiation before the law). As such, justice escapes the grasp of the present. The haunting of the undecidable is also in the assumption of presence and consciousness in the decision—a decision that could never be presently or fully just. A just decision is always urgent, while the third aporia is that justice is always "to come." The immediate need for justice demands a decision but the undecidability of justice defers its presence. Despite its aporetic experience, "incalculable justice *commands* calculation" (257).

Derrida's deconstruction of the law and justice provides an important perspective for the critical analysis of policy. Not only does Derrida posit that the law is not justice, he asserts that the law is necessary in order to enable the possibilities for justice. Building on Derrida's deconstruction of the law and the possibilities of justice, new materialisms understand the law and policy as apparatuses that performatively enact agential cuts and divisions. These enacted agential cuts and divisions are among the myriad forces that reconfigure assemblages of structural relations. Thus, there are always multiple policies that work intra-actively to produce the ontology of phenomena. For instance, first-generation college admissions or first-time home purchasing programs are policies that explicitly seek to enable social mobility; while, in contrast, certain policies may have inadvertent effects on possibilities for social mobility, such as legacy admissions or low-income (not asset-based) housing programs. In a time of stagnating salaries and high student-loan debt, first-generation college graduates are less likely to be able to qualify for low-income housing programs that do not account for high debt and low-assets holdings. Each of these policies as well as many other forces intra-actively and diffractively contribute to the reconfiguring of structural relations. It is for this reason I argue that policy analysis has to go beyond the deconstruction of a singular policy to consider the ways in which multiple laws and policies are intra-actively producing material reconfiguring possibilities and new phenomena. Given the overlap in the forces of these multiple policies, I argue that a diffractive reading and analysis of the policies will illuminate both how they are intra-acting and the diffracted patterns of differences—patterns that offer a better understanding of a reconfiguring system of structural relations than is provided by the more narrow lens of policy outcomes.

In light of the empirical results of multigenerational effects on SAT performance offered in chapter 4, I perform a diffractive analysis of college admissions practices with first-generation college and legacy applicants. I begin by reviewing the literature on the ontology of each admissions practice separately, then I diffractively read the ontology of each policy through the other so as to highlight the ways in which the two are intra-acting, as well as how the diffractive patterns both materially reconfigure future possibilities in college admissions while at the same time collectively doing the discursive and psychic work of meritocracy.

Review of First-Generation Students and College Recruitment

As more families than ever before have access to postsecondary education, more potential first-generation students are poised to enter college. However, less is known about first-generation students relative to other groups who have been traditionally underrepresented in higher education (e.g., black, Latinx, and low-income students). I open this review with an examination of how the existing higher education literature has defined first-generation college students and their relative overlap with other underserved groups. I then summarize the extant research on first-generation students' enrollment patterns in higher education, and their subsequent outcomes. Then, I examine the literature on institutions' admission policies and practices in their consideration of first-generation students.

Identifying First-Generation Students

Researchers, practitioners, and policymakers have used variations of the "first-generation" moniker in order to describe a group of students who come from families that have limited history or experience with higher education. One conservative approach defines first-generation students as those whose parents have never enrolled in college (Committee for Undergraduate Recruitment, Admissions, and Financial Aid 2013; Nuñez and Cuccaro-Alamin 1998; U.S. Department of Education 2012; Warburton, Bugarin, and Nuñez 2001), and therefore these students are considered first-generation college *goers*. Others (National Center for Education Statistics 2010) have also considered students whose parents enrolled in college but did not earn a degree or certificate as first-generation college *graduates*. A third and more inclusive definition recognizes the earning potential and other benefits accrued by those who have earned a bachelor's degree versus those who have not, and considers students whose parents have not received a bachelor's degree as first-generation *degree* holders (Baum, Ma, and Payea 2013).

Given that particular racial/ethnic and low-income groups have historically been excluded from certain segments of higher education, it is a near tautologous observation that many first-generation students overlap significantly with low-income students and students of color. A study on new college students who started in 2012 found that on average, 55 percent of dependent first-generation college goers come from families who earn less than $40,000, compared to 19 percent of students whose parents have a bachelor's degree. In contrast, 31 percent of students whose parents have a bachelor's degree also have incomes over $120K, compared to 6 percent of students whose parents have no more than a high-school diploma (U.S. Department of Education 2012). This is not surprising, as bachelor's degree holders earn 40 percent more in yearly wages, on average, than those with some college experience but no degree and 60 percent more than those with a high-school degree (Baum, Ma, and Payea 2013). In addition, greater shares of black and Latinx students are also first-generation college goers, and greater shares of white students are from families where at least one parent has a bachelor's degree. Only 28 percent of white college students are first-time college goers, compared to 33 percent Asian, 42 percent black, and 48 percent Latinx college students in 2012 (U.S. Department of Education 2012). In contrast, 44 percent of white and 45 percent of Asian college students come from homes where at least one parent has a bachelor's degree, compared to only 28 percent of black and 25 percent of Latinx college students.

The term "first-generation" is often used as a catch-all for students who are underrepresented in higher education: low-income students, students with low socioeconomic status, and students of color. However, while race, income, and first-generation status are related, first-generation status is its own distinct category and not wholly synonymous with poor students or students of color. Moreover, the ways in which researchers, practitioners, and policymakers define first-generation students could have implications for whether or not students whose parents may have some college experience but no degree, or even associate's degrees, are included in admissions considerations.

Recruitment

Colleges' efforts toward recruitment of first-generation students tend to take a back seat to efforts aimed at other groups. In 2012, the online journal *Inside Higher Ed* and the Gallup polling company administered a web survey to 576 college admission directors at two-year as well as public and private four-year institutions (with a 15 percent response rate). Roughly one-third (31 percent) of respondents indicated they were "very likely" to "increase recruitment efforts" for first-generation college students, as compared with minority students (44 percent) and full-pay students (31 percent). The level of recruitment interest varied by sector, as over half of two-year institutions indicated an interest in increasing their recruitment efforts (57 percent), followed by four-year public (34 percent) and only one in five four-year private (20 percent) institutions (Jaschik and Lederman 2012).

These survey results may be a reflection of the lack of incentives for colleges to aggressively recruit first-generation college students. First, the notion of diversity is typically characterized as the representation of students by race/ethnicity on a college campus. These are the data that have to be legally reported to the government for every institution that receives Title IV funding and are prominently displayed on college search websites (College Board 2013; College Confidential 2013; Peterson's 2013). Racial/ethnic minorities, moreover, are one of the groups that are designated as beneficiaries of affirmative action programs under the Equal Protection Clause of the Fourteenth Amendment, and therefore are given priority preference over first-generation applicants. Secondarily, and of growing importance, is the representation of low-income students on campus. This is usually captured by the percentage of students receiving Pell Grants, data readily available through the federal government. (In a speech, President Obama proposed using the percentage of Pell Grant recipients to measure performance-based funding in order to motivate institutions to enroll and graduate more low-income students.) However, first-generation college student data are not commonly collected or reported outside of the institutions themselves. Moreover, the share of first-generation college students is not factored into popular college rankings (Howard 2013; Morse and Flanigan 2013). Therefore, there are no legal, financial, or reputational carrots to encourage institutions to increase their applicant pool of first-generation students.

Admissions

An annual survey of colleges administered in 2010 by the National Association of College Admission Counseling (NACAC) reported that slightly more institutions found a student's first-generation status of "considerable importance" or "moderate importance" in the admissions process compared to alumni relations (29 percent versus 26 percent, respectively). In contrast, more institutions reported alumni relations of "limited importance" in the admissions process compared to first-generation status (35 percent versus 26 percent). Finally, more institutions reported that first-generation status was of "no more importance" than alumni relations (45 percent versus 40 percent). When considering survey responses by institution type, alumni relations were valued more by institutions that were private, smaller, or had low yield rates (i.e., the percentage of accepted students to enroll in the institution); institutions that were larger considered first-generation status as an important characteristic in admissions; and both first-generation and alumni relations were influential in the admissions process at more selective institutions (Clinedist, Hurley, and Hawkins 2011).

A survey of college admissions directors revealed that 9 percent would weight a student's first-generation status more heavily "if the right of colleges and universities to consider race and ethnicity in admissions decisions is scaled back [by the Supreme Court]"—although more two-year (13 percent) and public four-year (13 percent) colleges were willing to make that shift than private four-year institutions (6 percent; Jaschik and Lederman 2012).

The Other Side of the Coin: Legacies

In contradistinction to first-generation students, this section focuses on students who not only come from families that have had exposure to higher education, but are alumni of the very college to which the student is applying—the legacy applicant.

Elite College Admissions and Merit

As discussed in chapter 4, the concept of merit has changed over time to serve as the determining standard or rule to serve the interests of elite institutions. This included redefining their measures of merit in the early 1900s through *character* and other intangibles in order to weed out students they found not to fit their interest, such as Jewish and black students (Coe and Davidson 2011; Karabel 2005). Although merit would later be understood in a sense that supported equal opportunity, the lack of substantive financial aid programs and unbridled racism remained as barriers, regardless of whether this retooled standard of merit was met. The SATs helped shape the concept of merit.

One fallacy of admissions as a meritocratic process is that a number of other factors are considered that are beyond the control of the applicant and of which the applicant is perhaps oblivious (e.g., geography, high-school profile, legacy status). Golden (2007) estimates that in some universities, a paltry 40 percent of seats are doled out to students who are not "special admits" (e.g., legacy students or athletes). In conjunction with the increase in quantity and quality of applicants, admission into a selective institution becomes increasingly challenging. Additionally, certain admissions policies, such as early decision and early action, exclude students who cannot financially commit or are not savvy enough to understand their options. As a result, these policies disproportionately benefit those from wealthy backgrounds, where "on average, applying early increases the chances of admission to selective colleges the same amount as a jump of 100 points or more in SAT score" (Avery, Fairbanks, and Zeckhauser 2004, 16). Additionally, these admissions policies and practices increase the yield (and therefore the ranking) of selective institutions, but undermine access and meritocratic ideals.

The 1980s saw the advent of the *U.S. News and World Report* "America's Best Colleges" rankings, which fueled intense competition among institutions for the calculated prestige that previously had been merely implied. This also coincided with a sharp increase in fundraising activity for many institutions. Casting students as consumers, institutions jockeyed for funding to construct the best facilities, hire the best faculty, and attract the best students. Therefore, merit and endowment were closely linked, as funds were needed to create a suitable environment to remain competitive and attract the best students. While the national perceptions of merit were largely unchanged, competitive institutions began to align their definitions of merit with the metrics which would allow them to attain high rankings, paying particular attention to SAT scores and yield rates (Karabel 2005).

> One crucial component in the magazine's assessment was the percentage of applicants that an institution accepted—the lower the better, as the editors believed. *U.S. News* also tabulated the percentage of accepted students who chose to matriculate at that institution, a number it wanted to be as high as possible. (Steinberg 2002, 7)

So powerful were these rankings that increases in ranking were associated with increases in the quantity of applicants (Luca and Smith 2009).

The late 1990s onward brought a surge of applications through increases in high-school graduating classes (Bound, Hershbein, and Long 2009) and technologies that facilitated application submission (e.g., Common Application digital college application system). As a result, an increasing number of institutions enjoyed increases in selectivity, all the while only moderately increasing their freshman class sizes. This increase in selectivity translated to nearly half a standard deviation increase in the SAT scores required for admission (Bound, Hershbein, and Long 2009). Among the top twenty public universities, students in the seventy-fifth percentile in 2003 scored 52 points higher than those in the seventy-fifth percentile in 1986—roughly half of one standard deviation. At the top private institutions, the seventy-fifth percentile score increased by 42 points. In fact, one study found that a student with a combined SAT score of 1500 would have less than a 50 percent chance of getting into a very selective college (McDuff 2007).

The Legacy Advantage

Although less well-known than affirmative action, legacy admissions are a widespread policy that seems to be at odds with our society's achievement-oriented ideology (Bowen, Kurzweil, and Tobin 2005; Duffy and Goldberg 1997; Howell and Turner 2004; Megalli 1995). In an education policy address on November 21, 2002, Senator John Edwards made the following statement regarding legacy admissions policies:

There's no question many legacy students are highly qualified and tremendous additions to their schools. They can be admitted without any preferences, and they should be. Unlike affirmative action, which I support, the legacy preference does not reward overcoming barriers based on race or adding diversity to the classroom. The legacy preference rewards students who had the most advantages to begin with. It is a birthright out of eighteenth century British aristocracy, not twenty-first century American democracy. It is wrong.

Elite institutions have a longstanding tradition of admitting family members of alumni. Some staunchly defend the practice of giving legacies preferential treatment during the admissions process, using terms like "special bond" to characterize legacy students' relationship to their university and to expound upon their intangible assets—much as Christopher Eisgruber, the president of Princeton University, did in an interview (Schleifer 2013). In fact, Eisgruber stated, "That [legacy] preference is literally a tie-breaker in cases where credentials are about even." This was stated in defense of admitting nearly 30 percent of legacy students in contrast to a 7.4 percent overall admissions rate. Others justify legacy admissions with money; institutions argue that establishing and rewarding intergenerational familial ties increases their donor base. In short, it is believed that legacy parents give more money. Further, many argue that the money accrued through legacies can be used to fund the admittance of low-income students, or other benefits to be enjoyed by all, such as student centers and libraries. However, others point to the exceptionally low enrollment rates of low-income students at many of the selective institutions where legacy admissions are prevalent, in order to show such purported benefits are not actualized (Karabel 2005). In addition, recent research has indicated that legacy families do not in fact make larger donations than other families (Kahlenberg 2010).

Legacy admissions preserve a social hierarchy from a time when access was not equitably distributed. Therefore via their admissions history, the main beneficiaries of legacy status are mostly white students who do not need aid, and have relatively low academic profiles when compared to their schoolmates (Howell and Turner 2004; Wolniak and Engberg 2007). Dubbed "affirmative action for the rich" (Kahlenberg 2010; Leef 2008), legacy admission practices were met with increased scrutiny in response to litigation linked to affirmative action and race-based admissions policies in the 1990s, and many began to question the legitimacy of legacy admissions practices. Senator John Edwards, a longtime proponent of social justice and advocate for the poor, brought the issues surrounding legacy admissions into the fold of his 2004 presidential campaign platform (Golden 2003). In 2003, the late Senator Edward Kennedy introduced legislation to mandate reporting on legacies as a condition of receiving federal monies. His proposal, as part of the Higher Education Reauthorization Act, was met with much resistance, and a strong higher education lobby indefinitely buried the measure (Field 2009; Leef 2008).

Despite the lack of available data, it is estimated that legacy admissions make up 10 to 25 percent of most Ivy League schools' freshman classes each year (*Economist* 2004; Kahlenberg 2010; Larew 1991). Moreover, Massey and Mooney (2007) used a sample of approximately 3,924 fall of 1999 college freshmen in twenty-eight selective colleges from the National Longitudinal Survey of Freshmen (NLSF) to compare the academic performance of three affirmative action programs: athletics, legacy, and underrepresented minorities. Their study showed that legacy students were the only group for which SAT scores below the institution's mean SAT scores meant lower college GPAs.

A Diffractive Analysis of Both Admissions Policies

As intra-acting policies, first-generation and legacy admits produce diffractive patterns of reconfiguring structural relations in admissions. While their proximal interest may be different their distal purpose is the same. Proximally, the focus on first-generation admissions is to enable fairness and equity for those students whose parents were not college educated. For legacy admissions, the argument is to maintain "social bonds" and institutional donors. Although these two proximal aims are very different they both have the same enrollment management goal of enrolling as many students as possible, to generate the targeted tuition revenue. This often materializes in admissions decisions that will maximize the return to the institution in the long run.

Diffractively reading these two admissions policies through one another illuminates how the agential cuts and divisions of each policy apparatus reconfigure the determinate boundaries of what matters and what is excluded from mattering, enacting conditions of possibility and impossibility. A diffractive reading of policies is not limited to considering how the strengths of one policy might help the other, but rather highlights the ways in which seemingly different laws or policies are relationally and intra-actively producing phenomena. The prioritized interests of maintaining "social bonds" and institutional donors (of legacy admissions) renders the aims of fairness, equity, and institutional diversity (through first-generation admissions) secondary. We see this not just in the rationales of the stated aims in support of both but also in the statistical estimates. For instance, as we saw above, it is estimated that legacy students make up between 10 to 25 percent of freshman classes at Ivy League institutions. Although I was unable to locate a corresponding estimate for first-generation students, it is plausible to glean a rough estimate from the Educational Longitudinal Study of 2002 (https://nces.ed.gov/surveys/els2002/). Although the ELS:2002 does not provide data specific to Ivy League institutions, the 2006 PowerStats dataset estimates that 3.4 percent of the freshman classes at "very selective" institutions were students with parents who have a high-school diploma or less (U.S. Department of Education 2012). Moreover, these enrollment rates also suggest that first-generation students are between 68 to 92 percent *less* likely than legacy students to be admitted to very selective institutions. While these are very rough estimates (given the inaccessibility of better quality data), they still highlight one way in which the two admissions policies are relationally intra-acting at very selective institutions. Given the privileging of legacy students over first-generation students, this puts into question the institutions' commitment to the ideals of fairness, equity, and the social mobility promises of meritocracy.

The diffractive patterns of reconfigured structural relations from intra-acting admissions policies sustain the discursive and psychic work of meritocracy. By maintaining first-generation representation in selective institutions, the belief in the taken-for-granted ideals of meritocracy is upheld despite the marginalized existence of such students on very selective college campuses. Some may also say that the inherent contradiction between the two admissions policies is paradoxical, in that institutions cannot afford to provide opportunities without donations from their legatees. Although they represent opposites on the spectrum of social mobility, both first-generation and legacy admissions policies need one another in order to materially and discursively legitimate beliefs in ideologies of meritocracy, despite the ontological impossibility of meritocracy. Meritocracy assumes a system of fairness and equity based on an assumed universal "merit" that is imbued in the material of calculable rules, standard(ized) measurement apparatuses, and regulatory provisions. Like justice, fairness and equity are the incalculable, the infinite, the multiple, and the particular. Each applicant is different and requires a singular interpretation that no calculable rule or standard(ized) measure can guarantee. A decision generated by the pretended universality of "merit" for the singularity of each student applicant will always enact cuts and divisions that both reconfigure structural relations in college admissions while deferring the possibilities of fairness and equity. The two policies, which are coconstitutive based on their generational structure, relationally enact determinate boundaries that contribute to the myriad forces of both reconfiguring structural relations and material practices (e.g., images of bodily diversity) that legitimate discursive formations of and psychic beliefs in meritocracy.

As a social mobility policy, first-generation admissions practices seek to enable possibilities for applicants who come from families that historically have been marginalized from such opportunities. The empirical results we saw in chapters 3 and 4 demonstrate the ways in which processes of child development and college admissions test performance are a product of the inherited material–discursive forces of multigenerational inequality, thus underlining the important and necessary yet insufficient policies and practices of first-generation admissions. First-generation admissions are important and necessary in order to enable possibilities that would otherwise be constrained by the material–discursive forces of inherited inequality, yet they insufficiently address the multigenerational dynamics of inheritance. The above diffractive analysis suggests that first-generation applicants are not given enough attention in college admissions, especially in relation to the prioritized aristocratic practices of legacy admissions at very selective institutions. The meritocratic commitments to fairness and equity by society and institutions of higher education are compromised under current admissions practices where first-generation applicants receive marginal consideration in admission, let alone in their corporeal experience at many institutions.

This diffractive analysis of first-generation and legacy admissions practices is one instantiation of a new materialist approach to critical policy studies.

Lessons Learned from *Inheriting Possibility*

In light of the demonstrated utility of diffractive analysis for critical policy studies, I'd like to discuss the major lessons learned from this book project, *Inheriting Possibility*. Rather than "reflecting" on this book project I'd like to insert myself into its ontological fabric so as to account for my becoming with the assemblage of *Inheriting Possibility*. In other words, I'd like to consider how I have been intra-actively produced by and mutually constituted with *Inheriting Possibility* and the phenomena of social reproduction and quantitative inquiry.

Prior to working on *Inheriting Possibility*, I was situated in poststructuralist thought on the materiality of cultural constructions that merely "writes off" the epistemological accessibility of nature as always obscured by the discursive. My interest in deconstructing the nature/culture binary in this project drew me to new materialisms and their powerful implications for social theory and the philosophy of science on quantitative methods. As I have theoretically argued and empirically demonstrated, the identity and difference of nature and culture have greatly undergirded and limited social theories of social reproduction in education. The critical importance of accounting for the entanglement of the material and discursive and relational ontologies in the analysis of reproducing power relations sharply illuminated the complexities of social reproduction in parenting practices and youth SAT scores. The limits of quantification were also found to rest on the nature/culture binary, and that thinking beyond the limits opens up the performative possibilities for critical inquiry. The empirical results in chapters 3 and 4 demonstrate the ways in which ontologies of structural relations outlive human lives and produce multigenerational effects of inequality. Chapters 3, 4, and the Conclusion also demonstrate the analytic utility and power of diffractive analyses for the data of both critical social inquiry and policy studies. The combinatorial analytical utility of assemblages with diffractive analyses for the study of "difference" in social reproduction in chapter 3 shows that there are ways of performing comparative analyses without falling into the colonialist trap of pathology, deficiency, and depravity narratives of the marginalized but rather understanding the estimated "differences" as relational and connected. Lastly, *Inheriting Possibility* accentuates and draws attention to the critical importance of questions and methods of quantification for the new materialist analysis of power relations.

Although this project has, in part, focused on theories of social reproduction in education, the new materialist focus on process and the body
has important implications as well. Through assemblage theory, race,
gender, sexuality, class, and dis/ability are thought of not as identities or
characteristics of the human but rather as events that consist of relations
and connections, that intra-lace the material ontologies of the body with
discursive formations, and are imbricated in the material flow of events.
What is assumed in theories of social reproduction is a focus on social position and identity, a focus on moving from one position to another at the
cost of overlooking the rich and more important movement, process, and
flow in between. As Puar (2007) states:

> What is at stake in terms of biopolitical capacity is therefore not
> the ability to reproduce, but the capacity to *regenerate*, the terms of
> which are found in all sorts of registers beyond heteronormative
> reproduction. (211)

While Puar is referring more specifically to the problematic of reproductive futurity with children, the shift from social reproduction to regenerative capacity is even more apropos for research on education and
human learning and development. Shifting the analytical focus from position to process, regenerative capacities further enable the new materialist
analysis of power relations. The focus of such analyses is on "what capacities they can and cannot regenerate and what kinds of assemblages they
compel, repel, spur, deflate" (211). With the focus on analyzing capacities
that may or may not be able to regenerate, we can better understand the
dynamics and forces that are reconfiguring and designating what is materially possible and impossible. Regenerative capacity is an important concept for education and social policy as well as the movement, process, and
flow for/of social change.

As well as the critically important lessons learned from *Inheriting Possibility* on new materialisms and the quantum anthropologies of social
reproduction in education, there are two important critiques that I was
introduced to toward the completion of the book project. The first pertains to the epistemologies of black, brown, and maroon thinkers and the
ways in which they have already theorized on questions of the human,
relational ontologies, and the ontologies of land, place, and context. Alex
Weheliye (2014), for instance, argues that there seems to be an intellectual

amnesia when it comes to the contributions of black feminist scholars such as Hortense Spillers and Sylvia Wynter. While I introduced Weheliye's idea of racializing assemblages in chapter 3 I did not discuss the other critical and important part of his project. Weheliye argues:

> Black studies and other formations of critical ethnic studies provide crucial viewpoints, often overlooked or actively neglected in bare life and biopolitics discourse, in the production of racialization as an object of knowledge, especially in its interfacing with political violence and (de)humanization. (5)

The intellectual contributions of Spillers and Wynter have always engaged in questions on the human and in ways that address the shortcomings of Agamben's and Foucault's accounts of race and biopolitics.

In addition to black studies, my colleague Eve Tuck (2015) reminds us that many indigenous philosophies have always understood the ontologies of land, place, and context; the human's relational ontologies with the natural and spiritual world; and, by implication, their own epistemologies of science and mathematics. For instance, Angayuqaq Oscar Kawagley (2006) discusses the importance of balance and alignment between the natural, spiritual, and human realms of the Yupiaq worldview. Kawagley quotes Chief Seattle (1790–1866) as stating that "the earth does not belong to man, man belongs to earth. All things are connected like the blood that unites us all. Man did not weave the web of life, he is merely a strand in it. Whatever he does to the web, he does to himself" (15). In addition, Kawagley informs us that the best definition of the Yupiaq word for mathematics, *cugtaariyaraq,* is "the process of measuring and estimating in time and space" (51). Both of these examples have substantial resonance with the developments from new materialisms. I don't see these critiques as undermining or prohibiting the engagement of work in new materialisms but rather widening the possibilities for theoretical promiscuity of cultural studies in ways that more prominently configure the thought and theoretical strength of black, brown, and maroon thinkers.

The second critique concerns the extent to which new materialism is another iteration of social science appropriations from the physical sciences. As we learned in chapter 2, the development of social sciences goes back two hundred years to appropriations from the natural sciences by positivist philosophy. As social scientists, what do we gain and lose with this appropriation? What is carried over with such appropriations? Do these appropriations always hold for all intra-acting ontologies, or might there be limits? Engaging in this important line of questioning, Puar (2012, 64) states in a footnote:

> The danger of [Barad's] notion of "ontological realism" is that the effort to destabilize linguist essentialism may well privilege an essentialized truth produced through matter, a sort of ontological essentialism or materialist essentialism that uses a linguistic frame—performativity—to shore up the durational temporalities of matter.

The danger is a looming specter of positivism that maintains an assumption of "truth" as existing in the essentialism of natural phenomena. But, if phenomena are understood to be an assemblage of myriad forces, intra-acting in timespace, then the essentializing danger of matter as fixed and immutable is always held in critical tension. That is to say, the quantum conception of matter as unstable, nonfixed, and entangled with the discursive will always constitute this iteration of appropriation as something other than the seemingly similar appropriation of positivism. What remains to be understood is what the social sciences inherit from quantum physics, for instance, that may not hold or so easily fit. Or, does the transdisciplinary work of new materialisms implode the disciplinary divisions of the academy to render this questioning irrelevant? What we are learning in our era of computation, digital technology, and data analytics is the ever more clear posthumanist performativities of more-than-human ontologies such as that found in software culture and algorithms, and the ways in which they are profoundly affecting our lives.

The Computational Turn

Given the implications of *Inheriting Possibility* and the revolutionary turn toward computational culture and digital architectures, rather than closing with a "conclusion" I would like to consider the enfolding possibilities for critical inquiry. In recent decades, we have witnessed an astonishingly rapid growth in information and communication technologies. Developments in digital technologies have become ubiquitous in our lives and produce massive amounts of data at rates that are exponentially growing.

Indeed, in 2013 it was estimated that over 90 percent of the world's data had been produced in the previous two years (SINTEF 2013); and the growth of data production has shown no signs of letting up. The footprints of social life are more and more digitalized and available for examination.

Many of these technological advancements are based in computational analytics, mathematical algorithms, and statistics, and were developed for the many digital devices that inhabit our everyday lives. Digital technologies power smart phones, comprise the architecture of the Internet and social media, and manifest in the proliferation of software operating our computers. As Rob Kitchin (2014, xv) states, digital technologies "are materially and discursively reconfiguring the production, circulation, and interpretation of data, producing what has been termed 'big data.'" But, this "data revolution" has also leveraged the attention of many sectors of society, including the practices of govern-mentality.

Although the analytics of this data had its origin in computer science and business, it has increasingly become part of social science and policy research as well as practices of public policymaking and surveillance. In fact, on March 29, 2012, the Obama administration announced its Big Data Research and Development Initiative, which seeks to harness and utilize insights from the massive output of digital data to address the nation's challenges and social problems. Major global companies such as Facebook, Google, and IBM have been on the forefront of developing data analytics such as machine learning algorithms for the analysis of digital data in real time to inform corporate and public policy. For instance, IBM's Watson, a cognitive computing system, is designed to learn not just through interaction and trial and error, but to think and process like humans (e.g., observe, interpret, evaluate, and make decisions). IBM claims that Watson, unlike most computing systems, is able to process unstructured data that human ontologies read, interpret, and produce every day, such as books, articles, research reports, tweets, and blogs, along with the language-processing ability to recognize grammar, context, and culture in order to discern the author's "intent" (IBM Watson 2015). Watson is already being used to inform the law, policy, and medicine. These practices of digital technologies are already further enabling neoliberal and neoconservative political and economic interests, with the consequence of increasing social stratification and reconfiguring and reproducing power relations.

While the world is moving closer to the analytics of digital data, critical inquiry has maintained a hermeneutics of suspicion toward the critical epistemological possibilities of quantitative inquiry. *Inheriting Possibility* has not only deconstructed the modernist philosophy of science that has undergirded quantification but has reworked the onto-epistemological possibilities of quantitative inquiry for a critical new materialist project. In a 2016 special issue, "Alternative Ontologies of Number," for *Cultural Studies—Critical Methodologies,* my colleagues and coguest editors (Elizabeth de Freitas and Patti Lather) and I make the argument that if the previous paradigm in social inquiry might be described by the phrase "the discursive turn," then the next few decades will be characterized by the turn toward computation.

Critical studies and software studies scholars such as Luciana Parisi, Lev Manovich, Evelyn Ruppert, and Rob Kitchin have begun to do incredible work in this area, and a no-doubt massive amount of work remains unexcavated. How do we make sense of the "unreasonable effectiveness" of predictive analytics? In what ways are class structural relations reinforced and reconfigured by the practices of digital cultures? How have digital technologies enabled topological relations of global political economic forces that defy and transgress legally constituted geographic boundaries while adhering to the laws of place? In what ways do posthumanist performativities of what Parisi (2013) calls algorithmic "soft(ware) thinking" (i.e., algorithmic modes of thought, decision making, and mentality) interpellate social identities of "difference" such as race, gender, class, and sexuality? And in what ways do digital architectures enable the possibilities of challenging, contesting, and reimagining sociopolitical and historical conditions, particularly for the lives of the vulnerable and the marginalized?

Given the ubiquity of digital technology, critical scholarship cannot afford to maintain a hermeneutics of suspicion toward quantification. The mathematical algorithms that are doing the "thinking" of digital architectures (Parisi 2013) are materially and discursively reshaping our lives *in real time.* Critical scholarship must find ways of making interventions from within and through the quantitative reasoning of digital landscapes, and *Inheriting Possibility* provides one onto-epistemological instantiation. This is not simply a call for a new line of critical inquiry, but an urgent and necessary turn toward enabling possibilities.

Quantitative Methods and Results for Chapter 3

Methods

Sample and Data

These analyses employed data from the Child Development Supplement (CDS) to the Panel Study of Income Dynamics (PSID) (Hill, 1991). Given my interest in social reproduction and parenting, I analyze data that have an intergenerational or multigenerational structure. The PSID is a nationally representative longitudinal data set containing information on family economics, education, and composition of both families and of all individuals in those families, collected every year through interviews since 1968 and every other year starting in 1999. The CDS collected behavioral, psychological, and achievement data from 2,394 families from the PSID, with 3,563 children aged twelve and under in 1997.

In this study, in order to be included in the sample one either had to be a member of one of the original 1968 PSID families or marry into one of these families. The grandparent was the (biological or adoptive) parent of the (biological or adoptive) parent who was a participant in the PSID. Approximately half of the grandparents were paternal grandparents (N = 1138, 47 percent). Because the sample sizes of other racial/ethnic groups are relatively small, black (N = 1047) and white (N = 1192) children were the two groups of focus. Of the black children, 48 percent were females and of the white children 50 percent were females. The longitudinal family economic and child development data makes the PSID one of the richest datasets to study intergenerational and multigenerational processes of social reproduction.

Dependent Variables: Parenting Performativities

Parenting Dispositions and Practices

Parenting practices were measured with a battery of items on parenting in the CDS. Each item was factor analyzed constructing a close fit three factor structure, where an RMSEA of 0.05 or less and a CFI or TLI of 0.90 or higher indicates a plausible model. These three factors measured cultural practices, social relationship practices, and parental expressed affect toward parenting. The composite measure of parental cognitive stimulation and emotional warmth from the Home Observation for Measurement of the Environment scale (HOME; Caldwell & Bradley, 1984) was included as an additional dependent variable measure of parenting practices.

Independent Variables

Bodily Responses to Parental Gender Norms

The CDS contains eighteen items that measure parent's beliefs about gender roles, maternal employment, paternal involvement, childcare, and parental gender egalitarianism. These items were factor analyzed and included in the models as a measure of parental expressed responses to parental gender norms. Both measurement models of expressed responses to parental gender norms, affect toward parenting, and parenting practices had a close fit to the data (see CFA in Table 2).

Family Socioeconomic Background Measures

Permanent Income

Permanent income is an average of family income over multiple years to account for both simple measurement error and transitory shocks (Mazumder 2005). The parents' total family income was averaged over four years (1993, 1994, 1995, and 1996) to arrive at their permanent income estimate. The grandparents' permanent income was estimated over fifteen years: 1975 through 1989.

Wealth

As a liquid asset, the total net value of stocks/mutual funds was used for both parents in 1994 and grandparents in 1984.

Occupational Prestige

Occupational prestige was measured by the Hodge-Siegel-Rossi prestige score (see Nakao, Hodge, and Treas, 1990) for the parent head in 1997 and grandparent head in 1984.

Educational Attainment

The 1997 parent head and 1984 grandparent head educational attainment were measured in actual number of years up through seventeen years of education.

Control Variables

The parent's and grandparent's age in 1997 and 1984, respectively, were controlled for in the models as well as whether they were maternal or paternal grandparents, and the parent's and grandparent's marital status. The child's race, gender, and age in 1997 were controlled.

Analysis

The analysis for this study utilized multiple group structural equation modeling (SEM), which has been widely used in educational, psychological, and sociological research since the 1970s (Bollen, 1989; Kline, 2015). SEM is particularly the most appropriate approach to this analysis because several observed variables are indicators to measured variables (e.g., parenting performativities) while accounting for measurement error. SEM also helps simultaneously establish the direct and indirect associations of parent and grandparent socioeconomic resources on bodily responses to gender norms and parenting practices. The multiple group analyses of SEM enables the examination of the extent to which these processes vary by race and gender.

SEM, broadly speaking, consists of three stages: model specification, parameter estimation, and model fit estimation. In the model specification stage, I construct models that may account for the relationship among variables on the basis of their theoretical relationship derived from previous research and the models will be tested with the empirical data. The model specification is commonly divided into two portions: the measurement model that specifies the relationship between observed variables and latent variables (i.e., underlying factors) and the structural model that describes directional relationships among latent variables and observed variables.

I used a model-building approach to the structural portion of the model. I first fit the measurement model of parenting practices and parental bodily responses to gender norms. Then I did a multiple group analysis on the measurement model. Following the multiple group analysis of the measurement model, I then specified parenting practices to be endogenous to parental bodily responses to gender norms, then specified both to be endogenous to parent's socioeconomic resources, and finally grandparent's socioeconomic resources. The following tables present the results of these analyses.

Results

Table 1. Descriptive Statistics of PSID-CDS Analysis Variables									
	TOTAL SAMPLE					WHITE SAMPLE		BLACK SAMPLE	
	MEAN	SD	MIN	MAX	% MISSING	MEAN	SD	MEAN	SD
Child Age 1997	7.5	2.9	3.0	13.0	26.50%	7.4	2.9	7.5	2.9
Parent Age 1997	33.9	7.8	14.0	75.0	0.00%	34.5	7.0	33.3	8.6
Parent Married 1997	63%				0.08%	83%		41%	
P Head Education	10.9	2.3	0.0	15.0	4.00%	10.0	2.4	10.0	1.9
P Head Occupation	42.7	13.3	20.8	86.1	18.30%	46.5	14.0	37.9	10.6
P Permanent Income	$38,489	$45,254	$1,105	$780,976	0.00%	$52,489	$53,560	$23,075	$23,624
P Stocks/Mutual Funds	$0	$111,536	$0	$4,331,984	0.04%	$0	$153,019	$0	$7,550
GP Married 1984	68%				17.60%	85%		49%	
GP Age	47.6	11.0	16.0	82.0	17.80%	49.0	9.7	46.0	11.9
GP Head Education	11.0	3.3	0.0	17.0	17.90%	12.0	2.9	10.0	2.9
GP Head Occupation	34.5	10.8	16.8	73.5	41.10%	35.0	11.6	34.0	10.4
GP Permanent Income	$39,627	$29,264	$3,862	$309,705	11.10%	$52,954	$31,326	$26,914	$16,484
GP Stocks/Mutual Funds	$0	$22,291	$0	$400,000	27.40%	$0	$28,011	$0	$14,029
Cognitive Stimulation & Emotional Warmth	19.22	3.62	7.0	27.0	0.00%	20.3	3.4	18.0	3.5
Cultural Practices	0.0	0.6	-1.9	2.0	0.04%	0.2	0.6	0.0	0.6
Social Relationship Practices	0.0	0.9	-2.9	3.0	0.04%	0.3	0.8	0.0	0.9
Parental Embodied Expressed Response to Questions on:									
–Affect toward Parenting	0.0	0.4	-1.6	0.7	0.04%	0.0	0.3	0.0	0.4
–Gender Roles	0.1	0.6	-2.6	2.0	0.04%	0.1	0.6	0.0	0.6
–Parental Gender Egalitarianism	-0.1	1.0	-4.4	2.8	0.04%	-0.2	1.1	0.0	0.8
–Maternal Employment & Childcare	0.0	0.3	-1.2	1.2	0.04%	0.0	0.3	0.0	0.4
–Paternal Involvement	0.4	0.6	-2.0	2.4	0.04%	0.6	0.5	0.1	0.5
Total N	2563					1343		1220	

Note: P represents parents and GP represents grandparents

Table 2. Fits Indices for Structural Equation Models

MODELS	DF	SCF	Chi-Square	CD	TRd	RMSEA	CFI	TLI
CFA of Parenting Practices	218		987			0.03	0.91	0.94
CFA of Parenting Practices and Gender Ideology	1132		5194			0.037	0.93	0.92
Fully Constrained CFA	5352	0.93	13405			0.048	0.87	0.88
Parenting Practices by Gender*	5349	0.93	13201	6.28	36.54	0.048	0.88	0.88
Parenting Practices by Race & Gender*	5346	0.92	12947	4.49	58.13	0.047	0.88	0.88
Parental Gender Ideology by Gender*	5338	0.92	12759	2.92	72.21	0.047	0.88	0.88
Parental Gender Ideology by Race & Gender*	5514	0.91	13524	0.61	-936.15	0.048	0.88	0.88
Parental Gender Ideologies as Covariates	5499	0.87	13289			0.047	0.88	0.88
Dispositions toward Parenting as Covariate	5508	0.88	13238			0.047	0.88	0.88
Parent Socioeconomic Position as Covariate	6524	0.90	14052			0.042	0.88	0.88
Grandparent Socioeconomic Position as Covariate	7895	0.91	15356			0.042	0.86	0.86
Parental Gender Ideology Effects by Race*	7841	0.88	15173	5.85	116.63	0.042	0.86	0.86

* 95% Confidence interval does not include 0.

Note: SCF is the scaled correction factor; CD are weighted least squares adjusted degrees of freedom; TRd are weighted least squares adjusted Chi-Square; RMSEA is the root mean square error of approximation; CFI is the comparative fit index; and, the TLI is the Tucker-Lewis Index.

Table 3. Unstandardized Estimates (with Standard Errors) of Structural Equation Model								
	CULTURAL PRACTICE	SOCIAL RELATIONSHIPS	EMOT & COG STIMULATION	PARENTING AFFECT	GENDER ROLES	GENDER EGALITARIAN	MATERNAL EMP & CHILDCARE	PATERNAL INVOLVE
Affect toward Parenting	0.077 (0.060)	0.012 (0.094)	0.831 (0.198)*	—	—	—	—	—
Gender Roles	0.120 (0.077)	0.313 (0.139)*	0.350 (0.258)	0.227 (0.053)*	—	—	—	—
Parental Gender Egalitarianism	-0.090 (0.053)	-0.247 (0.100)*	-0.084 (0.166)	-0.133 (0.038)*	—	—	—	—
Maternal Employment & Childcare	0.113 (0.080)	0.335 (0.151)*	0.271 (0.246)	0.044 (0.049)	—	—	—	—
Paternal Involvement	0.044 (0.039)	0.035 (0.059)	0.034 (0.126)	0.124 (0.031)*	—	—	—	—
Child Age 1997	-0.100 (0.009)*	-0.033 (0.015)*	0.502 (0.020)*	-0.002 (0.005)	-0.005 (0.008)	-0.020 (0.012)	-0.004 (0.002)	-0.011 (0.012)
Parent Age 1997	0.002 (0.003)	-0.008 (0.007)	0.021 (0.011)	-0.004 (0.003)	-0.011 (0.005)*	-0.017 (0.007)*	-0.001 (0.002)	-0.011 (0.006)
Parent Married 1997	-0.006 (0.053)	0.212 (0.102)*	1.206 (0.161)*	0.096 (0.040)*	-0.271 (0.075)*	-0.393 (0.112)*	-0.012 (0.020)	-0.097 (0.097)
P Head Education	0.000 (0.011)	0.056 (0.021)*	0.134 (0.033)*	0.010 (0.008)	0.040 (0.014)*	0.035 (0.020)	0.000 (0.004)	0.080 (0.025)*
P Head Occupation	0.001 (0.002)	0.005 (0.003)	0.014 (0.006)*	0.001 (0.001)	-0.002 (0.002)	-0.003 (0.003)	0.000 (0.001)	0.000 (0.003)
P Permanent Income	0.005 (0.038)	0.174 (0.074)*	0.239 (0.115)*	0.030 (0.030)	0.172 (0.051)*	0.268 (0.078)*	0.002 (0.013)	0.182 (0.070)*
P Stocks/Mutual Funds	0.004 (0.005)	0.010 (0.010)	0.023 (0.018)	0.001 (0.004)	-0.014 (0.007)*	-0.018 (0.012)	-0.001 (0.002)	-0.004 (0.012)
Maternal Grandparents	0.045 (0.042)	0.108 (0.075)	0.276 (0.129)*	-0.003 (0.031)	-0.057 (0.050)	-0.159 (0.081)*	-0.024 (0.015)	-0.167 (0.087)
GP Married 1984	0.003 (0.003)	0.017 (0.006)*	0.016 (0.008)	0.006 (0.002)*	-0.004 (0.003)	0.000 (0.005)	-0.001 (0.001)	-0.003 (0.004)
GP Age	-0.004 (0.051)	0.103 (0.094)	-0.064 (0.162)	0.025 (0.039)	-0.074 (0.065)	-0.256 (0.099)*	-0.007 (0.017)	-0.052 (0.094)
GP Head Education	0.003 (0.007)	0.034 (0.015)*	0.067 (0.024)*	-0.003 (0.006)	0.011 (0.009)	-0.022 (0.015)	0.003 (0.003)	0.018 (0.014)
GP Head Occupation	0.001 (0.002)	-0.001 (0.003)	-0.006 (0.006)	0.003 (0.001)*	0.003 (0.002)	0.002 (0.003)	0.001 (0.001)	-0.002 (0.003)
GP Permanent Income	0.060 (0.045)	0.158 (0.089)	0.149 (0.136)	0.068 (0.033)*	0.052 (0.056)	0.145 (0.086)	-0.001 (0.015)	0.003 (0.080)
GP Stocks/Mutual Funds	0.008 (0.007)	-0.009 (0.011)	0.033 (0.021)	-0.008 (0.005)	-0.007 (0.008)	-0.032 (0.013)*	-0.002 (0.002)	-0.022 (0.014)

* 95% Confidence interval does not include 0.

Note: P represents parents and GP represents grandparents.

Quantitative Methods and Results
for Chapter 4

Methods

Data

This study employed data from National Longitudinal Survey of Youth 1997 (NLSY97) designed to document "the transition from school to work and from adolescence to adulthood" with a nationally representative sample of 8,984 children who were born during the years 1980 through 1984. Beginning with Round 1 in 1997, NLSY97 has collected annual data about youths' education and employment activities. The NLSY97 is, to our knowledge, the only national dataset that offers detailed reliable information on both family wealth and SAT scores for children. While the Transition into Adulthood Supplement to the Panel Study of Income Dynamics (PSID) is the only other data set that does collect SAT scores alongside measures of family wealth, the scores are self-reported, introducing additional measurement error; in addition the sample size of respondents that took the SAT is small. In contrast, the NLSY97 collected SAT scores from the high-school transcripts of a large sample of test-takers. This is discussed further in the variable description of the SAT. It is for these reasons that I use the NLSY97 over the PSID.

One of the unique aspects of the NLSY97 is that Round 1 of 1997 contains a parent interview that asked one parent of each youth who resided in the same household as the youth for extensive information on their marital and employment history as well as their spouse's. The responding parents also gave answers to questions about their children's lives as well as about the family in general, including parental income from Round 1 to 5 and family wealth in Round 1. This data is expected to provide more reliable information about the economic and social status of a family than that from youth interviews and enables researchers to explore intergenerational effects. Because of nonresponse, all youth with an eligible parent may not have provided information about parents; as a result, 7,942 children (88%) have information available from the parent survey.

In addition, NLSY97 collected information about educational achievement of youth through the transcript survey, which collected transcripts for NLSY youth who provided written permission to contact their high schools. The first phase of collecting transcripts of NLSY97 youth who were born in 1980 and 1981 began in 2000. In 2004, the transcript survey began the second phase, which collected transcripts of those who were born in 1982 to 1984. The transcript survey provides data on each course on a student's transcript, the grade in the course, the credit value of the course, and test scores on achievement tests such as the SAT. The transcript survey data are available for 6,232 NLSY97 youth (69%).

Participants

The original NLSY97 sample consists of 8,984 youth designed to nationally represent youth born between 1980 and 1984. In order to avoid complexity resulting from too many racial categories and to obtain reliable estimates in examining for differential associations of family wealth on SAT by race/ethnicity groups, the study sample was limited to white, black, and Hispanic/Latinx by dropping 417 youths (4.64%) who are not classified as white, black, or Hispanic/Latinx. In addition, given our focus on racial/ethnic differences in association with SAT performance, the heterogeneity of the Other category for race/ethnicity added too much noise. Given the special focus on the SAT, the study sample only includes youth who reported that they had taken the SAT during the years 1996 through 2003. Consequently, the final sample consists of 3,216 youth who had taken the SAT during the years 1996 through 2003 where 1,673 (52.0%) are female; 2,419 (77.7%) reside in urban centers; 1,731 (53.8%) are white; 859 (26.7%) are black; and 626 (19.5%) are Hispanic/Latinx.

Descriptive statistics of demographic variables for the original NLSY97 sample and the final study sample were with t-test and chi-square test indicating that the study sample and the original NLSY97 sample are not the same. Notably, families with youth in the study sample have better socioeconomic status than families with youth in the original NLSY97 sample. Compared to the original NLSY97 sample, the study sample consists of relatively more white and private school students with slightly more educated and affluent parents. These sample differences are to be expected since the population of SAT test-takers is relatively more privileged than the national population (Camara & Schmidt 1999; College Board 2012). Therefore, the study sample is a nationally representative sample of white, black, and Hispanic/Latinx youth who had ever taken the SAT rather than a national sample representing all youth.

Measures

SAT Scores

The SAT is a norm-referenced standardized measure of ability used as a high stakes test for college admissions. The SAT score data were drawn from the transcript survey of the NLSY97. These scores were reported directly to the test-taker's high school through the Score Reporting program of the SAT. The SAT scores are the scale score of the SAT verbal and quantitative reasoning subtests for children's last test administration of the SAT during the years 1996 through 2003. Although I aggregate SAT score data over this eight year time frame, the College Board equating program for the SAT ensures that a student's score on one edition of a test reflects the same ability as a score of another edition (College Board 2011). SAT subtest scores are reported on a 200 to 800 scale.

High-School Achievement

Course grade data were obtained by the transcript survey of NLSY97. Given that high-school transcripts employed a variety of types of course grades (e.g., letter grades or numbers), NLSY97 standardized various grading systems into a uniform grading system based on a predetermined conversion table (see NLSY97 User's Guide, Appendix 11, in the codebook supplement). In addition, NLSY97 created GPA variables taking credits earned for completed coursework into account by weighing credits with the Carnegie credit conversion method, which makes different credit systems across schools comparable. In the Carnegie credit system, "one Carnegie credit is defined as the credits earned for a class that meets every day for one period for an entire school year." Consequently, I used credit weighted GPA in English, foreign language, social science, mathematics, and life and physical sciences measured on a 4.3 GPA scale.

Family Wealth

Family wealth data were drawn from the parent survey of NLSY97 conducted in Round 1 of 1997, which asked responding parents to report the present value of assets and debts a family holds. The information about assets is comprehensive, including the present value of their dwelling, land, business partnership/professional practice, any real estate, bills and bonds (e.g., CDs, government savings bonds, or treasury bills), checking account, savings account, money market accounts, educational IRA accounts, other prepaid tuition savings accounts, pension or retirement savings, shares in publicly-held corporations or mutual funds, vehicles, and other assets including money owed by others, life insurance policies, and precious metals. In order to balance information about assets, NLSY97 also collected detailed information about debts including a mortgage, land contract, or any other type of loan that used their property as collateral, such as a second mortgage or a home equity loan, the amount owed on vehicles, educational loans for a child, and other debt including credit cards or bank loans.

Compared to other datasets collecting data on wealth, wealth data collected by NLSY97 are believed to be of high quality in that NSLY97 used an innovative survey method designed to "reduce the impact of item nonresponse and capture at least some information." When a responding parent was unable to ("don't know") or unwilling to ("refused") provide an exact value of wealth, a follow-up question asked them to choose a range from a predefined list that may appropriately reflect their wealth. By providing the best estimated values of wealth for item nonresponse, NLSY97 helps researchers impute the missing values with the most plausible values. In the study, the missing data were imputed with the middle point value within a range that responding parents chose.

In this study, I employed three measures of wealth. First, I created two asset-related variables: total illiquid assets and liquid assets. The illiquid assets include the home, land, business partnership/professional practice, any other real estate, and vehicle. The liquid assets encompass the rest of assets such as checking and savings account, stocks, and mutual funds. The third variable was a measure of total debt, which was the total sum value of all debt.

In the analysis, all wealth variables were transformed into the natural log form since the distribution of family wealth is positively skewed and has a nonlinear relationship with SAT scores.

Parental Income

It is widely known that a single-year income measure cannot adequately capture the economic status of a family because it may vary considerably due to transitory shocks to income from year to year, especially for low-income families. Hence, I decided to use a multiyear measure of income referred to as "permanent income" status (Blau and Graham 1990; Bowles, Gintis, and Groves 2005; Mazumder 2005). Permanent income more adequately reflects the overall economic status of a family. Information about income was obtained by the parent survey of Round 1 and the household income update data reported by responding parents from Round 2 to Round 5 of NLSY97. In Round 1, the parent survey gathered data on (pretax) earnings for responding parents and their current spouse or partner from a job, a farm, business, or professional practice, and (pretax) income from other sources including interest or dividend, child support payments, and various government programs during 1996. Although the parent survey was conducted only in Round 1 of 1997, NLSY97 conducted the household income update from Round 2 to Round 5. Consequently, our parental income measure is the total income of the parents averaged over five years. Permanent income was also log transformed in order to account for nonlinear relationships. It should be noted that the "income to needs ratio," which is frequently used, is not used here because I used family size as an exogenous variable.

Parents' Education

Data on parents' education were drawn from the parent survey that measures the years of completed schooling of parents who reside with children (i.e., children's residential parents include both biological and nonbiological parents).

Grandparents' Education

Data on grandparents' education were drawn from the parent survey that measures the level of educational attainment for the mother's mother and father and the father's mother and father. This question is not in years but based on completion of fourth grade, eighth grade, some high school, high school, associate's degree, bachelor's degree, master's degree, or PhD, MD, or JD. These categories were rescaled into average years of completion in order to measure number of years of completed schooling similar to parents' education. Then the maternal grandparents' education is based on the highest level of education between the mother's mother and father and the paternal grandparents' education was based on the highest level of education between the father's mother and father.

SAT Year of Administration

I include an SAT year of administration dummy variable referring to the year when children took the SAT in order to control for possible cohort effects. Reference year is 1998 when the most children took the SAT.

Mediator Variables

Parenting/Child Relationship

Parent/child relationship was measured by parent/youth relationship scale in Round 1 of NLSY97. The scale consists of the following eight items: (1) I think highly of him/her. (2) S/he is a person I want to be like. (3) I really enjoy spending time with him/her. (4) How often does s/he praise you for doing well? (5) How often does s/he criticize you or your ideas? (reverse coded) (6) How often does s/he help you do things that are important to you? (7) How often does s/he blame you for her problems? (reverse coded) (8) How often does s/he make plans with you and cancel for no good reason? (reverse coded). Each item was measured on a 5-point scale. The points to the eight items were summed to create the scale; scores on the scale range from 0 to 32 points, where higher scores mean a more positive relationship between parent and child. It is known that the scale has reliable internal consistency, given that Cronbach's alpha for mother/youth relationship and father/youth relationship were respectively .75 and .82 for the whole sample of Round 1 of NLSY97. In the final model, parent/child relationship was treated as a latent variable measured by a single indicator, parent/youth relationship scale with known reliability.

Home/Neighborhood Environment Risk

Home/Neighborhood Environment Risk was measured by the Physical Environment Risk Index of Round 1 of NLSY97. The index is composed of the following five items: (1) In the past month, has your home usually had electricity and heat when you needed it? (2) How well kept are most of the buildings on the street where the adult/youth resident lives? [Interviewer report] (3) How well kept is the interior of the home in which the youth respondent lives? [Interviewer report] (4) When you went to the respondent's neighborhood/home, did you feel concerned for your safety? [Interviewer report] (5) In a typical week, how many days from 0 to 7 do you hear gunshots in your neighborhood? For index creation, the NLSY97 coded each item into risk categories where 2 is high risk (for items #2 and #3), 1 is risk or moderate risk, and 0 is coded as no risk. Scores on the items were then summed to create a composite score for the Physical Environment Risk Index; the scores on the index range from 0 to 7 where higher scores point to a higher risk physical environment. In the final model, Home/Neighborhood Environment Risk was treated as an observed variable measured by Physical Environment Risk Index.

Enrichment Opportunities

Enrichment opportunities were measured by the Enriching Environment Index of Round 1 of the NLSY97. The index is composed of the following three items: (1) In the past month, has your home usually had a computer? (2) In the past month, has your home usually had a dictionary? (3) In a typical [school week/work week/week], did you spend any time taking extra classes or lessons, for example, music, dance, or foreign-language lessons? For index creation, NLSY97 coded each item, so that 0 is coded as no-enrichment and 1 is coded as enrichment. The items were then summed to create a composite score for the Enriching Environment Index; scores on the index ranges from 0 to 3 where higher scores indicate a more enriching environment. Enrichment opportunities was treated as an observed variable measured by the Enriching Environment Index.

Public/Private School

The school type (public vs. private) variable drawn from the transcript survey indicates the type of high school from which the children's transcript was primarily collected. In most cases, this is the last high school that the child attended. Public school was coded 0 and private school was coded 1.

Demographic Variables

I included several demographic variables. Of them, the race/ethnicity of the children consists of three categories: white, black, and Hispanic/Latinx. It was dummy coded in the analysis with reference category of white. Gender of children was also dummy coded with the reference category of male. Residential area of Round 1 is composed of two categories of urban or rural and coded as a dummy variable with urban as the reference category. Family structure measured in Round 1 has three categories of two-parent family, single-parent family, and other family including foster, adoptive, and no-parent family. It was dummy coded with the reference category of two-parent family. Finally, data about the number of family members was drawn from household size variable in Round 1 of NLSY97.

Analysis

The analysis in this study utilized structural equation modeling (SEM) which has been widely used in educational, psychological, and sociological research since the 1970s (Bollen, 1989; Kline, 2015). SEM is a particularly appropriate approach to this analysis because several observed variables are indicators of measured variables (e.g., SAT and high-school achievement) while accounting for measurement error. SEM also helps us simultaneously establish the direct and indirect associations of grandparents' education and parents' family wealth on SAT performance.

SEM, broadly speaking, consists of three stages: model specification, parameter estimation, and model fit estimation. In the model specification stage, I construct models that may account for the relationship among variables on the basis of the variable's theoretical relationship derived from previous research that can be tested with the empirical data. The model specification is commonly divided into two portions: the measurement model that specifies the relationship between observed variables and latent variables (i.e., underlying factors) and the structural model that describes directional relationships among latent variables and observed variables. As shown in Figure 15, our nine observed variables (SAT verbal score, SAT math score, mother/child relationship, father/child relationship, and five course grades) are believed to be indicators to four latent variables (high-school achievement, mother/child relationship, father/child relationship, and SAT performance) in our measurement model where each observed variable is connected to a single latent variable. The structural model, as depicted in Figure 16, specifies that observed family wealth, parental income, parental education, home/neighborhood risk, enrichment opportunities, public/private school attendance, and latent high-school achievement, mother/child relationship, father/child relationship each have direct associations on SAT performance, controlling for demographic covariates and SAT cohort effects represented by SAT year dummies. In addition, observed family wealth, parental income, and parental education have indirect associations on SAT via home/neighborhood risk, enrichment opportunities, mother/child relationship, father/child relationship, public/private school, and high-school achievement. I then fit a multiple indicator, multiple cause (MIMIC) model (Kline 2015) in order to examine for group differences between black, white, and Hispanic/Latinx students on SAT performance and high-school achievement.

I used a model-building approach to the structural portion of the model. I specified the initial structural model where parental income, parental education, and high-school achievement have direct associations with SAT performance, controlling for demographic covariates and SAT year of administration, and parental income and parental education have indirect associations on SAT performance via high-school achievement. The second structural model then added all the control variables to the model. The third model added the three wealth measures as covariates having direct and indirect associations (via high-school achievement) on SAT performance. The final model included maternal and paternal grandparents' education.

Given the degree of incomplete cases, especially for the SAT subtest variables, I employed multiple imputation, then deletion. Multiple imputation is a three-step incomplete case analytic method. In the first step, I employ Markov chain Monte Carlo methods in order to impute values for incomplete cases, producing ten imputed data sets. These ten imputed data sets were each analyzed by each structural equation model in the second

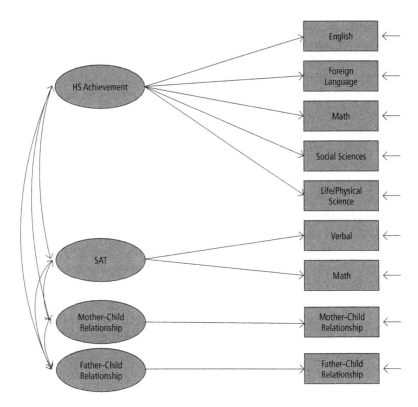

Figure 15. Measurement Model

step, producing ten structural equation model solutions. The ten structural equation model solutions were then concatenated in the third step, arriving at a model solution that is the pooled estimates of the ten SEMs. Multiple imputation is able to more reliably handle large degrees of missing data while also accounting for the uncertainty of single imputation (Little and Rubin 2002). Simulation studies have demonstrated the power of multiple imputation to reliably produce unbiased estimates even with extreme degrees of incomplete cases where the missing data mechanism is not at random (e.g., up to 70% missing data; Sinharay, Stern, and Russell 2001). However, there are substantial proportions of incomplete cases on SAT scores (i.e., 60.7%) and their mechanisms for missing could vary. For instance, SAT score incomplete cases could be due to the respondent mistaking the SAT for the PSAT or the ACT when asked whether they had

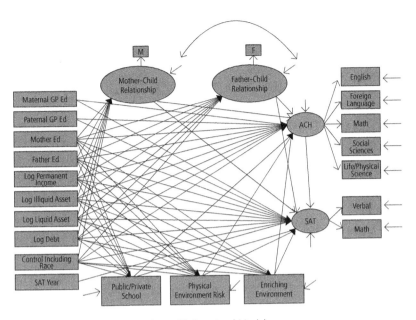

Figure 16. Structural Model

ever taken the SAT; or they could be a result of school administration data entry issues on the student's transcripts; or the youth may have never taken the SAT. Although it is possible that the pattern of missing SAT scores may not be missing at random, scholars have theoretically argued and empirically demonstrated that multiple imputation still results in little to no bias in parameter estimation (Schafer and Graham 2002; Sinharay, Stern, and Russell 2001). In fact, Schafer and Graham "believe that good performance is often achievable through likelihood or Bayesian methods without specifically modeling the probabilities of missingness" (154).

It is for these reasons that I employ multiple imputation, then deletion (MID; von Hippel 2007). MID includes the dependent variable (i.e., SAT scores) in the imputation model but only does the structural equation modeling on the cases that have SAT data. This approach uses the information of the incomplete SAT cases in order to better impute the model covariates while only conducting the analyses on the complete cases of SAT scores so as to reduce noise in estimation. Both the multiple imputation and structural equation modeling were conducted using Mplus (Muthén and Muthén 1998–2010).

Results

Table 4. Descriptive Statistics			
	TOTAL SAMPLE (N=3216)		
VARIABLE	MEAN [MEDIAN]	SD	% OF MISSING
SAT			
Verbal	504.27	109.95	60.70%
Math	502.37	111.49	60.70%
GPA			
English	2.90	0.69	27.18%
Foreign Language	2.97	0.79	39.37%
Math	2.74	0.72	27.36%
Social Sciences	2.94	0.72	27.74%
Life and Physical Sciences	2.82	0.71	28.23%
PARENTAL EDUCATION (YEAR)			
Father	14.00	3.25	30.91%
Mother	13.00	2.96	8.96%
GRANDPARENT EDUCATION (YEAR)			
Paternal Grandparents	12.00	4.71	45.02%
Maternal Grandparents	12.00	4.75	18.69%
INCOME ($)			
Permanent Income	54703.67 [43166]	48963.50	1.71%
WEALTH ($)			
Net Worth	142440.00 [78500]	158220.60	29.42%
Total Assets	224450.00 [150000]	267190.29	28.33%
Total Illiquid Assets	175620.00 [125000]	199165.35	20.21%
Total Liquid Assets	56980.00 [12400]	99163.40	25.25%
Debt	64920.00 [45000]	73801.99	18.35%
FAMILY SIZE			
Number of Family Members	4.46	1.41	0%
MEDIATORS			
Physical Environment Risk	1.09	1.30	47.14%
Enriching Environment	1.92	0.75	40.17%
Mother–Child Relationship	25.50	4.65	41.26%
Father–Child Relationship	24.96	5.37	53.11%

	WHITE (N=1731, 53.82% OF TOTAL SAMPLE)			BLACK (N=859, 26.71% OF TOTAL SAMPLE)			HISPANIC/LATINX (N=626,19.47% OF TOTAL SAMPLE)		
	MEAN [MEDIAN]	SD	% OF MISSING	MEAN [MEDIAN]	SD	% OF MISSING	MEAN [MEDIAN]	SD	% OF MISSING
	532.25	102.16	50.32%	441.81	92.85	73.69%	448.38	112.83	71.57%
	533.51	104.36	50.32%	424.20	82.84	73.69%	451.20	109.39	71.57%
	3.05	0.65	23.34%	2.63	0.69	30.97%	2.81	0.67	32.59%
	3.06	0.76	32.41%	2.72	0.82	49.59%	2.97	0.80	44.57%
	2.91	0.67	23.11%	2.45	0.73	31.43%	2.65	0.71	33.55%
	3.12	0.65	23.51%	2.65	0.74	32.13%	2.81	0.71	33.39%
	2.97	0.65	23.63%	2.54	0.74	33.06%	2.72	0.70	34.35%
	14.00	2.87	18.72%	12.00	2.13	54.02%	12.00	3.92	32.91%
	14.00	2.51	5.60%	12.00	2.08	14.44%	12.00	3.71	10.70%
	12.00	3.79	30.21%	12.00	4.67	69.62%	4.00	5.62	52.24%
	12.00	3.87	14.27%	12.00	4.23	23.98%	4.00	5.16	23.64%
	2416.44 [60420]	53521.45	1.44%	32567.58 [23690]	31975.89	2.68%	35782.49 [27150]	32964.64	1.12%
	72005.70 [108000]	178873.07	27.79%	47899.80 [20150]	84679.03	31.08%	55939.28 [14700]	101489.36	31.63%
	67418.16 [186375]	316722.27	26.75%	81182.34 [37500]	113041.30	29.69%	99807.51 [31814]	162637.58	30.83%
	05365.15 [154500]	233896.42	17.39%	69694.24 [37500]	91609.21	22.93%	89695.65 [43475]	127152.05	24.28%
	71252.64 [22500]	122405.43	24.67%	13244.34 [100]	36333.00	25.03%	15084.46 [0]	53485.25	27.16%
	73435.59 [56000]	82868.49	15.54%	31636.86 [9500]	48895.47	22.58%	39944.26 [8000]	58599.19	20.29%
	4.32	1.19	0%	4.46	1.67	0%	4.86	1.56	0%
	0.77	1.06	45.12%	1.66	1.53	48.78%	1.27	1.30	50.48%
	2.15	0.68	39.92%	1.69	0.76	41.79%	1.62	0.74	38.66%
	25.81	4.42	40.67%	24.98	4.99	43.42%	25.33	4.77	39.94%
	25.40	5.29	48.06%	23.70	5.68	64.96%	24.90	5.12	50.80%

Table 4. Descriptive Statistics *(continued)*

VARIABLE	TOTAL SAMPLE (N=3216)		
	MEAN [MEDIAN]	SD	% OF MISSING
GENDER			0%
Male	1543	47.98	
Female	1673	52.02	
FAMILY STRUCTURE			0.31%
Two Parents	2204	68.75	
Single Parent	844	26.33	
Adoptive, Foster, or No Parents	158	4.93	
RESIDENTIAL AREA			3.20%
Urban	2419	77.71	
Rural	694	22.29	
SCHOOL TYPE			25.22%
Public	2177	90.50	
Private	228	9.50	
YEAR OF SAT ADMINISTRATION			61.35%
1996	5	0.40	
1997	155	12.47	
1998	267	21.48	
1999	254	20.43	
2000	226	18.18	
2001	225	18.10	
2002	99	7.96	
2003	12	0.97	

WHITE (N=1731, 53.82% OF TOTAL SAMPLE)			BLACK (N=859, 26.71% OF TOTAL SAMPLE)			HISPANIC/LATINX (N=626, 19.47% OF TOTAL SAMPLE)		
MEAN [MEDIAN]	SD	% OF MISSING	MEAN [MEDIAN]	SD	% OF MISSING	MEAN [MEDIAN]	SD	% OF MISSING
		0%			0%			0%
863	49.86		389	45.29		291	46.49	
868	50.14		470	54.71		335	53.51	
		0.17%			0.23%			0.80%
1370	79.28		387	45.16		447	71.98	
310	17.94		380	44.34		154	24.80	
48	2.78		90	10.50		20	3.22	
		3.12%			4.19%			2.08%
1177	70.18		687	83.48		555	90.54	
500	29.82		136	16.52		58	9.46	
		22.65%			26.19%			30.99%
1159	86.56		605	95.43		413	95.60	
180	13.44		29	4.57		19	4.40	
		51.18%			73.92%			72.20%
4	0.47		1	0.45		0	0.00	
112	13.25		22	9.82		21	12.07	
176	20.83		49	21.88		42	24.14	
165	19.53		58	25.89		31	17.82	
163	19.29		33	14.73		30	17.24	
155	18.34		35	15.63		35	20.11	
65	7.69		22	9.82		12	6.90	
5	0.59		4	1.79		3	1.72	

Table 5. Measurement Model Estimates

FACTOR LOADING	UNSTANDARDIZED ESTIMATE	95% CONFIDENCE INTERVAL	
		LOWER 2.5%	UPPER 2.5%
SAT			
SAT Verbal	1.00	1.00	1.00
SAT Mathematics	1.07	1.00	1.14
ACHIEVEMENT			
English	1.00	1.00	1.00
Foreign Language	1.08	1.02	1.14
Math	0.92	0.87	0.97
Social Sciences	1.02	0.98	1.06
Life and Physical Sciences	0.98	0.94	1.02
RELATIONSHIP			
Mother–Child Relationship	1.00	1.00	1.00
Father–Child Relationship	1.00	1.00	1.00

Table 6. Structural Model Estimates

	SAT EST. (L95 | U95)	ACH EST. (L95 | U95)	LOG ILLIQUID ASSETS EST. (L95 | U95)	ENRICHING ENVIRONMENT OR EST. (L95 | U95)	PRIVATE SCHOOL OR EST. (L95 | U95)
High School Achievement	1.00	—	—	—	—
	(0.90 | 1.11)				
Father Education	0.01	0.03	0.05	1.12	1.11
	(-0.02 | 0.03)	(0.01 | 0.04)	(0.03 | 0.07)	(1.06 | 1.18)	(1.01 | 1.22)
Mother Education	0.03	0.01	0.04	1.04	1.04
	(0.01 | 0.05)	(0.00 | 0.02)	(0.02 | 0.07)	(0.99 | 1.09)	(0.96 | 1.14)
Log Parental Income	-0.02	0.01	0.17	0.94	1.01
	(-0.04 | 0.03)	(-0.01 | 0.04)	(0.10 | 0.23)	(0.86 | 1.03)	(0.87 | 1.16)
Log Liquid Assets	-0.02	0.01	0.09	1.04	1.00
	(-0.03 | 0.004)	(0.00 | 0.02)	(0.08 | 0.11)	(1.01 | 1.07)	(0.92 | 1.07)
Log Illiquid Assets	0.06	0.02	—	1.20	1.31
	(0.01 | 0.11)	(-0.01 | 0.04)		(1.08 | 1.32)	(1.11 | 1.55)
Log Debt	0.00	-0.01	0.13	1.00	0.96
	(-0.01 | 0.02)	(-0.02 | 0.00)	(0.11 | 0.14)	(0.97 | 1.03)	(0.91 | 1.01)
Black	-0.42	-0.24	-0.27	0.73	0.35
	(-0.55 | -0.31)	(-0.30 | -0.18)	(-0.40 | -0.14)	(0.55 | 0.95)	(0.21 | 0.58)
Hispanic/Latinx	-0.35	-0.04	-0.10	0.78	0.40
	(-0.53 | -0.27)	(-0.13 | 0.05)	(-0.25 | 0.04)	(0.58 | 1.06)	(0.22 | 0.71)
Family Size	-0.03	-0.01	-0.02	0.98	0.93
	(-0.06 | 0.01)	(-0.03 | 0.00)	(-0.06 | 0.02)	(0.91 | 1.06)	(0.80 | 1.07)

Table 6. Structural Model Estimates *(continued)*					
	SAT EST. (L95 | U95)	ACH EST. (L95 | U95)	LOG ILLIQUID ASSETS EST. (L95 | U95)	ENRICHING ENVIRONMENT OR EST. (L95 | U95)	PRIVATE SCHOOL OR EST. (L95 | U95)
Female	-0.39	0.26	—	1.36	0.92
	(-0.47 | -0.30)	(0.21 | 0.31)		(1.12 | 1.65)	(0.65 | 1.30)
Residential Area (Rural)	-0.05	0.00	0.23	1.03	0.79
	(-0.17 | 0.03)	(-0.06 | 0.06)	(0.13 | 0.33)	(0.83 | 1.29)	(0.54 | 1.14)
Single-Parent	0.02	-0.06	-0.77	0.62	0.81
	(-0.14 | 0.09)	(-0.14 | 0.01)	(-0.91 | -0.63)	(0.47 | 0.81)	(0.50 | 1.31)
Adoptive, Foster, No Parents	0.00	-0.24	-0.01	0.90	1.84
	(-0.23 | 0.30)	(-0.39 | -0.09)	(-0.26 | 0.24)	(0.52 | 1.54)	(0.91 | 3.73)
Mother-Child Relationship	-0.01	0.02			
	(-0.03 | 0.02)	(0.00 | 0.03)			
Father-Child Relationship	0.00	0.01			
	(-0.02 | 0.02)	(0.00 | 0.02)			
Physical Environment Risk	0.02	-0.03			
	(-0.02 | 0.10)	(-0.05 | 0.00)			
Enriching Environment	0.21	0.05			
	(0.11 | 0.26)	(0.00 | 0.10)			
Private School	0.13	0.01			
	(0.02 | 0.25)	(-0.07 | 0.08)			
Paternal Grandparent Ed.	0.04	0.00	-0.01	0.98	0.90
	(0.01 | 0.07)	(-0.02 | 0.02)	(-0.05 | 0.03)	(0.93 | 1.04)	(0.79 | 1.04)
Maternal Grandparent Ed.	0.00	0.00	0.02	1.04	1.02
	(-0.02 | 0.02)	(-0.02 | 0.01)	(-0.01 | 0.05)	(0.99 | 1.09)	(0.91 | 1.13)
SAT Year (1996)	0.39				
SAT Year (1997)	-0.17				
	(-0.27 | 0.03)				
SAT Year (1999)	-0.21				
	(-0.31 | -0.05)				
SAT Year (2000)	-0.14				
	(-0.27 | -0.004)				
SAT Year (2001)	-0.04				
	(-0.18 | 0.09)				
SAT Year (2002)	-0.17				
	(-0.34 | 0.02)				
SAT Year (2003)	-0.32				
	(-0.81 | 0.11)				

Note: All coefficients are unstandardized. Coefficients for Private School are odds ratios. The estimates for SAT performance need to be multiplied by 200 to return them to the original SAT score scale.

Acknowledgments

THIS PROJECT AND thing-in-the-making is an assemblage of a myriad of experiences, thinkers, conversations, mentors, friends, and family. Although it wouldn't be possible without them, it would be impossible to acknowledge them all. Thus, if I miss anyone or anything please know that there is a trace of your influence in the pages of this book.

As a regular café-goer, I am indebted to at least three cafés where I wrote much of this book: Manhattanville, Double Dutch, and Astor Row Café. The awesome employees, great coffee, dope music, cool people I've met, and excellent conversations were all productively helpful.

Several people so substantially contributed to the book's quality and successful completion that I must extend my gratitude. Carol Ross of HyperLife Editing Services did incredible work editing the entire manuscript. Any errors are mistakes of my own. I had an awesome graphic designer of information, Joel Katz, who made all of the graphs in chapters 3 and 4 more easily legible and aesthetically more pleasing.

The two anonymous reviewers provided very thorough, helpful, and really important challenges, feedback, and suggestions that substantially sharpened this thing-in-the-making. Most important, I extend my deep gratitude to my editor at the University of Minnesota Press, Pieter Martin, for not only his interest in this project but patience, feedback, and formative suggestions and ideas. Each of these people significantly added to the quality of this book.

Many thanks to my supportive institutional home and colleagues in the School of Social Policy and Practice at the University of Pennsylvania. This book benefited from the work and feedback of a number of former students: Julianne Oothoudt, Deepa Vasudevan, Xiaoge Zhang, Nan Zhou, and students in my course Policy and "Difference" in Postmodernity.

I'm also very appreciative to my colleagues and conversation partners, some of whom read various parts of the work, providing helpful and important feedback, enhancing the arguments and making them accessible for a broader audience. These people include Ed Brockenbrough, Gerald Campano, Elizabeth de Freitas, David Eng, Nessette Falu, Ken Gergen, TJ Ghose, Wilfredo Gomez, Kris Gutierrez, Shaun Harper, Korina Jocson, David Kazandjian, Patti Lather, Carol Lee, Lisa Mazzei, Na'ilah Nasir, Lisa (Leigh) Patel, Awilda Rodriguez, Jerry Rosiek, Deborah Thomas, Eve Tuck, Deepa Vasudevan, and I am sure many more I am forgetting. A special thanks to Vivian Gadsden and Zeus Leonardo for their unwavering support for the direction of my scholarship and to Korina Jocson for being a regular sounding board, conversation partner, and friend.

This project began in January 2011 when I decided that I would pursue a book project that would deconstruct the nature/culture binary, work through deconstruction to reconceptualize theories of inheritance and social reproduction in education, and, through this work, philosophically rethink methods of quantitative inquiry. As with many projects, there is often at least one major rupturing (or diffracting) moment. That came less than twelve months later when my colleague (and now dean) John L. Jackson received a set of books in return for reviewing a book for Duke University Press. Among those books was Vicki Kirby's *Quantum Anthropologies*. John began reading this book and texted me to say that I needed to read it because it was doing much of what I was talking about and moving toward. I ordered and read it immediately, and John and I discussed it together. The new materialist deconstruction that Kirby develops in *Quantum Anthropologies* opened new windows of possibility for my project in ways that I had only imagined and didn't have the theoretical knowledge and language to develop. I don't take this event to have been random but rather purposive in pushing me to make an ontological turn in my work and produce an incredibly sharper project as a result. Vicki Kirby read an earlier version of part of this project and provided the very hard but necessary critique it needed in order to sharpen the work and make the fuller ontological turn that new materialists are pushing. I only hope I have even partially met her expectations. I am grateful. Moreover, I am profoundly appreciative to my colleague John L. Jackson. He was a tremendous sounding board for my arguments and listened, provided feedback, and had the courage to ask the difficult questions that sharpened and were formative.

I have been fortunate to have a mentor who has pushed, challenged, supported, encouraged, listened, and provided the necessary feedback that has been tremendously formative in my personal and intellectual development. Edmund W. Gordon provided both the embrace and challenge that is necessary for productive mentorship from the first moment we met. In that first meeting, he planted the very important intellectual seeds on critical theory and epistemology in measurement, which I would come to take up in my scholarship. I thank him immeasurably for his ongoing mentorship, guidance, and unwavering support.

Of course I would be remiss if I didn't extend my special appreciation to my family in a book on inheritance. Andrea Williams, Augustine Román, and David Román have each been significant actors in the genesis of my becoming understanding of the world. Antonio Williams, Shelly Román, Taina Román, Tasha Phillips, Stephanie Román, Olivia Khouri, and Zoe Román have each been formative in important ways.

Finally, I extend immense gratitude to my partner and best friend, Denise Pillott, and my son, Elijah. This book has not been without sacrifice and I am profoundly grateful for their patience, love, and support. I have learned a lot from both of them and this composite project is as much their making as it is mine.

This book is dedicated to my son, Elijah.

Notes

1. Inheriting Possibility

1. Capital, according to Bourdieu, is both material and non-material. As a form of material resources, economic capital includes one's income, assets, home, business, etc. He also posited three forms of non-material capital: social, cultural, and symbolic capital. Bourdieu (1986) defines social capital as "the aggregate of the actual or potential resources which are linked to possession of a durable network of more or less institutionalized relationships of mutual acquaintance and recognition—or in other words, to membership in a group—which provides each of its members with the backing of the collectively-owned capital, a 'credential' which entitles them to credit, in the various senses of the word" (p. 21). Thus, the value of one's social capital is contingent on the size of one's social networks and the value of economic and cultural capital one possesses. Both social and economic capital can be converted into/enabled by cultural capital. Cultural capital is manifested in three states: embodied, objectified, and institutionalized. The embodied state of cultural capital is habitus. The objectified state is the material forms of culture such as books, magazines, art, or music. The institutionalized state refers to the degrees or certifications conferred by dominant institutions of schooling. Finally, symbolic capital is a function of prestige, fame, and reputation. Each form of capital socially structures and is socially structured differently, and is enacted differently, based on the social field.

2. Foucault's (1972) discursive theory is a deployment of enouncements via a sequence of semiotic signs. Discourse is not what is said but rather the sociohistorical material conditions that both constrain and enable possibility. For Foucault, discursive acts are situated in cultural and historical context, constrained by power, and the meaning-making and knowledge that emerges from discourse is a product of power and ideology. Thus, the knowledge and ideology of power is always working in everyday discursive acts; power not only produces the subject but also works through the subject.

3. Theoretically, space has been conceptualized and understood in various ways in the social sciences. In *Capital*, Marx's conceptualization of space was reduced to the economic determinism of social classes. Pierre Bourdieu described

social space as "a field of forces, i.e., as a set of objective power relations that impose themselves on all who enter the field," yet not reducible to the actions and interactions of agents in space (1985, 724). Bourdieu's conceptualization focused more on the structuring forces of space and the produced social divisions and less on the practices within space and their mediation and constitution of space. Alternatively, Michel de Certeau (1984) explained the distinction between place and space pointing toward the practices as the primary distinction. He suggested that place is a location whereas space is a "practiced place" determined by subjects in the history of place and the users of it. Although de Certeau gives more attention to the mediating processes of practices within space he does not adequately account for the production and reproduction of space itself whereby social divisions are mediated and embodied via inheritance.

4. Inheriting Merit

1. As an iteration of the Elementary and Secondary Education Act of 1965, NCLB requires that schools be evaluated based on the overall performance of their student body on state selected standardized summative assessments. States define proficiency levels and schools are expected to perform at or above those levels. If they do not then they are expected to make adequate yearly progress until proficiency levels are achieved. When adequate yearly progress is not met then the school is identified for school improvement and when not met for five consecutive years then the school may be closed, completely restructured, or turned into a charter school.

Bibliography

Alaimo, S., and S. Hekman. 2008. *Material Feminisms*. Bloomington: Indiana University Press.

Althusser, L. (1971) 2001. *Lenin and Philosophy and Other Essays*. New York: Monthly Review Press.

Avery, C., A. Fairbanks, and R. Zeckhauser. 2004. *The Early Admissions Game: Joining the Elite*. Cambridge, Mass.: Harvard University Press.

Barad, K. 2007. *Meeting the Universe Halfway: Quantum Physics and the Entanglement of Matter and Meaning*. Durham, N.C.: Duke University Press.

Baum, S., J. Ma, and K. Payea. 2013. *Education Pays 2013: The Benefits of Higher Education for Individuals and Society*. New York: The College Board.

Becker, G. 1964. *Human Capital: A Theoretical and Empirical Analysis with Special Reference to Education*. Chicago: University of Chicago Press.

Becker, Gary, and Nigel Tomes. 1979. "An Equilibrium Theory of the Distribution of Income and Intergenerational Mobility." *Journal of Political Economy* 87, no. 6: 1153–89.

———. 1986. "Human Capital and the Rise and Fall of Families." *Journal of Labor Economics* 4, no. 3: S1–S39.

Bennett, J. 2005. "The Agency of Assemblages and the North American Blackout." *Public Culture* 17, no. 3: 445–465.

Bennett, J. 2010. *Vibrant Matter: A Political Ecology of Things*. Durham, N.C.: Duke University Press.

Berger, Peter, and Thomas Luckmann. 1967. *The Social Construction of Reality: A Treatise in the Sociology of Knowledge*. New York: Anchor.

Blau, Francine D., and John W. Graham. 1990. "Black-White Differences in Wealth and Asset Composition." *Quarterly Journal of Economics* 105: 321–339.

Blau, Peter M., and Otis Dudley Duncan. 1967. *The American Occupational Structure*. New York: John Wiley.

Block, J. H. 1983. "Differential Premises Arising from Differential Socialization of the Sexes: Some Conjectures." *Child Development* 54, no. 6: 1335–54.

Bollen, K. 1989. *Structural Equations with Latent Variables*. New York: John Wiley & Sons.

Bonilla-Silva, E. 1997. *Racism without Racists: Color-Blind Racism and Racial Inequality in Contemporary America.* 3rd ed. Lanham, Md.: Rowman & Littlefield.

Bound, J., B. Hershbein, and B. T. Long. 2009. "Playing the Admission Game: Student Reactions to Increasing College Competition." NBER Working Paper Series 15272. Cambridge, Mass.: National Bureau of Economic Research. http://www.nber.org/papers/w15272.

Bourdieu, Pierre. 1977. *Outline of a Theory of Practice.* New York: Cambridge University Press.

———. (1979) 1984. *Distinction: A Social Critique of the Judgment of Taste.* Cambridge, Mass.: Harvard University Press.

———. 1986. "The Forms of Capital." In *Handbook of Theory and Research for the Sociology of Education,* ed. J. G. Richardson, 241–58. Westport, Conn.: Greenwood Press.

———. (1980) 1990. *The Logic of Practice.* Stanford, Calif.: Stanford University Press.

———. 1991. *Language & Symbolic Power.* Cambridge, Mass.: Harvard University Press.

Bourdieu, Pierre, and Jean-Claude Passeron. 1977. *Reproduction in Education, Society, and Culture.* 4th ed. Thousand Oaks, Calif.: Sage Publications.

———. 1979. *The Inheritors: French Students and Their Relation to Culture.* 2nd ed. Thousand Oaks, Calif.: Sage Publications.

Bowen, W. G., M. A. Kurzweil, and E. M. Tobin. 2005. *Equity and Excellence in American Higher Education.* Charlottesville: University of Virginia Press.

Bowles, Samuel, and Herbert Gintis. 2002. "The Inheritance of Inequality." *Journal of Economic Perspectives* 16: 3–30.

Bowles, Samuel, Herbert Gintis, and Melissa O. Groves. 2005. *Unequal Chances: Family Background and Economic Success.* New York: Russell Sage Foundation.

Briggs, D. 2009. "Preparation for College Admission Exams." 2009 NACAC Discussion Paper. Arlington, Va.: National Association for College Admission Counseling.

Butler, Judith. 1990. *Gender Trouble.* New York: Routledge.

———. 1993. *Bodies That Matter: On the Discursive Limits of "Sex."* New York: Routledge.

———. 1997. *Excitable Speech: A Politics of the Performative.* New York: Routledge.

Caldwell, B., and R. Bradley. 1984. *Home Observation for Measurement of the Environment.* Little Rock: University of Arkansas.

Calhoun, C. 1993. "Habitus, Field, and Capital: The Question of Historical Specificity." In *Bourdieu: Critical Perspectives,* ed. E. Lipuma, M. Postone, and C. Calhoun. Chicago: University of Chicago Press.

Camara, W. J., and A. E. Schmidt. 1999. "Group Differences in Standardized Testing and Social Stratification." *College Board Report (99–5)*. New York: College Board.

Carter, Prudence. 2003. " 'Black' Cultural Capital, Status Positioning, and Schooling Conflicts for Low-Income African American Youth." *Social Problems* 50, no. 1: 136–55.

Chan, Tak Wing, and Vikki Boliver. 2013. "The Grandparents Effect in Social Mobility: Evidence from British Birth Cohort Studies." *American Sociological Review* 78: 662–78.

Charles, C., V. Roscigno, and K. Torres. 2007. "Racial Inequality and College Attendance: The Mediating Role of Parental Investments." *Social Science Research* 36, no.1: 329–52.

Cherlin, Andrew J., and Frank F. Furstenberg. 1992. *The New American Grandparent: A Place in the Family, a Life Apart.* Cambridge Mass.: Harvard University Press.

Clark, K. 1965. *Dark Ghettoes: Dilemmas of Social Power.* Hanover, N.H.: Wesleyan University Press.

Clinedist, M. E., S. F. Hurley, and D. A. Hawkins. 2011. *2011 State of College Admission.* Arlington, Va.: National Association for College Admission Counseling.

Coe, D. L., and J. D. Davidson. 2011. "The Origins of Legacy Admissions: A Sociological Explanation." *Review of Religious Research* 52, no. 3: 233–47.

Cohen, C. J. 1999. *The Boundaries of Blackness: AIDS and the Breakdown of Black Politics.* Chicago: University of Chicago Press.

Cole, M., and S. Scribner. 1974. *Culture and Thought.* New York: Wiley.

College Board. 2011. "SAT Reasoning Test—Scores & Reports." http://professionals.collegeboard.com/testing/sat-reasoning/scores/reports.

College Board. 2012. *2012 College-Bound Seniors: Total Group Profile Report.* New York: The College Board.

College Board. 2013. "Big Future—College Search." https://bigfuture.collegeboard.org/college-search.

College Confidential. 2013. "College Search." http://www.collegeconfidential.com/college_search.

Collins, P. H. 2000. "Gender, Black Feminism, and Black Political Economy." *Annals of the American Academy of Political and Social Science* 568: 41–53.

Committee for Undergraduate Recruitment, Admissions, and Financial Aid. 2013. *Report to the University Committee* (CFC 130313). Madison, Wisc.: Committee for Undergraduate Recruitment, Admissions, and Financial Aid.

Common, with Adam Bradley. 2011. *One Day It'll All Make Sense.* New York: Atria Books.

Comte, A. 1988. *Introduction to Positive Philosophy,* edited by Frederick Ferré. Indianapolis, Ind.: Hackett Publishing Company.

Conant, J. B. 1940. "Education for a Classless Society." *The Atlantic Monthly* (May).

Conley, Dalton. 1999. *Being Black, Living in the Red: Race, Wealth, and Social Policy in America*. Berkeley: University of California Press.

Conley, D., and R. Glauber. 2008. *Wealth Mobility and Volatility in Black and White*. Washington, D.C.: Center for American Progress.

Coole, D., and S. Frost. 2010. *New Materialisms: Ontology, Agency, and Politics*. Durham, N.C.: Duke University Press.

Crary, J. 1990. *Techniques of the Observer: On Vision and Modernity in the Nineteenth Century*. Cambridge, Mass.: MIT Press.

Crenshaw, K. 1993. "Mapping the Margins: Intersectionality, Identity Politics, and Violence against Women of Color." *Stanford Law Review* 43: 1241–99.

Cronbach, L. J. 1988. "Five Perspectives on Validation Argument." In *Test Validity*, eds. H. Wainer and H. Braun. Hillsdale, N.J.: Erlbaum.

Crouse, J., and D. Trusheim. 1988. *The Case Against the SAT*. Chicago: University of Chicago Press.

Daston, L. 1988. *Classical Probability in the Enlightenment*. Princeton, N.J.: Princeton University Press.

de Certeau, Michel. (1980) 1984. *The Practice of Everyday Life*. Berkeley: University of California Press.

Deleuze, Gilles, and Félix Guattari. 1987. *A Thousand Plateaus: Capitalism and Schizophrenia*. Minneapolis, Minn.: University of Minnesota Press.

Demo, D. H., and M. J. Cox. 2000. "Families with Young Children: A Review of Research in the 1990s." *Journal of Marriage and the Family* 62, no. 4: 876–895.

Derrida, Jacques. (1972) 1982. *Margins of Philosophy*. Chicago: University of Chicago Press.

———. (1996) 1998. *Monolingualism of the Other; or, the Prosthesis of Origin*. Stanford, Calif.: Stanford University Press.

———. (1967) 1998. *Of Grammatology*. Baltimore, Md.: Johns Hopkins University Press.

———. 2002. "Force of Law: The 'Mystical Foundation of Authority.'" In *Acts of Religion: Jacques Derrida*, ed. G. Anidjar, 230–98. New York: Routledge.

———. (1995) 2008. *The Gift of Death and Literature in Secret*. Chicago: University of Chicago Press.

Derrida, Jacques, and Elisabeth Roudinesco. (2001) 2004. *For What Tomorrow . . . : A Dialogue*. Stanford, Calif.: Stanford University Press.

Dixon-Román, Ezekiel. 2012. "Introduction: Social Space and the Political Economy of Education Conceived Comprehensively." In *Thinking Comprehensively About Education: Spaces of Educative Possibility and Their Implications for Public Policy*, ed. Ezekiel Dixon-Román and Edmund W. Gordon, 1–13. New York: Routledge/Taylor & Francis.

———. 2013. "The Forms of Capital and the Developed Achievement of Black Males." *Urban Education* 48, no. 6: 828–62.

———. Forthcoming. "Multigenerational Inequality and Social Differences in Reading Skills Development: A New Materialist Perspective."

Dixon-Román, Ezekiel, H. Everson, and J. J. McArdle. 2013. "Race, Poverty, and SAT Scores: Modeling the Influences of Family Income on Black and White High School Students' SAT Performance." *Teachers College Record* 115, no. 4: 1–33.

Dixon-Román, Ezekiel, and Kenneth J. Gergen. 2013. "Epistemology in Measurement: Paradigms and Practices — Part I. A Critical Perspective on the Sciences of Measurement." http://www.gordoncommission.org/rsc/pdfs/dixonroman _gergen_part1_epistemology_measurement.pdf.

Dixon-Román, E., and M. Kim. Forthcoming. "Assessing Wealth: Family Assets, Race, and SAT Performance."

Dorans, N. 2004. "Freedle's Table 2: Fact or Fiction." *Harvard Educational Review* 74, no. 1: 62–79.

Dorans, N., and K. Zeller. 2004. *Examining Freedle's Claims and His Proposed Solution: Dated Data, Inappropriate Measurement, and Incorrect and Unfair Scoring* (No. RR-04–26). Princeton, N.J.: Educational Testing Service.

Duckworth, A. L., C. Peterson, M. D. Matthews, and D. R. Kelly. 2007. "Grit: Perseverance and Passion for Long-Term Goals." *Journal of Personality and Social Psychology* 92, no. 6: 1087–1101.

Duffy, E. A., and I. Goldberg. 1997. *Crafting a Class: College Admissions and Financial Aid, 1955–1994.* Princeton, N.J.: Princeton University Press.

Dumais, S. 2002. "Cultural Capital, Gender, and School Success: The Role of Habitus." *Sociology of Education* 75, no. 1: 44–68.

Dumais, Susan A. 2006. "Early Childhood Cultural Capital, Parental Habitus, and Teachers' Perceptions." *Poetics* 34: 83–107.

Duncan, G. J., and J. Brooks-Gunn. 1997. *Consequences of Growing Up Poor.* New York: Russell Sage Foundation.

Duncan, Greg J., Kjetil Telle, Kathleen Ziol-Guest, and Ariel Kalil. 2011. "Economic Deprivation in Early Childhood and Adult Attainment: Comparative Evidence from Norwegian Registry Data and the U.S. Panel Study of Income Dynamics." In *Persistence, Privilege, and Parenting: The Comparative Study of Intergenerational Mobility,* ed. T. Smeeding, R. Erikson, and M. Jäntti. New York: Russell Sage Foundation.

During, Simon. (1993) 1999. *The Cultural Studies Reader.* 2nd ed. London: Routledge.

Economist. 2004. "The Curse of Nepotism: A Helping Hand for Those Who Least Need It." Lexington. *The Economist,* January 8. http://www.economist.com/ node/2333345.

Edwards, J. 2002. "Education Policy Address." University of Maryland, College Park, November 21. http://www.gwu.edu/~action/2004/edwards/edw112102sp.html.

Elert, G. 1992. *The SAT: Aptitude or Demographics?* http://hypertextbook.com/eworld/sat.shtml.

Eliot, L. 2010. "The Myth of Pink and Blue Brains." *Educational Leadership* 68, no. 3: 32–36.

Erikson, Robert, and John H. Goldthorpe. 1992. *The Constant Flux: A Study of Class Mobility in Industrial Societies.* Oxford: Clarendon Press.

Ermisch, J., M. Jäntti, and T. Smeeding, eds. 2012. *From Parents to Children: The Intergenerational Transmission of Advantage.* New York: Russell Sage Foundation.

Everson, H., and R. Millsap. 2004. "Beyond Individual Differences: Exploring School Effects on SAT Scores." *Educational Psychologist* 39, no. 3: 157–172.

Fausset, R., and A. Blinder. 2015. "Atlanta School Workers Sentenced in Test Score Cheating Case." *New York Times,* April 15. http://www.nytimes.com/2015/04/15/us/atlanta-school-workers-sentenced-in-test-score-cheating-case.html?_r=0.

Featherman, David L., and Robert M. Hauser. 1978. *Opportunity and Change.* New York: Academic Press.

Field, K. 2009. "Sen. Edward Kennedy, Longtime Champion of Higher Education, Dies at 77." *Chronicle of Higher Education.* http://chronicle.com/article/Sen-Edward-Kennedy-Longti/48175/.

Foucault, Michel. 1972. *The Archaeology of Knowledge; and, The Discourse on Language.* New York: Vintage Books.

Foucault, Michel. 1980. *Power/Knowledge: Selected Interviews and Other Writings, 1972–1977.* New York: Pantheon Books.

Frazier, E. F. 1939. *The Negro Family in the United States.* Chicago: University of Chicago Press.

Freedle, R. 2003. "Correcting the SAT's Ethnic and Social-Class Bias: A Method for Reestimating SAT Scores." *Harvard Educational Review* 73, no. 1: 1–43.

Gergen, Kenneth J., and Ezekiel Dixon-Román. 2014. "Social Epistemology and the Pragmatics of Assessment." *Teachers College Record* 116, no. 11: 1–22.

Gluckman, P., and M. Hanson. 2005. *The Fetal Matrix: Evolution, Development, and Disease.* Cambridge, U.K.: Cambridge University Press.

Goering, John, and Judith D. Feins. 2003. *Choosing a Better Life? Evaluating the Moving to Opportunity Social Experiment.* Washington, D.C.: Urban Institute Press.

Golden, D. 2003. "Family Ties: Preference for Alumni Children in College Admission Draws Fire." *Wall Street Journal,* January 15, Al.

———. 2007. *The Price of Admission: How America's Ruling Class Buys Its Way into*

Elite Colleges—And Who Gets Left Outside the Gates. New York: Three Rivers Press.

Gordon, E. W. 1999. "Human Social Divisions and Human Intelligence: Putting Them in Their Place." In *Education and Justice: A View from the Back of the Bus,* ed. E. Gordon. New York: Teachers College Press.

Gossip Girl. 2007–2012. The CW television series. Developed by Stephanie Savage and Josh Schwartz.

Gould, S. J. 1981. *The Mismeasure of Man.* New York: W. W. Norton.

Guinier, L., and G. Torres. 2002. *The Miner's Canary: Enlisting Race, Resisting Power, Transforming Democracy.* Cambridge, Mass.: Harvard University Press.

Gutiérrez, K. D., and B. Rogoff. 2003. "Cultural Ways of Learning: Individual Traits or Repertoires of Practice." *Educational Researcher* 32, no. 5: 19–25.

Hacking, I. (1975) 2006. *The Emergence of Probability: A Philosophical Study of Early Ideas About Probability Induction and Statistical Inference.* 2nd ed. Cambridge, U.K.: Cambridge University Press.

Hamer D. H., S. Hu, V. L. Magnuson, N. Hu, and A. M. Pattatucci. 1993. "A Linkage between DNA Markers on the X Chromosome and Male Sexual Orientation." *Science* 261, no. 5119: 321–27.

Hames-García, M. 2008. "How Real Is Race?" In *Material Feminisms,* ed. S. Alaimo and S. Hekman. Bloomington: Indiana University Press.

Harraway, D. 1985. "Manifesto for Cyborgs: Science, Technology, and Socialist Feminisms in the 1980s." *Socialist Review* 80: 65–180.

Hernstein, R., and C. Murray. 1996. *The Bell Curve: Intelligence and Class Structure in American Life.* New York: Free Press Paperbacks.

Hill, Martha S. 1991. *The Panel Study of Income Dynamics: A User's Guide, Volume 2.* Thousand Oaks, Calif.: Sage Publications.

Hill, N. E. 2001. "Parenting and Academic Socialization as They Relate to School Readiness: The Roles of Ethnicity and Family Income." *Journal of Educational Psychology* 93, no. 4: 686–97. doi:10.1037/0022-0663.93.4.686.

Hill, S. A., and J. Sprague. 1999. "Parenting in Black and White Families: The Interaction of Gender with Race and Class." *Gender & Society* 13, no. 4: 480–502.

Hofferth, S. L., and J. E. Sandberg. 2001. "How American Children Spend Their Time." *Journal of Marriage & Family* 63, no. 2: 295.

Hoffmeyer, J. 2008. *Biosemiotics: An Examination into the Signs of Life and the Life of Signs.* Scranton, N.J.: University of Scranton Press.

Holland, P. 2003. *Causation and Race.* ETS Research Report RR-03-03. Princeton, N.J.: Educational Testing Service.

Horn, J. L., and R. B. Cattell. 1966. "Refinement and Test of the Theory of Fluid and Crystallized General Intelligences." *Journal of Educational Psychology* 57: 253–70.

"How Not to React When Your Child Tells You That He's Gay." 2014. Video posted to YouTube, August 27. https://www.youtube.com/watch?v=1df_i26wh-w.

Howard, C. 2013. "Ranking America's Top Colleges 2013." http://www.forbes.com/sites/carolinehoward/2013/07/24/ranking-americas-top-colleges-2013/.

Howell, Cameron, and Sarah E. Turner. 2004. "Legacies in Black and White: The Racial Composition of the Legacy Pool." *Research in Higher Education* 45: 325–51.

Hu, S., A. M. Pattatucci, C. Patterson, et al. 1995. "Linkage between Sexual Orientation and Chromosome Xq28 in Males but Not in Females." *Natural Genetics* 11, no. 3: 248–56.

Hurwitz, M. 2011. "The Impact of Legacy Status on Undergraduate Admissions at Elite Colleges and Universities." *Economics of Education Review* 30, no. 3: 480–92.

IBM Watson. 2015. IBM Watson website. http://www.ibm.com/smarterplanet/us/en/ibmwatson/index.html.

Jackson, John L. 2008. *Racial Paranoia: The Unintended Consequences of Political Correctness.* New York: Basic Books.

———. 2013. *Thin Description: Ethnography and the African Hebrew Israelites of Jerusalem.* Cambridge, Mass.: Harvard University Press.

Jaschik, S., and D. Lederman. 2012. *The 2012 Inside Higher Ed Survey of College and University Admissions Directors.* Washington, D.C.: Inside Higher Ed, Gallup.

Jensen, Arthur R. 1969. "How Much Can We Boost IQ and Scholastic Achievement?" *Harvard Educational Review* 39, no. 1: 1–123.

Jensen, Arthur R. 2000. "Testing: The Dilemma of Group Differences." *Psychology, Public Policy, and Law* 6: 121–127.

Johnson, Jamie. 2003. *Born Rich.* Directed by Jamie Johnson, produced by Jamie Johnson and Dirk Wittenborn. Wise and Good Film, LLC.

Journal of Blacks in Higher Education Foundation. 1998. "Why Family Income Differences Don't Explain the Racial Gap in SAT Scores." *Journal of Blacks in Higher Education* 20: 6–8.

Juster, R. P., N. G. Smith, É. Ouellet, S. Sindi, and S. J. Lupien. 2013. "Sexual Orientation and Disclosure in Relation to Psychiatric Symptoms, Diurnal Cortisol, and Allostatic Load." *Psychosom Med* 75, no. 2: 103–16.

Kahlenberg, R. 2010. *Affirmative Action for the Rich: Legacy Preferences in College Admissions.* Washington D.C.: Century Foundation.

Kalil, Ariel, Mary Pattillo, and Monique Payne. 2004. "Intergenerational Assets and the Black/White Test Score Gap." In *After the Bell: Family Background, Public Policy, and Educational Success,* ed. D. Conley and K. Albright. New York: Routledge.

Karabel, Jerome. 2005. *The Chosen: The Hidden History of Admission and Exclusion at Harvard, Yale, and Princeton.* Boston, Mass.: Mariner Books.

Kawagley, A. O. 2006. *A Yupiaq Worldview: A Pathway to Ecology and Spirit.* 2nd ed. Long Grove, Ill.: Waveland Press.

Keister, Lisa A. 2004. "Race, Family Structure, and Wealth: The Effect of Childhood Family on Adult Asset Ownership." *Sociological Perspectives* 47: 161–187.

Khan, Shamus R. 2011. *Privilege: The Making of an Adolescent Elite at St. Paul's School.* Princeton, N.J.: Princeton University Press.

Kincheloe, J. L., S. R. Steinberg, and A. D. Gresson. 1996. *Measured Lies: The Bell Curve Examined.* New York: St. Martin's Press.

Kirby, Vicki. 2011. *Quantum Anthropologies: Life at Large.* Durham, N.C.: Duke University Press.

Kitchin, Rob. 2014. *The Data Revolution: Big Data, Open Data, Data Infrastructures and Their Consequences.* Thousand Oaks, Calif.: Sage Publications.

Kline, R. 2015. *Principles and Practice of Structural Equation Modeling.* 4th ed. New York: Guilford Press.

Kuhn, Thomas. 1996. *The Structure of Scientific Revolutions.* 3rd ed. Chicago: University of Chicago Press.

Lamont, Michele, and Annette Lareau. 1988. "Cultural Capital: Allusions, Gaps, and Glissandos in Recent Theoretical Developments." *Sociological Theory* 6, no. 2: 153–68.

Lamott, Anne, and Sam Lamott. 2012. *A Journal of My Son's First Son.* New York: Riverhead Books.

Lareau, Annette. 2003. *Unequal Childhoods: Class, Race, and Family Life.* Berkeley: University of California Press.

Lareau, Annette, and Erin M. Horvat. 1999. "Moments of Social Inclusion and Exclusion: Race, Class, and Cultural Capital in Family-School Relationships." *Sociology of Education* 72, no. 1: 37–53.

Larew, J. 1991. "Why Are Droves of Unqualified, Unprepared Kids Getting into Our Top Colleges? Because Their Dads Are Alumni." *Washington Monthly,* June 1991: 10–15.

Lave, J., and E. Wenger. 1991. *Situated Learning: Legitimate Peripheral Participation.* New York: Cambridge University Press.

Lee, Carol. 2001. "Is October Brown Chinese? A Cultural Modeling Activity System for Underachieving Students." *American Educational Research Journal* 38, no. 1: 97–142.

Lee, J. S., and N. Bowen. 2006. "Parental Involvement, Cultural Capital, and the Achievement Gap among Elementary School Children." *American Educational Research Journal* 43, no. 2: 193–218.

Leef, G. 2008. "Legacy Admissions—Affirmative Action for the Rich?" The John

William Pope Center for Higher Education Policy, February 19. http://www .popecenter.org/news/article.html?id=1966.

Lefebvre, Henri. (1974) 1991. *The Production of Space.* Translated by Donald Nicholson-Smith. Malden, Mass.: Blackwell Publishing.

Lemann, N. 1999. *The Big Test: The Secret History of the American Meritocracy.* New York: Farrar, Straus, and Giroux.

Leonardo, Zeus. 2013. *Race Frameworks: A Multidimensional Theory of Racism and Education.* New York: Teachers College Press.

Lewis, Oscar. 1966. "The Culture of Poverty." *American* 215, no. 4: 19–25.

Little, R. J. A., and D. B. Rubin. 2002. *Statistical Analysis with Missing Data.* 2nd ed. Indianapolis, Ind.: John Wiley & Sons.

Lubrano, Alfred. 2005. *Limbo: Blue-Collar Roots, White-Collar Dreams.* Hoboken, N.J.: John Wiley & Sons.

Luca, M., and J. Smith. 2009. "The Market for Rankings." http://citeseerx.ist.psu .edu/viewdoc/download?doi=10.1.1.343.3531&rep=rep1&type=pdf

Lytton, H., and D. M. Romney. 1991. "Parents' Differential Socialization of Boys and Girls: A Meta-analysis." *Psychological Bulletin* 109, no. 2: 267.

Macklemore, and Ryan Lewis. 2012. "Ten Thousand Hours." On *The Heist* studio album. Macklemore LLC.

Mandara, Jelani, Fatima Varner, Nereira Greene, and Scott Richman. 2009. "Intergenerational Family Predictors of the Black-White Achievement Gap." *Journal of Educational Psychology* 101, no. 4: 867–78.

Mare, Robert D. 2011. "A Multigenerational View of Inequality." *Demography* 48, no. 1: 1–23.

Marx, Karl. 1906. *Capital: A Critique of Political Economy.* Vol. 1, *The Process of Capitalist Production.* Chicago: Charles Kerr.

Massey, Douglas S., and Nancy A. Denton. 1994. *American Apartheid: Segregation and the Making of the Underclass.* Cambridge, Mass.: Harvard University Press.

Massey, D. S., and M. Mooney. 2007. "The Effects of America's Three Affirmative Action Programs on Academic Performance." *Social Problems* 54, no. 1: 99–117.

Massumi, Brian. 2002. *Parables for the Virtual: Movement, Affect, Sensation.* Durham, N.C.: Duke University Press.

Mauss, Marcel. [1950] 1990. *The Gift: The Form and Reason for Exchange in Archaic Societies.* New York: W. W. Norton.

Mayer, Susan E., and Leonard M. Lopoo. 2008. "Government Spending and Intergenerational Mobility." *Journal of Public Economics* 92, 139–158.

Mazumder, Bhashkar. 2005. "The Apple Falls Even Closer to the Tree Than We Thought: New and Revised Estimates of the Intergenerational Inheritance of Earnings." In *Unequal Chances: Family Background and Economic Success,* ed. S. Bowles, H. Gintis, and M. O. Groves, 80–99. New York: Russell Sage Foundation and Princeton University Press.

Mazzei, L. 2013. "Materialist Mappings of Knowing in Being: Researchers Constituted in the Production of Knowledge." *Gender and Education* 25, no. 6: 776–85.

McDuff D. 2007. "Quality, Tuition, and Applications to In-State Public Colleges." *Economics of Education Review* 26, no. 4: 433–49.

McLoyd, V. 2008. "The Impact of Economic Hardship on Black Families and Children: Psychological Distress, Parenting, and Socioemotional Development." *Child Development* 61, no. 2: 311–46.

Megalli, M. 1995. "So Your Dad Went to Harvard: Now What About the Lower Board Scores of White Legacies?" *Journal of Blacks in Higher Education* 7: 71–73.

Messick, S. 1988. "The Once and Future Issues of Validity: Assessing the Meaning and Consequences of Measurement." In *Test Validity,* eds. H. Wainer and H. Braun. Hillsdale, N.J.: Erlbaum.

Mezey, N. 2001. "Law as Culture." *Yale Journal of Law and the Humanities* 13: 35–67.

Michell, J. 1999. *Measurement in Psychology: A Critical History of a Methodological Concept.* New York: Cambridge University Press.

Mills, Charles. 1997. *The Racial Contract.* Ithaca, N.Y.: Cornell University Press.

Morse, R., and S. Flanigan. 2013. "How *U.S. News* Calculated the 2014 Best Rankings." http://www.usnews.com/education/best-colleges/articles/2013/09/09/how-us-news-calculated-the-2014-best-colleges-rankings.

Moynihan, Daniel. P. 1965. *The Negro Family: The Case for National Action.* Washington, D.C.: Office of Policy Planning and Research, U.S. Department of Labor.

Mustanski, B. S., M. G. Dupree, C. M. Nievergelt, S. Bocklandt, N. J. Schork, and D. H. Hamer. 2005. "A Genome Wide Scan of Male Sexual Orientation." *Human Genetics* 116, no. 4: 272–78.

Muthén, L. K., and B. O. Muthén. 1998–2010. *Mplus User's Guide.* 6th ed. Los Angeles: Muthén & Muthén.

Nakao, K., R. W. Hodge, and J. Treas. 1990. "On Revising Prestige Scores for All Occupations." *General Social Survey Methodological Report 69.* Chicago: NORC.

Nasir, N. S., and G. B. Saxe. 2003. "Ethnic and Academic Identities: A Cultural Practice Perspective on Emerging Tensions and Their Management in the Lives of Minority Students." *Educational Researcher* 32, no. 5: 14–18.

National Association for College Admission Counseling. 2008. *Report of the Commission on the Use of Standardized Tests in Undergraduate Admission.* Arlington, Va.: National Association for College Admission Counseling.

National Center for Education Statistics. 2010. *Profile of Undergraduate Students: 2007–08* (NCES 2010–205). Washington, D.C.: U.S. Department of Education, National Center for Education Statistics. http://nces.ed.gov/pubs2010/2010205.pdf.

National Geographic. 2013. "Visualizing Race, Identity, and Change." September. http://proof.nationalgeographic.com/2013/09/17/visualizing-change/.

National Public Radio. 2011. "From Pre-Med to Teacher: A New Kind Of Healing." *Weekend Edition Sunday,* October 30. http://www.npr.org/2011/10/30/141779097/from-pre-med-to-teacher-a-new-kind-of-healing.

Nuñez, A., and S. Cuccaro-Alamin. 1998. *First-Generation Students: Undergraduates Whose Parents Never Enrolled in Postsecondary Education* (NCES 98–082). Washington, D.C.: National Center for Education Statistics.

Omi, Michael, and Howard Winant. (1994) 2014. *Racial Formation in the United States.* Berkeley: University of California Press.

Parisi, Luciana. 2013. *Contagious Architecture: Computation, Aesthetics, and Space.* Cambridge, Mass.: MIT Press.

Perry, Imani. 2011. *More Beautiful and More Terrible: The Embrace and Transcendence of Racial Inequality in the United States.* New York: New York University Press.

Peters, H. Elizabeth. 1992. "Patterns of Intergenerational Mobility in Income and Earnings." *Review of Economics and Statistics* 47: 456–466.

Peters, J. F. 1994. "Gender Socialization of Adolescents in the Home: Research and Discussion." *Adolescence* 29, no. 116: 913.

Peterson's. 2013. "College Search." http://www.petersons.com/college-search/.

Pew Research Center. 2015. "Political Polarization." http://www.pewresearch.org/packages/political-polarization/.

Phillips, M., J. Brooks-Gunn, G. J. Duncan, P. Klebanov, and J. Crane. 1998. "Family Background, Parent Practices, and the Black-White Test Score Gap." In *The Black-White Test Score Gap,* ed. C. Jencks and M. Phillips, 103–45. Washington, D.C.: Brookings Institution Press.

Piketty, Thomas. (2013) 2014. *Capital in the Twenty-First Century.* Cambridge, Mass.: the Belknap Press of Harvard University Press.

Poovey, Mary. 1998. *A History of the Modern Fact: Problems of Knowledge in the Sciences of Wealth and Society.* Chicago: University of Chicago Press.

Porter, Theodore. 1995. *Trust in Numbers: The Pursuit of Objectivity in Science and Public Life.* Princeton, N.J.: Princeton University Press.

Powers, D. E. 1993. "Coaching for the SAT: A Summary of the Summaries and an Update." *Educational Measurement: Issues and Practice.* Summer: 24–39.

Puar, Jasbir. 2007. *Terrorist Assemblages: Homonationalism in Queer Times.* Durham, N.C.: Duke University Press.

———. 2012. "I Would Rather Be a Cyborg Than a Goddess: Becoming-Intersectional in Assemblage Theory." *philoSOPHIA* 2, no. 1: 49–66.

Rees, Dee. 2011. *Pariah.* Written and directed by Dee Rees, produced by Nekisa Cooper. Focus Features.

Ridge, J. M. 1974. "Mobility in Britain Reconsidered." Working Papers No. 2, *Oxford Studies in Social Mobility*, Oxford: Clarendon Press.

Ridgeway, C. L. 2011. *Framed by Gender: How Gender Inequality Persists in the Modern World*. New York: Oxford University Press.

Roberts, D. 2011. *Fatal Invention: How Science, Politics, and Big Business Re-Create Race in the Twenty-First Century*. New York: New Press.

Robinson, K., and A. L. Harris. 2014. *The Broken Compass: Parental Involvement with Children's Education*. Cambridge, Mass.: Harvard University Press.

Rogoff, Barbara. 2003. *The Cultural Nature of Human Development*. New York: Oxford University Press.

Rogoff, Natalie. 1953. *Recent Trends in Occupational Mobility*. New York: Free Press.

Roksa, Josipa, and Daniel Potter. 2011. "Parenting and Academic Achievement: Intergenerational Transmission of Educational Advantage." *Sociology of Education* 84: 299–321.

Rotman, Brian. 2000. *Mathematics as Sign: Writing, Imagining, Counting*. Stanford, Calif.: Stanford University Press.

Rubinowitz, Leonard S., and James E. Rosenbaum. 2000. *Crossing the Class and Color Lines: from Public Housing to White Suburbia*. Chicago: University of Chicago Press.

Saenz, V. B., S. Hurtado, D. Barrera, D. Wolf, and F. Yeung. 2007. *First in My Family: A Profile of First-Generation College Students at Four-Year Institutions Since 1971*. Los Angeles, Calif.: Higher Education Research Institute.

Santelices, M. V., and M. Wilson. 2010. "Unfair Treatment? The Case of Freedle, the SAT, and the Standardization Approach to Differential Item Functioning." *Harvard Educational Review* 80, no. 1: 106–33.

Saussure, Ferdinand de. 1910. *Course in General Linguistics*. Peru, Ill.: Open Court.

Schafer, J. W., and J. L. Graham. 2002. "Missing Data: Our View of the State of the Art." *Psychological Methods* 7, no. 2: 147–177.

Schleifer, T. 2013. "Eisgruber '83 Defends Legacy Admissions, Grade Deflation at New York Alumni Event." *The Daily Princetonian*, October 7. http://dailyprincetonian.com/news/2013/10/at-new-york-alumni-event-eisgruber-83-defends-legacy-admissions-grade-deflation/.

Schultz, T. W. 1961. "Investment in Human Capital." *The American Economic Review* 51, no. 1: 1–17.

Selden, S. 1999. *Inheriting Shame: The Story of Eugenics and Racism in America*. New York: Teachers College Press.

Shapiro, Thomas. M. 2005. *The Hidden Cost of Being African American: How Wealth Perpetuates Inequality*. New York: Oxford University Press.

Sharkey, Patrick. 2008. "The Intergenerational Transmission of Context." *American Journal of Sociology* 113: 931–69.

———. 2010. "The Acute Effect of Local Homicides on Children's Cognitive Performance." *Proceedings of the National Academy of Sciences* 107, no. 26: 11733–38.

———. 2013. *Stuck in Place: Urban Neighborhoods and the End of Progress toward Racial Equality.* Chicago: University of Chicago Press.

Sharkey, Patrick, and Felix Elwert. 2011. "The Legacy of Disadvantage: Multi-generational Neighborhood Effects on Cognitive Ability." *American Journal of Sociology* 116, no. 6: 1934–81.

Sieczkowski, C. 2013. "Dad's Note to Gay Son About Coming Out Might Make You Cry." *Huffington Post,* March 15. http://www.huffingtonpost.com/2013/03/15/dads-note-to-son-coming-out_n_2883194.html

Sinharay, S., H. S. Stern, and D. Russell. 2001. "The Use of Multiple Imputation for the Analysis of Missing Data." *Psychological Methods* 6, no. 4: 317–329.

SINTEF. 2013. "Big Data—For Better or for Worse." http://www.sintef.no/home/corporate-news/big-data—for-better-or-worse/.

Smith, M. 2006. *How Race Is Made: Slavery, Segregation, and the Senses.* Chapel Hill: University of North Carolina Press.

Smeeding, T. M., R. Erikson, and M. Jäntti, eds. 2011. *Persistence, Privilege, and Parenting: The Comparative Study of Intergenerational Mobility.* New York: Russell Sage Foundation.

Solon, G. 1992. "Intergenerational Income Mobility in the United States." *American Economic Review* 82, no. 3: 393–408.

Spillers, Hortense. 2003. *Black, White, and In Color: Essays on American Literature and Culture.* Chicago: University of Chicago Press.

Steele, Claude M., and Joshua Aronson. 1995. "Stereotype Threat and the Intellectual Test Performance of African Americans." *Journal of Personality and Social Psychology* 69, no. 5: 797–811.

Steinberg. J. 2002. *The Gatekeepers: Inside the Admissions Process of a Premier College.* New York: Penguin Publishing Group.

Steinmetz, G., ed. 2005. *The Politics of Method in the Human Sciences.* Durham, N.C.: Duke University Press.

Swimme, B. T., and M. E. Tucker. 2011. *Journey of the Universe.* New Haven, Conn.: Yale University Press.

Taguchi, H. L. 2012. "A Diffractive and Deleuzian Approach to Analyzing Interview Data." *Feminist Theory* 13, no. 3: 265–81.

Tuck, Eve. 2015. "Re-visioning Social, Re-visioning Context, Re-visioning Agency." Presented at the Annual Meeting of the American Educational Research Association in the session "New Materialisms and Ontologies of Social Context: Critical Inquiry on Equity and Education."

U.S. Department of Education and National Center for Education Statistics. 2012.

"2011–12 National Postsecondary Student Aid Study." PowerStats computation. http://nces.ed.gov/datalab/powerstats/default.aspx.

Varenne, H., and R. McDermott. 1999. *Successful Failure: The School America Builds*. Boulder, Colo.: Westview Press.

von Hippel, P. T. 2007. "Regression with Missing Ys: An Improved Strategy for Analyzing Multiply Imputed Data." *Sociological Methodology* 37: 83–117.

Walter, M., and C. Anderson. 2013. *Indigenous Statistics: A Quantitative Research Methodology*. Walnut Creek, Calif.: Left Coast Press.

Warburton, E. C., R. Bugarin, and A. Nuñez. 2001. *Bridging the Gap: Academic Preparation and Postsecondary Success of First-Generation Students*. Washington, D.C.: National Center for Education Statistics.

Warren, John R., and Robert M. Hauser. 1997. "Social Stratification Across Three Generations: New Evidence from the Wisconsin Longitudinal Study." *American Sociological Review* 62, no. 4: 561–72.

Weheliye, Alexander. G. 2014. *Habeas Viscus: Racializing Assemblages, Biopolitics, and Black Feminist Theories of the Human*. Durham, N.C.: Duke University Press.

Willis, Paul. 1977. *Learning to Labor: How Working Class Kids Get Working Class Jobs*. New York: Columbia University Press.

Wilson, William. J. 1987. *The Truly Disadvantaged: The Inner City, the Underclass, and Public Policy*. Chicago: University of Chicago Press.

Wolniak, G. C., and M. E. Engberg. 2007. "The Effects of High School Feeder Networks on College Enrollment." *Review of Higher Education* 31, no. 1: 27–53.

Wyly, Elvin. 2009. "Strategic Positivism." *Professional Geographer* 61, no. 3: 310–22.

Wynne, B. 2005. "Reflexing Complexity: Post-genomic Knowledge and Reductionist Returns in Public Science." *Theory, Culture, and Society* 22, no. 5: 76–94.

Wynter, Sylvia. 2001. "Towards the Sociogenic Principle: Fanon, Identity, the Puzzle of Conscious Experience, and What It Is Like to Be Black." In *National Identities and Sociopolitical Changes in Latin America,* eds. A. Gomez-Moriana and M. Duran-Cogan. New York: Routledge.

Yeung, Wei-Jun Jean, and Kathryn M. Pfeiffer. 2009. "The Black-White Test Score Gap and Early Home Environment." *Social Science Research* 38: 412–37.

Žižek, Slavoj. 2014. *Event: A Philosophical Journey Through a Concept*. Brooklyn, N.Y.: Melville House Publishing.

Zuberi, Tukufu. 2001. *Thicker Than Blood: How Racial Statistics Lie*. Minneapolis, Minn.: University of Minnesota Press.

Zuberi, Tukufu., and Eduardo. Bonilla-Silva. 2008. *White Logic, White Methods: Racism and Methodology*. Lanham, M.D.: Rowman & Littlefield.

Zwick, R. 2004. "Is the SAT a "Wealth Test"? The Link between Educational Achievement and Socioeconomic Status." In *Rethinking the SAT in University Admissions,* ed. R. Zwick. New York: Routledge Falmer.

Index

Ezekiel J. Dixon-Román is associate professor of social policy in the School of Social Policy and Practice at the University of Pennsylvania. He coedited *Thinking Comprehensively about Education: Spaces of Educative Possibility and Their Implications for Public Policy.*

CPSIA information can be obtained
at www.ICGtesting.com
Printed in the USA
BVOW11s1427110817
491777BV00016B/79/P